THE
MARKETING
GAME

This book is dedicated to my parents, Roger and Della Schulz, who have always believed and supported me in all my endeavors; and to my beautiful wife, Brook, whom I love and cherish with all my heart.

THE
MARKETING
GAME

HOW THE WORLD'S BEST COMPANIES *PLAY TO* **WIN**

ERIC SCHULZ

FORMER DIRECTOR OF MARKETING FOR
THE COCA-COLA COMPANY

AND MARKETING MANAGER FOR
PROCTER & GAMBLE
THE WALT DISNEY COMPANY

KOGAN
PAGE

The following are trademarks of Schulz Consulting: The Marketing Game™, Secrets of the Game™, Knowledge Mining™, The Six Deadly Sins of Advertising™, The ABC's of Strategic Positioning™, The Four Plagues of Consumer Promotion™, Been There, Done That™, Sleeping Sickness™, Trinkets and Trashitis™, Oddsitis™, The Three Ingredients of Greatness™, The Octopus Planning Matrix™, The Three Incarnations of Public Relations™, The Big Bang Theory™.

The following are trademarks of the Eureka! Institute and used with permission: Eureka!™, 666™, Jump Start Your Brain™, Mind Dumpster™, Pin Pricks™, Stimulus Response™, Catalog City™, Tabloid Tales™.

Brain Programs Copyright © 1991, 1992, 1993 by Doug Hall used with permission.

Many of the designations used by manufactures and sellers to distinguish their products are claimed as trademarks. Where those designations have appear in this book and Adams Media was aware of a trademark claim, the designations have been printed in initial capital letters.

This publication is designed to provide accurate and authoritative information with regard to the subject matter covered. It is sold with the understanding that the publisher is not engaged in rendering legal, accounting, or other professional advice. If legal advice or other expert assistance is required, the services of a competent professional person should be sought.
—From a *Declaration of Principles* jointly adopted by a Committee of the American Bar Association and a Committee of Publishers and Associations

First published in the United States by Adams Media Corporation in 1999
First published in Great Britain in 2000

Apart from any fair dealing for the purposes of research or private study, or criticism or review, as permitted under the Copyright, Designs and Patents Act 1988, this publication may only be reproduced, stored or transmitted, in any form or by any means, with the prior permission in writing of the publishers, or in the case of reprographic reproduction in accordance with the terms and licences issued by the CLA. Enquiries concerning reproduction outside these terms should be sent to the publishers at the undermentioned address:

Kogan Page Limited
120 Pentonville Road
London N1 9JN

© Eric Schulz, 1999, 2000

The right of Eric Schulz to be identified as the author of this work has been asserted by him in accordance with the Copyright, Designs and Patents Act 1988.

British Library Cataloguing in Publication Data

A CIP record for this book is available from the British Library.

ISBN 0 7494 3198 9

Printed and bound in Great Britain by Biddles Ltd, Guildford and King's Lynn

ACKNOWLEDGMENTS

There are many individuals who have helped me on this journey. My biggest thanks go to Lisa Clements, my dear friend, colleague, and personal editor who kept peeking over my shoulder, dropping hints, and offering ideas for improvements during the writing of the book. She was invaluable as my second set of eyes to make sure topics were covered thoroughly and that everything made sense, flowed properly, and conformed to standard English (as you'll see, I have a tendency to make up words—"Schulzie-isms" as Lisa likes to call them).

I would also like to thank my agent Julie Castiglia and Adams Media Corporation for working together to publish the book. I appreciate their enthusiastic support of the project.

And last, but certainly not least, I'd like to acknowledge the many great marketing minds with whom I have had the pleasure to work through the years, who have taught me much of what I am sharing with you. Particular thanks go to Dr. Pete Clarke of the Marriott School of Management at Brigham Young University, the best teacher I ever had; Doug Hall, my friend and mentor; Mark Upson, who gave me my first "break" and hired me at Procter & Gamble; Sergei Kuharsky, the best boss I've ever worked for; Brendan Harris, the smartest marketing mind I've ever encountered; Grant Harrison, a tremendously creative promotions genius; and other friends and colleagues too numerous to mention who have sat around offices with me on numerous occasions after hours to debate marketing theory. These late-night sessions were the seed inspiration for many of the insights contained in this book.

CONTENTS

Acknowledgments v

Introduction. xi

PART 1: Development and Planning

1. Mission IS Possible 3
Creating a vision of success within the organization.

> Most businesses today exist in a state of controlled chaos—time constrained, under stress, with employees carrying tremendous workloads. This chapter explains the secrets to developing a clear, actionable working mission statement and operating charter to define objectives and responsibilities within an organization, creating a vision and measurable goals leading to success.

2. Mo' Better Brainstorming 17
Using Stimulus Response to increase productivity and generate great new ideas.

> There are two ways to generate new ideas. The most popular is the "suck" method of creativity, which assumes that all great ideas already exist in your head and all you have to do is somehow coax them out. For most this is a very short experience. The better way to ideate is Stimulus Response, which surrounds you with a wide and varying range of stimuli and uses your brain as a coprocessor to make new connections and develop ideas. This secret brainstorming technique has been proven to be five times more effective at developing new ideas than standard methods.

3. What Consumer Research Won't Tell You 27
Finding strategic consumer insight outside traditional research methods.

> Traditional market research can only take you so far. To create intellectual competitive advantage, marketers must learn how to develop the discipline of strategic learning in everyday life. This chapter reveals secrets top marketers teach their marketing personnel to learn things about their consumers that the competition never knows.

4. The Best-Kept Secret of Branding 41
Developing a relevant yet unexpected strategic positioning.

> Brand strategy development is the most difficult task marketers face. Creating a strategic positioning statement defines what your brand will stand for and affects the entire consumer communication effort for your product. This chapter unveils the secrets to creating a relevant-yet-unexpected brand positioning statement that establishes competitive advantage.

5. The New Products Underworld 57
Increasing your chances of new product success.

> Should you continue to invest in research and development to create new products and line extensions in-house? No. Most of the big boys are secretly buying their new ideas from outside vendors. This chapter will offer insight into the burgeoning industry of new-product think tanks.

PART II: Marketing Cornerstones

6. How You Can Know That the Price Is Right. 75
Maximizing profitability can be a difficult journey.

> Making money is what it's all about—but pricing is trickier than it looks. Depending upon the price sensitivity of consumers in the product category, a difference of even pennies can drastically affect sales volume and impact the bottom line. The chapter reveals pricing models designed to optimize profitability.

7. Unfair Advantage: How to Own a Category 89
Offering the right product mix to consumers.

> Large companies often dominate a single product category with several products that compete for market share. This chapter reveals how top consumer goods marketers analyze product mix to optimize consumer appeal, build share, and neutralize competitors. It demystifies the shrouded world of generics, fighter brands, and premium brands, revealing different strategies to use, depending upon your company's market position.

8. Simple Steps to Powerful Packaging 105
Creating differentiation and specialness through packaging initiatives.

> This chapter discusses the hidden truths of how companies willing to break the paradigm and create unique packaging have developed competitive advantage.

9. Solving the Merchandising and Distribution Mystery . . 121
Putting your product in the right place for consumers.

> Everything communicates something about your product to consumers, including where they see it being sold. The store environment and how it is merchandised creates a powerful image about your brand in the mind of the consumer—more powerful than even your advertising message. This chapter unveils merchandising secrets and offers distribution strategy tips.

PART III: Consumer Communication

10. Cracking the Code to Great Advertising. 137
The keys to getting great results from your ad agency

> In this chapter we reveal the secrets to creating breakthrough advertising and dealing with advertising agencies/creative teams to produce an ad campaign that not only looks good, but works.

11. The Six Deadly Sins of Advertising 153
Common mistakes to avoid at all costs.

> An analysis of hundreds of hours of TV ads and thousands of print campaigns has revealed six secret no-no's that consistently kill campaigns.

12. Solving the Public Relations Puzzle. 165
It's not about finding dancing elephants to wear your brand name on TV.

> Many public relations people think that their job is to get their product's name in the newspaper or on TV. Wrong. PR has to be integrated with the overall marketing plan and deliver messages strategically aligned to the brand positioning. This chapter defines what great public relations is and its place in the overall marketing mix.

PART IV: Promote, Promote and Promote

13. The Hush-Hush World of Trade Promotions 183
What you can do besides paying feature, display and slotting allowances.

> Many retailers won't execute promotions anymore—but it can be done if you know the right buttons to push! This chapter reveals how to create great and effective trade marketing strategies and tactics.

14. What You Don't Know about Consumer Promotions. . . 201
Create brand personality, competitive advantage and boost sales.

> Companies spend big chunks of their annual marketing budgets on consumer promotions. Most think of promotions as a way to get a short-term volume increase and don't spend a lot of time thinking about the long-term implications. This is a *big* mistake. Consumer promotions can be used to effectively create brand personality, build competitive advantage, *and* stimulate sales, with results that can last long past the promotional window.

15. The Secrets to Effective Sports Sponsorships 221
Attaching your name to big-time sports is expensive stuff—Here's how to make it pay off.

> Corporations spend millions of dollars each year sponsoring sports—why? How does it pay off? Most of the time, it doesn't. It's not about putting your name in front of people—that's old-school thinking. Here's an in-depth evaluation and discussion of the benefits of sports marketing and the secrets of how to make it work effectively for your brand—through strategic linkage to a brand's core consumer benefits.

16. Concealed Tactics for Leveraging Alliances 241
Making partnerships work for you.

> Many companies form strategic alliances with properties—from concert tours to Miss America pageants to TV programs. This chapter discusses the secrets of how to find alliances, what rights you need to execute effectively, and how to leverage the alliance's imagery for your benefit.

17. What Coke Doesn't Want You to Know about Special Events 259
Secret tactics for getting noticed and standing out in a crowd.

> At most major events there are swarms of people and sponsors camped out on every square inch of free space, competing for consumer attention. This chapter reveals secret strategies developed by Coca-Cola for creating effective and cost-efficient presence at special events—signage, covert tactics, and grassroots efforts.

18. The Hidden Benefits of Licensing 271
A bigger opportunity than T-shirts and coffee mugs.

> The biggest untapped opportunity for many companies is licensing—through offering your brand to others or via acquiring the rights to use others' names/likenesses in association with your brand. This chapter outlines secrets of how to effectively use licensing—leveraging image, creating brand awareness, generating new profit centers and line extensions.

Parting Thoughts 285

Feedback 285

Index 286

INTRODUCTION

I F YOU'VE EVER SUSPECTED YOUR COMPETITION KNEW SOMETHING YOU DIDN'T, you were probably right. But not anymore. The Marketing Game breaks the code of silence to teach you the covert strategies and marketing secrets that have been powering the machines of the world's most savvy marketers for the past decade.

Successful companies don't owe their greatness to luck. They're on top because they know more about their consumers than the competition and they execute their marketing efforts better. As you read *The Marketing Game,* you too will acquire the strategic tools these top companies use to stand out from the crowd. You'll be taught how to apply the strategies and tactics to market your business more effectively. And along the way, you'll find secrets like this one to help you get ahead of the competitive crowd.

Secrets of the Game

Virtually every strategic principle and tactic that works for large corporations can also be used to effectively market other businesses or products, no matter the size.

Any strategy or consumer learning that works within a particular category can usually be applied successfully to other unrelated products that share the same consumer dynamic.

For example, any product that is part of the morning wake-up routine can learn from other morning products and apply the insight—especially if those other products have absolutely nothing else in common. Think about Coast soap. The advertising message promises *Shower in the morning with Coast soap, and you'll feel refreshed and alive because of its tingling feeling and fresh smell.* Could a local coffeehouse craft a hybrid of this strategy? It seems plausible that an effective positioning could be developed by promising that *the great taste and smell of Joe's coffee will help you start your day feeling refreshed and alive*—in effect, stealing the strategy of Coast! Such a positioning would definitely give Joe's coffeehouse a unique consumer niche in the marketplace.

Congratulations. You've now learned the simplest secret within the corporate marketing world.

Secrets of the Game

Stealing ideas from other companies isn't taboo—it's smart business, and it happens every day!

The businesses and brands that are most successful are always looking at what other brands, companies, and products are doing with their marketing, and trying to learn what is effective and what isn't. They take what works, twist it into their own idea, and apply it to their business. There are very few genuinely original strategies. Most great thoughts are hijacked from somewhere else and just executed better in a different way. *The Marketing Game* provides you with a one-stop resource for finding these great ideas that you can commandeer for your business, whether it's a delicatessen, a pizza parlor, or a multinational corporation.

The insights you'll find in this book primarily come from learning I've gained through my work over the past decade at marketing giants such as The Procter & Gamble Company, The Walt Disney Studios, and The Coca-Cola Company. While at these terrific corporations I've had the privilege and honor of working on many high-profile business initiatives. At Coke, I was in charge of worldwide Olympic marketing behind the 1996 Summer Games in Atlanta, the largest and most expensive integrated global marketing campaign ever executed by any company in history. At Disney, I conceived the direct-to-video concept, which has grown into a huge segment of the home video marketplace. At Procter &

Gamble, I was blessed with being able to work on brands such as Folgers Coffee, Citrus Hill Orange Juice, Hawaiian Punch, and Duncan Hines. I had the opportunity to author the national introductory marketing plan for Folgers Coffee Singles; made the original recommendation to add a pouring spout to the Citrus Hill Orange Juice cartons (which is now standard on all major brands); and spent a Memorial Day weekend in my apartment, cooking about a hundred different versions of microwavable brownies, which ultimately led to the creation of the Duncan Cups line of microwave desserts.

While the work on these megabrands has been fascinating and rewarding, I've also had the honor of working on smaller and underappreciated brands such as Texsun juices and Special Olympics. The breadth of insight from these polar opposites has demonstrated to me how every sound marketing strategy can be utilized effectively no matter the size of the budget or the type of business. Great marketing strategies, if executed properly, can work just as well for a hometown shoe repair shop as they can for Coca-Cola Classic.

As we make our way through each chapter, we'll look at many examples of both good and bad marketing executions. I've found it's easier to comprehend a strategy when you can visualize its application in a real-life or a hypothetical situation. My apologies to those companies and brands that I've used as real-life bad examples, but if the shoe fits, I'm afraid that for now you have to wear it. If you work at one of these places and are reading this book, maybe you can use some of the insights to improve your efforts!

You should also notice that the chapters are arranged in such a way that at the beginning, we look at planning and development strategies, then move to marketing fundamentals and consumer communication, then finally end up talking at length about different kinds of promotions. There is logic to the madness. Think of this analogy: If you are going to build a house, the easy part—the *fun* part—is imagining what the finished house will look like. But before you start dreaming about brick walkways and Jacuzzi bathtubs, the first thing you do is plan your foundations, plumbing, and electrical circuits. Only after thoughtful preparation do you actually begin pouring the concrete and pounding nails.

Marketing is the same. You must build systematically, however appealing it might be to leap ahead and start inventing promotions or competitive tactics. *Random acts of marketing don't work.* You can't just jump in and start swinging the promotion hammer, improvising as you go. You must plan and build on a solid strategic foundation; then you can worry about execution (and you can feel confident that your executions will work). If you follow the step-by-step layout of the chapters, you won't miss anything, and you will be able to develop great plans for your business.

I have tried to limit the amount of marketing jargon and buzzwords, writing *The Marketing Game* in plain language to make it easy to understand. Some of the basic principles you are about to learn are taught in MBA programs and business schools throughout the world, but this book includes unique strategic twists I've learned in the business trenches that they don't teach you in grad school. These insights optimize the basic strategies for effectiveness in today's ever-changing marketing environment.

I respect your time and truly appreciate that you are investing some of your busy life into reading what I've got to say. I have tried to be succinct when writing each chapter. Every page and every story has a purpose in demonstrating the key strategies and illustrating their usefulness. I urge you to stay focused as you move through the book, or you may miss some of the key insights.

One last thing and we'll get on with it. Once you enter the world of *The Marketing Game*, you will find that the way you think about marketing will be changed forever. I hope you enjoy the journey.

DEVELOPMENT AND PLANNING

Mission IS Possible

CREATING A VISION
OF SUCCESS WITHIN THE
ORGANIZATION

I T IS ALWAYS SURPRISING TO ME that so many businesses keep most of their employees in the dark about the company's overall business objectives or the CEO's vision for growth. Everyone shows up for work and does what he or she was hired to do in their own private corner of the building, picks up a paycheck, then goes home. Very few people outside top senior management really know the big picture or understand how any one particular job or initiative affects the company objective as a whole.

It's true of any group effort that if you don't all know where you are going, you have a slim chance of arriving anywhere at all. Management consultants recognized this fact in the mid 1990s and began suggesting that companies develop corporate mission statements to help their employees and shareholders understand their ultimate goal. The results are often long, flowery, well-written prose. For example, here is the published corporate mission statement of Hallmark:

This is Hallmark.
We believe that our products and services must
enrich people's lives and enhance their relationships.
That creativity and quality in our concepts, products and
services are essential to our success.
That the people of Hallmark are our Company's
most valuable resource.
That distinguished financial performance is a must, not as an end
unto itself, but as a means to accomplish our broader mission.
That our private ownership must be preserved.

Pretty as a Hallmark card, isn't it? I'm sure the senior management and a gaggle of consultants invested a lot of time and thought into developing this corporate mission. It sounds nice and it makes you feel all warm and fuzzy about the company.

Now, step back for a moment and think. If you are in senior management at Hallmark or any other company, would you publish your company marching orders for all the world to see? Do you think that Hallmark's competitors at Gibson Greeting Cards or American Greetings might read Hallmark's annual report?

Corporate mission statements are a smoke screen! They're simply feel-good mottos developed for public consumption. Inside the company walls, employees often operate with a very different agenda and a very defined mission.

Secrets of the Game

The world's best marketing companies have all developed secret internal missions that are called working mission statements.

Working mission statements are strategic tools to focus employees on the ultimate objective and clearly map out the road to success. They define "what you do" in a single crisp, clear, and memorable sentence. Given what I know about Hallmark, its working mission statement might be something like this:

The working mission of Hallmark is:

1) to create unique, high-quality products that enrich lives and enhance relationships;
2) to reflect this warm, friendly spirit of Hallmark products in our stores.

You might think this statement says as much—or as little—as the long, public version. But this statement makes clear that product development is the number one priority and that products must be unique to Hallmark (not available anywhere else), describes a little about what the products do and how they make consumers feel, and addresses the store environment. Best of all, every employee could memorize it in thirty seconds—which is the reason to have a working mission statement in the first place: to give employees an understanding of the strategic goals of the company.

INTERNAL GOAL SETTING

Secrets of the Game

Every department develops a departmental mission to focus their employees on the role that their group plays in meeting the working mission of the overall organization.

The company also creates operating charters for each department to specify measurable goals and objectives for its work group.

The most successful companies spend time and energy continually improving their internal systems—from internal communications to organizational structure to reporting structures. They clearly define their working mission. They also do two other very important things:

1. The departmental mission and operating charter becomes a single document that precisely delineates what everyone within each department in the organization is ultimately

trying to achieve, at the same time setting measurable goals and defining limitations; and

2. Departmental mission and operating charters reduce the chances of bad decisions and dropped balls.

Without a well-defined set of objectives, many businesses find themselves recalling the old saying, "I have seen the enemy and it is me." Well-meaning individuals working on their own agendas, and with only a partial understanding of the company's larger goals, can greatly damage both the morale of other employees and the company's overall ability to succeed. They are so intent on checking off priorities on their own private list, they have very little time or interest in the goals of their coworkers. This tendency toward working in isolation is a particularly thorny problem in many privately held or family-owned businesses, where employees often have the leeway to carve out their own fiefdoms.

THE GOLD STANDARD

Even the most well organized marketing companies still get tangled in unclear operating systems, usually during internal upheavals such as reorganizations or the development of new departments. At Coca-Cola, we introduced the concept of a departmental mission and operating charter shortly after I arrived to assume the responsibility of Director of Worldwide Olympic Marketing. With Atlanta, the home of the Coca-Cola Company, hosting the 1996 Olympics, the Games became an agenda item for almost every meeting. I quickly discovered that I was a very popular guy. I'd never felt so wanted, being invited to dozens of meetings each day. It seemed that every department within the company wanted to have its fingers in the Olympic rings.

Instead of powerful synergy, we were on the verge of absolute business chaos. Marketing initiatives poured in literally by the hundreds. Some ideas sounded good, but they were all over the map—community projects, promotion ideas, requests for Olympic athlete appearances, Olympic pins, and Coke/Olympic merchandise. And that wasn't the half of it. Outside vendors submitted ideas by the thousands. I received a proposal from one consultant for Coke to build an Eiffel Tower in downtown Atlanta to commemorate the Games. Another wanted me to fund the building of the world's tallest totem pole of peace. Still another wanted me to fill the skies over Atlanta with a fleet of Coca-Cola hot air balloons during the Games.

The craziest idea came from a Frenchman who had actually built an airplane that was an exact replica of Charles Lindbergh's "Spirit of St. Louis." He had painted the plane to look like a Sprite bottle and named it "The Spirit of Sprite." His plan was to reenact Lindbergh's famous New York–to–Paris flight on the eve of the Olympic Games. He wanted me to sponsor him for one million dollars. Needless to say, that historic flight was never made.

It didn't take long to see that unless I defined with senior management exactly where Olympic Marketing fit in the *big picture*, then determined what my group was specifically responsible for delivering, a thousand different projects would be springing up all over the company, with no overall objective and no strategic synergy. Worse still, any spurned department could argue—with some reason—that my decisions were unfair, unsound, or just plain dumb.

To define our role, our management team sequestered itself off-site for two days and created a mission statement and operating charter for the Olympic Marketing Department. The mission statement defined our overall goal. The operating charter took a broad-stroke view in:

    a. Defining the areas in which the Olympic Marketing Department had authority to operate;
    b. Listing the tasks we would accomplish;
    c. Defining our aspirations;
    d. Specifying how we would measure success; and
    e. Waving warning flags about issues beyond our control that could impede our ability to complete the tasks as planned.

While this sounds like we must have been writing a book, we weren't. The whole document was only one page long.

The Olympic Marketing Mission and Operating Charter was printed and widely dispersed throughout the Coca-Cola system so that everyone else knew what they could and could not expect from our group, and it helped them to shape their proposals to fit our objectives.

The Olympic Marketing Mission and Operating Charter clearly defined our goals as a company and focused my team's efforts on the job at hand. It worked like a charm. The 1996 Coca-Cola Olympic effort was the biggest and most successful global marketing initiative in the company's history. During the eight months in which the system was executing Olympic initiatives, worldwide volume increased 9 percent, global profits increased 22 percent, and Coca-Cola's stock value increased 32 percent. Why did it work? Because the Olympic Marketing Mission and Operating Charter allowed us to unite the corporate system in one theme, one look, and one objective, and to work cooperatively to achieve spectacular business results.

The point is simple. Most companies don't have a clearly defined working mission. In today's evolving business environment, not only do you need a clear, succinct, and well-defined working mission statement for the company, but each department needs to develop its own mission that identifies its role in supporting the company goals.

CREATING A WORKING MISSION STATEMENT

Now that you're a believer in the value of the mission statement, let's take a look at how to write your own.

Secrets of the Game

The working mission statement should answer the question "what do you do?" It is no more than one sentence, must be easily understood, and should be memorizable by everyone within your organization.

There are three steps to building a working mission statement:

1. List two or three ideas that you think sum up your job activities.
2. List a core principle for which you will stand.
3. Write down who you are working to help.

For example, if you were the operator of a fast-food hamburger restaurant, the three ideas that sum up your job activities could be: 1) prepare high-quality fast food; 2) provide quick and friendly customer service; and 3) operate a clean, safe, and inviting restaurant. The core principle for which you stand could be: excellence. And who you are working to help would be: our customers. Now put it all together:

> The working mission of our restaurant is to prepare high-quality fast food, provide quick and friendly customer service, and operate a clean, safe, and inviting restaurant with excellent service for our customers.

Just think of the possibilities and what a difference it would make if every employee could recite this working mission by memory and then perform their job in accordance with it!

As another example, assume you are a marketing manager for a car-rental agency. The three ideas that sum up your job activities could be: (1) provide clean, quality cars; (2) friendly, no-hassle service; and (3) fast, accurate transactions. The core principle for which you stand could be: being the most efficient company in the car-rental business. Who you are working to help: our customers. Again, put it all together:

> The working mission of our agency is to provide clean, quality cars, friendly, no-hassle service, and fast, accurate transactions to be the most efficient company in the car-rental business for our customers.

CREATING THE OPERATING CHARTER

Operating charters are no more difficult to write than mission statements but may be even more important in saving your sanity—and your job. Here's how to write a good one.

Secrets of the Game

The operating charter should be the foundation of your business plan. It defines the areas in which you have authority to operate, lists the tasks you will accomplish, defines your aspirations, identifies how you will measure success, and waves warning flags to issues beyond your control that could impede your ability to complete the task as planned.

Operating Charter

Specifically, an operating charter contains the following elements:

Scope. Defines the parameters in which you work. Is it a particular geography, a particular brand, a particular customer? Be as specific as possible.

Primary objectives. List no more than six clearly stated roles your area will provide to the overall organization. These should include primary job responsibilities, areas where your group will provide leadership, and places where your group will provide assistance to others within the organization.

Secondary objectives. List no more than two other clearly stated roles that are "hoped for" but not mandatory to meet business success.

Aspirations. List no more than three dreams you hope your work can accomplish within the organization (both short- and long-term).

Quantifiable measures of success. List quantifiable means you will use to track whether or not you are accomplishing what you set out to do.

Constraints. List external factors you cannot control that could negatively influence your ability to meet all of the objectives as stated above.

Here is an example of a mission statement and operating charter for a typical marketing department.

Marketing Department Working Mission and Operating Charter

Working Mission: To increase shareholder wealth by creating volume-building and image-enhancing marketing plans, aligned to consumer needs, that increase sales, profitability, consumer brand loyalty, and long-term equity for our brands.

Scope: Soaps and detergents manufactured by our company and sold within the United States and Canada.

Primary objectives:
- To develop and widely communicate a strategic consumer positioning statement for each brand, aligned to consumer needs and brand benefits.
- To develop and execute consumer research for each brand and to widely communicate findings throughout the company.
- To develop a variety of strategically aligned promotion initiatives (with the assistance of the promotions department) to meet the needs of the consumer, increasing purchase frequency and enhancing consumer brand loyalty/increasing long-term brand equity.
- To develop an annual business plan for each brand and assume ultimate responsibility for delivering the agreed-upon profit and volume.
- To lead coordination within the company of all communication vehicles related to our brands—advertising, public relations, packaging, promotions.
- To help the sales organization create programs to meet retailers' needs.

Secondary objectives:
- To seek incremental revenue-generating opportunities through special events or licensing.
- To communicate learning and best practices to others within the organization.

Aspirations:
- To establish a new gold standard for marketing practices.

- To be a net exporter of talent to other company organizations.
- To be viewed by the system as functional experts possessing unparalleled consumer insight into our brands.

Quantifiable measures of success:
- Meeting or exceeding agreed-upon volume and profit goals as established in the annual business plan.
- A 7 percent increase in consumer purchase intent/brand loyalty.
- A 9 percent increase in consumer brand equity versus competitive brands.

Constraints:
- Inability due to financial reallocation to execute all agreed-upon programs.
- Unforeseen competitive forces.
- Sales organizational focus and time pressure.

WHY CHARTERS WORK

The day-to-day operations at many businesses can best be described as a state of controlled chaos. Employees are rushing to meet deadlines, crushed under heavy workloads, feeling the constraints of too little time. While a sense of urgency is necessary to keep business moving, employees must also feel a sense of direction. Through the process of defining a working mission statement for both the company and each department and by creating an operating charter, you can:

1. Define management and employee expectations of your business goals and paint a vision of the road to success;
2. Set parameters and define authority that individuals in your department have the right to exert within the organization as a whole; and
3. Focus everyone's time, energy, and resources on single-mindedly accomplishing the stated goals.

Developing the working mission statement, department mission, and operating charter is a very painful and time-consuming process. You need to face reality and become very specific about what you can and cannot do. You must focus, prioritize, and determine the goals and responsibilities that meet the overall needs of the company, with a eye to maximizing business results.

THE OPERATING CHARTER VS. THE BUSINESS PLAN

As you can see, the operating charter is more than bullet points pulled out of your business plan. The operating charter is different in several distinct ways. First, the charter is the view of your business from 20,000 feet. It gives the big picture for your work group. Second, it paints the core tasks you will accomplish in broad strokes, not in the detail demanded by a business plan. Third, it should be only one page long, so that it can be tacked up on the wall over everyone's desk as an easy reference for what your group is striving to achieve.

This may seem like a silly idea, but it works. By having the operating charter in plain sight of all employees every day, it keeps everyone focused on the strategic goals and helps them make decisions on a daily basis, prioritizing tasks. Many times during each day of my Coke Olympic journey I would reference the operating charter to help me decide what tasks to tackle (and more importantly, which to ignore). During the rush of business, it is very easy to get caught up in tasks that feel urgent but don't move the priorities ahead. The operating charter helps you sort the necessary from the minutia and focuses time and efforts to get better business results.

Secrets of the Game

To ensure success within an organization, you must take responsibility for your own well-being. Even if your company does not operate under the auspices of a mission or operating charter, create one for your area.

The principles behind the success of mission statements and operating charters can be felt from the boardroom to the secretarial pool. And the wonderful by-product of creating these statements is that they can actually get you promoted. Here's how: First, they provide a clear, agreed-upon objective that you can use to ward off those wild goose chases that seem to be the natural offspring of upper management meetings. Your boss will be much more likely to support your priorities if they have been established up front, and if he or she is convinced that they make sense to advance the business. Second, you have a powerful negotiating tool when you walk in at year's end with a clear statement of what you aimed to achieve and quantitative evidence that you succeeded.

One of the senior managers at Coca-Cola was so fanatical about having missions and charters defined, he took it all the way down to the individual job level and challenged every employee to develop a one-sentence working mission statement for his or her particular job. He would approach employees in the halls and ask "What do you do?" If they couldn't give the answer in one succinct statement, he skewered them. While his tactic may have been a bit harsh, the strategy is right. If everyone in your organization knows and can state in three simple sentences the company working mission, his or her department's mission, and his or her personal job mission, your business will run much more efficiently and effectively. This rule is as important for a small company as it is for a multinational corporation.

Think back to the hypothetical Hallmark example at the beginning of this chapter. If you were the Marketing Brand Manager for Hallmark Cards, you might create the following definitions:

Company working mission: The working mission of Hallmark is:

1) to create unique, high-quality products that enrich lives and enhance relationships;
2) to reflect this warm, friendly spirit of Hallmark products in our stores.

Marketing department mission: The mission of the Hallmark Marketing Department is to create consumer-relevant and brand-aligned marketing initiatives that drive volume, increase consumer preference and build brand equity for Hallmark products.

My personal job mission: My job is to create consumer insistence for Hallmark products.

That, my friends, is strategic clarity, and it is what every company or business must strive to achieve.

CHAPTER SUMMARY

- It is important for all employees to understand the working mission of the company.
- In today's evolving business environment, not only do you need a clear, succinct, and well-defined working mission statement for the company, but each department needs to develop its own mission that identifies its role in supporting the company goals.
- A mission statement is built with three elements:

  1. Two or three ideas that you think sum up your job activities,
  2. a core principle for which you will stand, and
  3. who you are working to help.

- Operating charters work hand-in-hand with the mission statement for your work group. The charter is a document that outlines the goals and objectives of your department. It is no more than one page long and becomes the foundation upon which your group operates.
- Your operating charter is the view of your business from 20,000 feet and is more than just bullet points pulled out of your business plan. It gives the big picture for your work group.
- Operating charters help to define what you do—and more importantly, what you don't do. The charter helps keep everyone focused on the ultimate goals.
- Even if your company doesn't use mission statements and operating charters, develop one for your work area. It will help at annual review time to get you raises and promotions by offering a clear and measurable assessment of your accomplishments!

Mo'
Better
Brainstorming

USING STIMULUS RESPONSE TO
INCREASE PRODUCTIVITY AND
GENERATE GREAT NEW IDEAS

I OFTEN GET INVITED by different corporations to participate in on-site brainstorming sessions to help dream up
new marketing and promotion ideas. I love the art of
strategic creativity, so I jump at the chance whenever offered.

Many times, the session is hosted by a moderator provided
through the client's advertising agency. The group meets in a staid
office conference room somewhere on the corporate campus.
Typically some toys like Play-Doh or blocks are tossed out on the
tables in a feeble attempt to create a playful environment. Then the
corporate participants march in—often in the middle of a work-
day for an hour or two session—dressed in their business suits,

the men with neckties smartly tight around their collars, with corporate decorum and rank in full effect.

Unfortunately, most of the time, these sessions provide very little out-of-the-box thinking by the corporate participants. They produce run-of-the-mill ideas. The one or two outsiders like me usually out-produce the entire corporate team by a 10-to-1 margin. The question I am asked by my corporate clients in the follow-up meeting from these sessions is always the same—if we have a bunch of very smart people in the room, why does the brainstorming exercise fail to produce great creative results?

The answer lies in the brainstorming methodology and the environment. To get breakthrough creative results, you have to break out of traditional paradigms. Great ideas aren't usually found sitting around a corporate conference table at two o'clock in the afternoon.

BRAINDRAINING

My friend Doug Hall has a great way of describing the problem. He calls this typical corporate method of brainstorming "braindraining," or the "suck" method of creativity. This method presupposes that all great ideas already exist within the gray matter of one's brain, and all you have to do is somehow siphon the ideas out. People sit down in a room, think, sweat, use their brains as reference libraries, and try to squeeze out a few hard-thought ideas. For most, this is a very short and laborious experience.

THE GOLD STANDARD

STIMULUS RESPONSE

The alternative method of creativity, which I ascribe to and Doug purveys at his Eureka! Ranch new products think tank, uses the brain as it was intended—to absorb and process stimuli, then make new connections. This method is called Stimulus Response. In his book *Jump Start Your Brain,* Doug writes:

With the Eureka! Stimulus Response method, your brain is used more like a processing computer and less like a reference library. Instead of withdrawing ideas from a finite collection of thoughts, your brain reacts off stimuli to create new associations, new Eureka!'s.

Stimuli act as a fertilizer for your brain; they set up the chain reaction of ideas, many with the potential for brilliance. Stimuli can be anything you see, hear, smell, taste, or touch. Stimuli is anything that spurs your brain to make new connections, new associations, and new-to-the-world ideas.

Validation studies by Dr. Arthur VanGundy of the University of Oklahoma, one of the nation's leading authorities on the creative process, have found that the Stimulus Response method cranks out over 1,000 percent more new ideas than the aforementioned Braindraining technique used by the average corporation. Going further, the studies concluded that Stimulus Response generated 558 percent more "super-smart" ideas with above-average marketplace potential. Said another way, it can make your brain five times more effective at coming up with the "Big Idea."

PREPARING FOR BRAINSTORMING SUCCESS

There are three keys to creating an atmosphere where great brainstorming can occur. First, *provide an environment that's fun.* Get out of the corporate office. When I was at Coca-Cola, I held my creative sessions at a place called Dave & Buster's. It is an adult's playground, with thousands of video games and virtual reality simulators. We'd rent out the back room, do some creative exercises, then go out into the game room to play for a while before coming back in to create again. Fun is critical to the creative process. A University of Maryland study indicates that when people are laughing, they're three to five times better at generating successful ideas.

Music is also crucial to the process. Loud, upbeat, and eclectic are the best. My favorite CDs are *ESPN Jock Jam* and others that offer the theme songs of TV shows. Food is important as well. M&Ms, soft drinks, coffee, and anything laced with sugar, to keep the blood racing, work great as snacks and munchies.

Second, *bring lots and lots of stimuli to provoke ideas*. Stimuli can be anything you can see, smell, taste, or touch. Magazines, toys, products, pictures, and lists of interesting words can all work wonders. It is important to keep feeding the brain with stimuli for the duration of the session. If you are planning on doing a full-day creative session, you'll need about one thousand different stimuli to maximize your effectiveness.

Third, *invite creative people who don't work for you to participate*. You need to seed both business sense and nonsense into the invitees. Why have people that don't work in your business there? Simple. Remember when you first started your job and you came in all fired up with exciting new ideas? Then you started learning the business: corporate culture, personal agendas, and biases, and were told by others what you could and could not do. Over time, those new ideas dried up. One day you woke up and discovered that you'd been beaten into the mold of corporate conventionalism.

This is not an unusual transformation. In fact, it's often part of the company system. Corporate culture makes its employees fit like pegs into holes. Employees learn what their job is and stop thinking. They perform the task to which they are assigned. Only rebels continue to press for new ideas. But over time, most rebels abandon the company out of frustration. It's a strange dichotomy. Corporations need these free spirits to spur them on, but the system can't handle them because they don't fit with the culture.

You need outside thinkers who are unbridled by the confines of corporate conventionalism. It's the only way to get out-of-the-box thinking.

Secrets of the Game

The recipe for brainstorming success is simple: blend together people who know everything about your business with a healthy serving of creative folks who know absolutely nothing about what you do. Pour fun sauce all over and serve in a wild and loud environment with lots of stimuli, great music, and munchies!

CREATING THE PERFECT BRAINSTORMING SESSION

There are a few very important steps to take at the beginning of the brainstorming session to foster the creative environment. First, *tell everyone to show up in casual clothes.* Absolutely no ties are allowed. Neckties are nothing more than tourniquets that decrease blood flow to the brain. Heck, T-shirts, shorts, and bare feet are the preferred attire for brainstorming. Comfortable clothes are important in allowing each individual to feel free of restraints and be relaxed.

Second (and this one is absolutely critical), *the playing field must be level among all participants.* Vice presidents and other corporate muckity-mucks must store their egos in their pockets and participate sans titles. Everyone in the session must feel equal to everyone else—from CEO to administrative assistant. There are no titles in brainstorming sessions, just people all having fun working together to create. High-ranking executives must be made aware of this philosophy before arriving at the session so that they can help facilitate the leveling process with their underlings.

Third, *you must have a curriculum developed for the day with a full itinerary of different creativity exercises* (you'll find a bunch of great ones in just a moment).

Fourth, *you must have a moderator that can motivate the group and keep the energy at a frenetic level.* One executive coming out of a Stimulus Response brainstorming session remarked that "it seemed at times like a train wreck in there. But the amazing thing is that the chaos really was quite structured and we got a lot of great ideas."

Fifth, *as the brainstorming session commences, the participants should be assigned to small groups of no more than five or six people to work on each exercise.* Studies have shown that small groups are much more effective at creating new ideas than individuals working alone or larger groups. Groups should be reorganized after each exercise to create different connections and exposure to different thinking styles.

And finally, *you should break after each exercise and have a spokesperson for each group report back the highlights of their brainstorming.* This breather gives everyone in the session the opportunity to use the seeds of ideas generated to build on for even better ideas. After three exercises, take a thirty-minute break for everyone to unwind and relax, then fire it back up.

THE TRUTHS OF BRAINSTORMING

Over the years, I have found that for me to be most effective at brainstorming, I have to remember what it was like to be five years old. All of a sudden, this mundane world is a fantastic new adventure. I start feeling things I haven't felt since childhood. Once I get rid of preconceived notions and business sense, my ideas run wild and true creativity can bubble to the surface.

GREAT BRAINSTORMING EXERCISES

When conducting a brainstorming session, you have only one rule: *All* ideas are sacred and great—protect the newborns.

The analogy is simple. Sometimes when a child is born, he looks a little funny; squishy, or blotchy, or hairy, or pointy-headed. The wonderful thing is that often these ugly babies grow up to be attractive adults. For the same reason, we don't kill ugly ideas during the brainstorming session. While they may appear to be hideous and deformed when first uttered, sometimes this is where "Big Ideas" are born. When the brainstorming is in session, every idea is a great idea, no matter how outlandish or ridiculous.

There are hundreds of different exercises that have been developed for brainstorming. Here are six of my favorites. They all originate from Doug Hall and are used extensively at Eureka! Ranch. For more great exercises and brainstorming ideas, get his book *Jump Start Your Brain,* published by Warner Books. It contains a plethora of great exercises, plus a wealth of creative knowledge from the master marketing inventor himself.

Exercise #1: Mind Dumpster (Individual Exercise)

This exercise is critical to starting a brainstorming session. At most sessions, participants have already thought up some ideas before they get there. Until everyone can get these preconceived ideas dumped out, their brains are constipated and nothing else can be thought of.

Pass out a handful of 3" × 5" cards to each individual. Give the group five minutes for everyone to "dump" the ideas they came into the session with on the cards, one idea per card. This helps "flush" everyone's mind so that creativity can begin. Turn on some loud music and let them dump!

Exercise #2: Stimuli One-Step

Provide each group with a box of miscellaneous stimuli collected from the grocery store. The objective of the exercise is to make direct connections between the stimuli and the task. Rifle through the stimuli quickly, making quick connections.

This exercise may appear too ridiculously simple to yield worthwhile results, but you'll change your mind once you try it. Often the simplest, most straightforward paths are the most effective.

Exercise #3: 666

The objective of this exercise is to force-associate related elements.

On a piece of paper, create three separate columns containing six words, thoughts, ideas, or product attributes—anything that might be used to describe the task and a few that don't relate at all. Label the three columns "Red," "Blue," and "White." Now pass out to each group three dice—a blue, a red, and a white one.

Roll the dice. Look at the number that comes up on each, and look to the word or idea that corresponds in each color's column. Force yourself to make associations between those three unrelated thoughts. When the ideas wane, reroll the dice and force-associate another three ideas. Use the combinations that emerge with each toss as starting-gate stimuli. They don't have to be taken literally. It's to stimulate thoughts outside of normal thought patterns.

Exercise #4: Catalog City

Get a stack of different catalogs and pass them out to each group for stimuli. Use the photography and products as stimuli to get outside the box.

Exercise #5: Tabloid Tales

This exercise pushes you to the extremes. It takes the spirit of P. T. Barnum and the rank exploitativeness of the *National Enquirer* and applies it to the task at hand.

The objective is to make your task larger than life. To emphasize, magnify, and overstate various aspects of your task to create new applications for individual elements, new approaches to improving the total package, or new solutions for your task.

First, hand out copies of the supermarket rags—*National Enquirer, Weekly World News,* or others—to each group. Then list four thoughts about your task or problem in the middle of a piece of paper. Find ways to make them more provocative—sensationalize them. Distort one aspect, then another. Look for facts that spark exaggeration. Use the tabloid rags as stimuli. Where has Elvis been spotted? Force-associate the wild, the bizarre, the eye popping.

Exercise #6: Pin Pricks

This is a devilishly fun exercise where you take on the persona of a madman. The objective is to spot vulnerabilities in your competition and turn them into advantages for you—to engage in one-upsmanship, to make the other guy gnash his teeth, pull out his hair, and curse the day he was born.

To start the exercise, identify competitive candidates, anyone with whom you compete for time, sales, dollars, or attention. Map out a plan to gig your rival in any one of the following ways:

- What is your competition's greatest source of pride?
- Who could endorse your effort, and in so doing most annoy your competition?
- How could you change your product to annoy the competition?
- What customers could you steal to bother them?
- How could you irritate competitors by changing pricing or sizing?
- What elements of your competitors' product, packaging, marketing, or advertising could you learn from?

- What humorous or outrageous claim could you make to drive the competition crazy?
- How could you shame them into taking steps they'd rather not?

BRAINSTORMING IMAGINATIVELY

Your only limitation is your own imagination. There are literally thousands of different ways you can brainstorm effectively. The key is to provide your mind with stimulation. Get out of your comfortable everyday environment. Go someplace where creativity abounds. When I need an injection of creativity, I go to the Walt Disney World Resort. At EPCOT they have a ride I just love. It's a silly ride called "Journey into Imagination." It features a jovial inventor and his little purple friend "Figment." The theme song chorus that plays throughout the ride says something like this:

> Imagination . . .
> A dream can come true
> With a spark from me or you.

Any marketer would be well served to commit this verse to memory and use it as the starting place for developing all marketing initiatives. As you work to develop your imaginative power through repeated Stimulus Response brainstorming sessions, your capacity to be a better marketer will increase significantly.

CHAPTER SUMMARY:

- Most corporate brainstorming exercises fail to produce out-of-the-box thinking as a result of the brainstorming methods used.
- The most common technique of brainstorming is brain-draining, which presupposes all great ideas already exist in one's head and all you need to do is somehow suck them out. This is a very short exercise for many.

- Stimulus Response brainstorming techniques have been validated to produce up to five times more "Big Ideas" than braindraining.
- It is critical to have both people who know everything about your business and those who know absolutely nothing about it in order to get great idea generation in your brainstorming session.
- Protect the newborns! There will be plenty of time to shoot down ideas after the session is over. I've never yet seen an organization that isn't adept at killing ideas. During the session, every idea is a great idea, no matter how ludicrous or whacked out it may be.

What Consumer Research Won't Tell You

FINDING STRATEGIC CONSUMER
INSIGHT OUTSIDE TRADITIONAL
RESEARCH METHODS

I WISH I HAD A DIME for every time someone called me up, bursting with excitement over some brilliant new product idea they just had. Inspiration strikes in some strange and wonderful places; washing the dog, looking for car keys, flipping the remote. The thought emerges, "Gee, I wish someone would invent something to make my dog smell better, or find my keys, or keep my remote handy." Presto, the idea is hatched, and the product begins to take shape.

Sometimes the concept is pretty good, and often the inventor has already dreamed up a catchy name, like "Smooch Your Pooch Sweet-Smelling Shampoo." But marketing a successful product should never begin with a focus group of one. The problem with many of these home-grown inventions is the inventor becomes so intoxicated with his idea that he starts building momentum before he tests the concept. He violates the most important rule of The Marketing Game: Honor Thy Consumer.

Everything in The Marketing Game begins and ends with the consumer. Before you can sell your product—before you even develop a product—you must understand what the consumer wants and design your offering to meet his or her needs. *You* may want a dog that smells like the Rose Queen, but do other consumers share your desire—and more importantly, will they pay for it? If your product concept is on the mark, then your job is simply finding the best way to communicate that you've got the goods consumers want. It's a basic concept: You can't create a need that isn't there, and you can't argue consumers out of what they want.

STANDARD RESEARCH METHODS

Knowing that the consumer is at the heart of every marketing decision, researchers have invented ingenious techniques to get in tune with the consumer, from focus groups, phone and mail surveys, concept testing, and in-home trial and mall intercepts to proprietary panels, Internet panels, and purchase diaries. Consumers have been ambushed, bar coded, spied upon, and even hypnotized in the quest for information. Companies pour millions of dollars into research every year to help them understand what consumers are thinking and how the marketplace is changing.

But here's the big question: If you are looking at the same studies and doing the same types of research as your key competition, how is it possible that you will gain insights different from—and better than—theirs? The answer: you can't.

CREATING INTELLECTUAL COMPETITIVE ADVANTAGE

Top companies understand this fact and force their marketing personnel to go further than standard methodologies, to gain broader and deeper consumer understanding. This is where they *create* competitive advantage. They teach their marketers how to beat competition at the consumer learning game, where all good marketing begins.

So how do the top companies get better information than the competition? By spending millions, right? Wrong.

Secrets of the Game

Top marketing companies teach their marketing personnel to gain strategic consumer insight through everyday life . . . watching TV commercials, browsing in stores, and talking with friends and families.

It sounds too ordinary to be true, doesn't it? Paying attention in everyday life is nowhere near as exciting as launching a half-million-dollar research project, complete with one-way mirrors and hidden video. But don't be fooled by the trappings of research. Top companies know the best way to gain real-world experience is in the real world, and they've made a science of it.

THE DISCIPLINE OF REAL-WORLD LEARNING

At Procter & Gamble, the company rule is if you travel to another city, for business or pleasure, you are required to visit at least three stores that carry your brands and competitive brands. You walk in, look around, analyze the situation, and submit a report of those visits upon your return. Why? One reason is to try to pick up any competitive activities or test-market products that have been slipped into a market, but the primary purpose is to teach the discipline of in-store, walk-around learning. There isn't much to inspire new thinking in the typical office cubicle, but a store is filled with a wealth of stimulation to help you develop wonderful new ideas.

P&G isn't the only company that thinks this way. In 1995, Coca-Cola held a marketing summit that brought together all two thousand of the worldwide Coke marketing personnel. The summit was three days of workshops, discussions, and lectures designed to teach the marketing team how to be better marketers.

How much of the meeting was spent talking about Coca-Cola and soft drinks? None. The entire three days was dedicated to analyzing other industries and other product categories!

David Stern, the commissioner of the NBA, gave a talk about the transformation of the league from the 1970s to the 1990s. James Carville and Mary Matalin discussed U.S. presidential political campaign strategy. A rocket-propulsion engineer gave a speech on the evolution of the jet engine. The group broke into teams and developed a marketing plan for the city of West Palm Beach, Florida.

Not one minute was spent talking about Coca-Cola or any other soft drinks. Why? Because you need to stimulate your mind with information and marketing strategies from other walks of life if you are going to develop breakthrough ideas for your business. You will not develop revolutionary thoughts sitting around conference tables, staring at your peers and your own products. You must vigorously pursue new stimulation and learning from sources far and wide, and then relate the learning and make connections back to your business.

IDEA CROSS-POLLINATION FROM OTHER PRODUCT CATEGORIES

When I worked at Walt Disney Home Video, I taught the real-world observation habit to my brand team. Every Friday for lunch I would pile them into my car and we'd drive to several stores to look around—not to shop, but to learn. We'd drop by the video departments and investigate new products, wander over into the toy and book areas, and then explore other parts of the store to see how different companies were marketing their wares.

We'd pick a different product category every week and go study it—detergents, deodorants, soup, motor oil, frozen foods—it didn't matter what the category was. We'd talk about the brand offerings, hypothesizing about the strategic insights that might have led to product development, their packaging, and different line extensions. We'd analyze which brands were doing it right and which were lagging. By performing this exercise on a weekly basis, we were forced to think strategically and stay alert about what was happening in a variety of different businesses. This information cross-pollinated our thinking and helped us recognize opportunities we otherwise would have missed.

For example, one Friday afternoon we found ourselves in the toy department at a Kmart store during a huge sale of Disney plush toys. Consumers were buying the toys by the armful. We noticed that no Winnie the Pooh characters were available. Several consumers were asking the store clerks if the Poohs were sold out. When we returned to the office we made a few calls to our friends in Disney Consumer Products and discovered that there were no Winnie the Pooh plush toys available to the Kmart store, because Sears held an exclusive twenty-five-year license on Pooh merchandise. We also discovered that this license was expiring in just a few months and would not be renewed.

That afternoon we began dreaming up an idea for our Winnie the Pooh videos. On the day that the Sears license expired, we launched a nationwide Pooh video and plush promotion, packaging our videos and Pooh plush characters together in a single box. They sold like hotcakes. All four SKU's turned up on the Top 10 Video Bestseller list. In just three weeks, we sold twenty times more Winnie the Pooh videos than we had in the previous twelve months. By being aware of an unmet consumer need in a completely different product category (plush toys), we were able to produce huge profits for our video division.

INSIGHT REQUIRES CORRECT INTERPRETATION

An important thing to remember is that consumer insight is only as good as its interpretation. How many times have you walked out of a meeting with a group of people and then had an argument over what was said? Everyone heard the same conversation, yet many came away with a different point of view: "I thought so and so said this" or "I thought so and so said that."

The same dynamic is true in the art of interpreting consumer insight. Your research probably won't produce a clear, single message, shining like a beacon from the heavens to guide your way. Much of what you learn will be open to interpretation, and many different interpretations may be legitimate. Your challenge is to resist the "eureka!" impulse of latching on to one message (usually the one you *want* to believe) and ignoring the other, possibly contradictory, bits of information. It is important to keep an open mind and consider the information from many different viewpoints to try and understand the full spectrum of what you have heard or seen. The more open you are, the better you will be at making connections between your observations and your business.

I remember a P&G colleague of mine coming home from a business trip to Seattle back in 1987. In his walk-around observations he picked up on a new trend of sit-down coffeehouses developing in that area. That "trend" is now a huge nationwide chain called Starbucks. You might guess that the Folgers brand people looking at the information concluded that Folgers business was selling coffee in grocery stores, so they dismissed Starbucks as noncompetitive. What do you suppose that noncompetitive brand has done to Folgers volume over the last dozen years now that the Starbucks chain has over fifteen hundred stores and has spawned a new line of grocery-store coffee?

AND THE HUMBLE SHALL INHERIT THE KNOWLEDGE

Many marketers have a tremendous arrogance about themselves and their brands. They somehow believe that they are smarter than everybody else and that the people working for their competition are bozos. They mistakenly think that analyzing competition can offer very little insight about how they can be better marketers.

To the contrary, the smartest thing you can do is to learn everything you can about your competition and the product category in which you compete. You need to know what product benefits are driving consumers. And if you *are* a genius, your research will only confirm that fact.

Secrets of the Game

Top marketing companies have adopted a new mental model about competitive understanding to break through the status quo and advance to a higher plane of consumer insight. This new mental model is called Knowledge Mining.

Knowledge Mining is an in-store learning exercise to develop profound understanding about what steers consumer purchase decisions within a product category. It analyzes the different product attributes and consumer benefits offered throughout the category by various products and helps marketers define the qualities that lead to purchase. Just as important, it reveals which product benefits are least associated with product purchase in the category.

Through the Knowledge Mining exercise, this in-store learning becomes a strategic road map that paints a clear picture of the consumer's psychological landscape. What is he or she responding to? What benefits or attributes tempt a consumer to pick up the product and put it in their shopping cart? Why are so many products in the same category ignored?

Naturally, if you understand the benefits and product attributes that drive purchase within your category, you've taken a quantum leap in understanding your consumer. Unfortunately, very few marketers have this depth of insight. Most just jump into the fray and start concocting as many marketing efforts as the budget will bear—coupons, price reductions, advertising, promotions. They perform what I call random acts of marketing, trying this, trying that, learning along the bumpy way. They have no clear strategic knowledge or vision to guide them, because they don't really know *for sure* why consumers buy their product or competing products.

Knowledge Mining is such an effective and powerful tool, I've detailed a step-by-step guide on how to do it yourself. It takes a little time to master, but the results are invaluable. I hope you'll take full advantage of the exercise—you'll be delighted, and probably surprised, with what you learn.

THE GOLD STANDARD

KNOWLEDGE MINING EXERCISE

To perform a Knowledge Mining exercise that develops the guiding strategic principles for a product category, you do the following:

Step 1: *Assemble a list of all the product attributes and consumer benefits you believe drive consumer purchase in the category.*

Where can you find this? It's easy. It's all waiting for you in stores. Go look at the product descriptions that different marketers use on their packaging for all sorts of different items. It's all there. Make a list by writing down all of the benefits and product attributes the different products use to sell the consumer. If at all possible, try to find out which items are the best-sellers and which are not selling well, as this will help you later in the process. This process works for any business, from bike shops to private schools.

Step 2: *Take the "Product Attributes and Consumer Benefits" list and type it up. Make thirty-one copies (we'll call this our survey sheet). Next, randomly select thirty different items in your product category. One by one, using a separate survey sheet for each product, read the packages and dissect the attributes and benefits—put a check mark next to each of the attributes or benefits on your survey sheet that is used in selling that product to consumers.*

Step 3: *Take your thirty product-survey sheets and sort them in rank order, best-selling products to worst selling products.*

If you can find sales data to help you, that would be extremely useful—but it isn't critical. Do the best you can in sorting the thirty sheets according to your perception of best-selling to worst-selling. Often times you can tell by looking at the store shelves which products are selling and which are not. Put the best-sellers on top, the worst-sellers on the bottom.

Step 4: *Write on each of the sheets in the top right-hand corner a number. On the best-seller sheet you should write the number 30. On the next-best-seller sheet, 29, and so on until you get to the worst-seller, which will be 1.*

Step 5: *Take the remaining clean copy of your survey sheet. Go through the thirty filled-out surveys one-by-one. For each attribute and benefit associated with each product, write on your new survey sheet next to that attribute the number you listed in the right-hand corner (the best-seller/worst-seller numbers from 30 to 1).*

Step 6: *Add up the totals for each product attribute and benefit.*

The resulting grand totals reveal which of the product attributes and benefits are most associated with products that sell (the highest numbers) and those that are not (the lowest numbers), revealing which are driving consumer purchase, and exposing those that are not.

Through analysis of these findings, you will be able to develop a list of guiding principles for your product category. On the flip side, you will also see which attributes to avoid in your product marketing efforts.

THE ASSUMPTION TRAP

Even the world's most successful marketing companies periodically fall into the assumption trap, confident that they know enough to sell their product without pursuing new information to challenge their assumptions. I was snagged in the trap only a few months into my first brand management job at Procter & Gamble, working on the fledgling Citrus Hill Orange Juice brand. The brand was struggling, a distant third in the race against Tropicana and Minute Maid. P&G held leadership in about 90 percent of the product categories in which it did business. The third-place status of Citrus Hill had put the brand directly in the cross-hairs of senior management. They wanted Citrus Hill to ascend to the top of the orange juice heap—*fast.*

The brand group and research team at the Winton Hill lab were frantically working on what they do best—product upgrades. Their consumer research had revealed that consumers wanted great-tasting orange juice. The lab team developed and improved Citrus Hill until the juice won blind taste tests against all competitors—particularly Tropicana and Minute Maid. "Aha!" we crowed. "Now we can beat the competition. We have the best-tasting orange juice in the world."

We invested heavily in a new advertising campaign to tell consumers that Citrus Hill tasted better than any other orange juice and prepared to declare victory. Management was giddy with anticipation, and expectations ballooned. The new advertising aired. Everyone was ready with tall glasses of juice in hand, awaiting the next AC Nielsen sales reports to toast our triumph. The day approached, the envelope was opened and the mood suddenly darkened. Nothing had happened to sales. Consumers not only hadn't stampeded the juice aisles to pick up this new super juice; they hadn't even taken a sip.

The knee-jerk response from management was that the advertising copy wasn't delivering the message effectively. As often happens, the blame fell on the ad agency. Copy testing of advertising became a self-fulfilling prophecy, and so the brand invested more money to create more advertising to tell consumers that Citrus Hill tasted great. Again with much hoopla, the new ads began airing.

One month later, the same result. No consumer response. "How could this be?" the brand group kept asking. "All of our consumer research tells us that 'good taste' is the most important thing to consumers in choosing their orange juice." This cycle of trying to reposition Citrus Hill based on taste preference continued for several more years, until finally P&G surrendered and pulled the brand from the marketplace.

WHAT CONSUMERS SAY VERSUS WHAT THEY MEAN

Why did Citrus Hill fail? If you reviewed all of the traditional research, the positioning of Citrus Hill lined up precisely with what consumers were telling the brand group—"good taste" was the most important thing in selecting their juice brand; "freshness," "good nutrition for the family," and "orange juice helps brighten the morning" were secondary benefits. All these promises were built into the Citrus Hill positioning and expressed in the advertising copy and on the packaging. The brand group had used every logical and methodical tool in the P&G research arsenal to understand why consumers should prefer Citrus Hill, yet came up empty.

What the brand group finally came to recognize is that purchase decisions aren't always based on the rational criteria consumers offer in focus groups and research. Among competitive products, there is often very little difference in quality and product performance. This parity is especially true in categories in which the product is a commodity—such as orange juice or coffee. In this instance, while "good taste" was very important, most consumers didn't think their current orange juice tasted bad or needed to taste better. Consumers believed "100 percent orange juice" is "100 percent orange juice"—so how could there be a difference in taste between the brands? The Citrus Hill "better taste" positioning didn't strike a chord of credibility. Most consumers felt the brand they were currently buying tasted great. So consumers weren't lying—taste was the most important thing to them. Nevertheless, that wasn't the differentiating criterion upon which their purchase decision rested.

Ignoring the segment of buyers who based their purchase decision only on low price (not a profitable segment in which to be a player), the brand team came to learn that "freshness" was the product benefit upon which most consumers made their ultimate purchase decision. Many consumers believed that fresh juice was better juice—and they didn't believe that juices made from concentrate, like Citrus Hill, could be as healthy or fresh tasting.

The competitive "fresh," not-from-concentrate juices knew they had a consumer advantage and played it up—even though, in reality, the processing and freezing methods of Citrus Hill made it more nutritious than many "fresh-picked" brands. Category leader Tropicana's advertising featured an anonymous hand plucking a ripe orange from a tree and inserting a straw, a pair of lips sucking on the straw with obvious pleasure, and the tag line "You just can't pick a better juice—for just picked freshness, pick Tropicana Pure Premium." Game over. Citrus Hill did not have a "fresh picked" product offering, and Tropicana had the perfect product and positioning, aligned to the consumers' desire for "fresh" orange juice.

Had the Knowledge Mining methodology been developed at that time, Citrus Hill might have had a fighting chance to develop a not-from-concentrate product before millions had been wasted on research, product development, and advertising on the losing promise of "great taste."

> ### Secrets of the Game
> You must understand the hierarchy of the product attributes and benefits that drive consumer purchase within your product category *before* making any marketing decisions. You must prove conventional wisdom and reveal illusions and fallacies through the development of guiding strategic principles.

The benefits of Knowledge Mining are many. The insight gained can be used to ensure that you optimize your product positioning and that advertising messages are focused on the product attributes and benefits that drive consumer purchase. It can tell you the best way to communicate with consumers, guide new product development and steer promotion planning. Best of all, Knowledge Mining is *free*. You can do it in a couple of days of just wandering around stores.

Being a better marketer means you have to be smarter and work harder than everybody else. Consumer insight is tough. You have to dig to find it. But it pays off in the end with better marketing plans that can truly make your products different, better, and special to consumers.

Give it a shot. Start looking at the world more strategically and analytically. I know for a fact you'll have fun. It's a great way to keep your mind sharp.

CHAPTER SUMMARY

- Consumer understanding is the foundation of all marketing. You must go beyond standard research methodologies in order to get learning that is better than your competitors'.
- Before you can sell your product—before you even develop a product—you must understand what the consumer wants and design your offering to meet his or her needs.
- Top marketers teach their marketing personnel to gain strategic consumer insight through everyday life—watching TV commercials, browsing in stores, and talking with friends and family.

- The best way to stimulate new ideas is to cross-pollinate and transfer ideas from other product categories.
- An open mind is critical to interpreting consumer understanding. Resist the temptation to latch onto what you want to hear, discarding other, contradictory information.
- Knowledge Mining is a terrific in-store learning exercise that can advance marketers to a higher plane of consumer insight by developing operating principles within a product category. The results of the exercise paint a clear picture of the consumer psychological landscape.
- You must understand the hierarchy of product attributes that drive consumer purchase within your product category, and focus on those when delivering your message to consumers.

The Best-Kept Secret of Branding

DEVELOPING A RELEVANT YET
UNEXPECTED STRATEGIC
POSITIONING

Suppose you are responsible for developing a marketing campaign for a terrific new car. Where do you begin? You could tell consumers about its luxurious interior and its sporty new look. You could boast about horsepower, safety, handling ability, roominess, or high-tech engineering. Or you could create a product image to appeal to a particular type of driver. Is it big and luxurious like a Cadillac, or irreverent fun like a Miata? Is it as safe and practical as a minivan, or as zippy and well-made as a Volkswagen Beetle?

If you were to produce a TV commercial about this car, you'd have thirty seconds to tell consumers why they should buy it. If your commercial was any good, it would define *who you want to buy your car* and *what the most compelling reasons are that they should want it*. You don't have enough time to say that the car is luxurious, roomy, has fine Corinthian leather, is fast, sporty, fun to drive, well engineered and sounds great—and you probably can't appeal to everyone watching the commercial. So before you review the first commercial storyboard, you would have to make tough choices about what your product is and who it's for.

The way marketers define what it is they want to say about their product and who they are targeting to buy it is accomplished through the development of what's called a strategic positioning statement. This statement is the foundation of all of your consumer communications, including advertising, pricing, packaging, merchandising, promotions, public relations—anything that reaches the consumer will be shaped by this statement. But despite its far-reaching effects, it isn't an opus; it is a simple, clearly stated sentence—yes, just *one* sentence—that defines whom to target and what to say.

Think you need more than just one sentence to contain your thoughts? Then you're trying to say too much, and your message is surely becoming diluted. If you can't say it simply, your consumer can't understand it.

THE ART AND DISCIPLINE OF POSITIONING

Successful marketing companies hone the development of strategic positioning statements to a fine art. They have files full of case studies to indicate what type of strategies work and what type fail. And let's face it, product managers at these companies are very busy people. So how long do you suppose they spend on that one little positioning statement? Forty-five minutes? An entire afternoon?

Try months. Part of the effort is agonizing over every word to make sure that the strategic positioning statement is powerful, compelling, and specific. The real work and worry comes in analyzing the roads not taken. If you position your lipstick as old-time glamour, it can't also be youthful and new, so you'd better be sure that glamour has the bigger audience and stronger appeal. If you position sunglasses as the choice of the stars, you can't also be unbreakable sports lenses or the most comfortable fit. These difficult choices make strategy development the most troublesome task in marketing. It involves more than creative thinking in a vacuum; you must collect and analyze information and consumer learning from every available source, then boil it all down to a simple, clear, consumer-focused positioning that will maximize your product's consumer appeal. Everything the consumer knows and believes about the product is driven from the strategic positioning statement. There is no margin for error.

THE ABC'S OF STRATEGIC POSITIONING

The thinking you invest in your strategic positioning statement is hard work, but the statement itself is as easy as ABC.

Audience

Benefit

Compelling reason why (this is actually sentence #2 of the statement)

It's that easy. Undisciplined marketing managers try to hedge their bets by writing the positioning statement as broadly as possible. They hate to make choices about their target audience (wouldn't *all* consumers love this?) or their key benefit (it slices, dices, does the dishes, and walks the dog!). The road not taken haunts them, so they position their product squarely at the fork—it's a great product for every consumer and every occasion!

Resist this trap. If your product stands for everything, it stands for nothing. Don't be afraid to define your product in the clearest, most intriguing terms possible. Only then will consumers appreciate your benefit and become loyal to your product.

Secrets of the Game

Top marketers go beyond traditional thinking when developing their strategic positioning statements. They push to find a clear, *relevant yet unexpected* strategic positioning statement that creates a meaningful point of difference and competitive advantage for their product.

The best way to comprehend the power of the *relevant yet unexpected* idea is to look at the results of some great contemporary marketing campaigns that capture this concept.

One of my favorites is that of Dow Bathroom Cleaner. You've seen the commercials for years, with the little Scrubbing Bubbles racing around the bathtub to give it a clean shine. The strategic positioning statement for Dow Bathroom Cleaner is likely something like this: "For homemakers, Dow Bathroom Cleaner is the easy way to get a great, clean shine for your tub and tile. That's because only Dow Bathroom Cleaner contains Scrubbing Bubbles, which cut through the dirt and grime clean to the shine, so you don't have to!"

Note the ABC's of the strategy as follows:

a. *Target audience:* homemakers
b. *Unique benefit:* the easy way to get a great, clean shine for your tub and tile
c. *Compelling reason why:* because only Dow Bathroom Cleaner contains Scrubbing Bubbles, which cut through the dirt and grime so you won't have to!

This brand positioning has been effective at keeping Dow Bathroom Cleaner in a market leadership position for years, and effectively creates a distinct point-of-difference through the use of Scrubbing Bubbles—a relevant yet unexpected way to address consumers about the product's efficacy. Think about every other household cleaner. Does any bring a clearer visual as to what the product does than Dow Bathroom Cleaner? No. Dow's brand team has created a distinct and defensible point of difference by talking about their product in the most intriguing terms possible.

Toyota recently introduced a set of TV commercials that are unique to the car category. One commercial features a shiny new car parked in a lot, with a child's voice begging Mom to let him buy the car, just like a four-year-old begs his Mom for a candy bar in the grocery store. The positioning statement that led to this advertising was likely something like this: "For male car buyers ages 18–45, shiny new Toyota cars are the ultimate in desirability. That's because they are designed with a sense of playfulness that awakens the inner child and reminds us of how much fun driving a brand-new car can be."

Note the ABC's of the strategy as follows:

a. *Target audience:* consumers ages 18–45
b. *Unique benefit:* Toyota cars are the ultimate in desirability.
c. *Compelling reason why:* because Toyota cars are designed with a sense of playfulness that awakens the inner child and reminds us of how much fun driving a brand-new car can be.

Now think how differently the advertising would look if the positioning strategy had been this: "For unmarried males ages 18+, Toyota cars are the cool toy that makes you irresistible to women. That's because any man looks better in a hot new Toyota."

Analyze both strategies. Does it define the target audience? Does it communicate a clear consumer benefit? Is the "reason why" compelling and believable? Notice that both are *relevant yet unexpected*. These two radically different positioning statements define the same product in very different ways. So why did the brand team at Toyota choose the first strategy? Because that's the one their consumer research led them to believe would produce the most sales.

DEVELOPING A UNIQUE MARKET POSITION

To delve deeper into "relevant yet unexpected," let's think about Michelin tires. Recall their advertising campaign featuring a baby inside a Michelin tire, with the copy "Michelin: Because so much is riding on your tires." The strategic positioning statement that led to this execution could be: "For parents with young children, Michelin is the safest tire you can buy to protect the lives of your loved ones. That's because dual-wall Michelin tires perform exceptionally well in all weather conditions, gripping the road so you won't have accidents."

Michelin has a specific target, a clear benefit, and a compelling, believable reason why. Through the insightful strategic decision to use babies as the way to define your loved ones, Michelin came up with a relevant yet unexpected way to create consumer appeal versus other tire companies.

Now, consider for a moment how different the advertising would look and feel if the strategy were something like this: "For adults 18–45, Michelin tires give you the best performance in any driving situation. That's because dual-wall Michelin tires perform exceptionally well in all weather conditions, gripping the road so you won't have accidents."

The second strategy could easily—and logically—have been chosen as the positioning statement. After all, it has the same "reason why" and all the consumer research probably revealed that performance is a compelling consumer benefit. But, alas, this is pretty much how every competitive tire brand is positioned.

So why did the marketing team at Michelin choose the first statement? Because their research, their observations, and their gut instincts told them that the strongest emotional tie consumers have to their tires involves safety for the children they chauffeur (think of all those "Baby on Board" signs that used to be so popular and you'll have to agree). Sure, consumers want good performance, but most of them aren't revving fine-tuned sports cars on slippery mountain roads. They're too busy carpooling or taking the kids to soccer practice.

Here's a fun exercise: Watch a television commercial; then try to restate what you saw in the words of a strategic positioning statement and analyze how well the strategy works. You'll be amazed at the number of bad marketing campaigns you will discover—ones that have no clear target, no clearly stated consumer benefit, no believable "reason why." Only rarely will you jump out of your chair and see one that is exceptionally adept at executing a relevant yet unexpected strategy—and nine times out of ten that product will be a category leader!

DEFINING A TARGET AUDIENCE

I can't think of any product that can be marketed to the population en masse. Even water has an image and an audience, depending on the brand. If you want to deliver your message, you have to know to whom it is you're talking. The target is usually described in demographic terms (teens, young adults 18–35, parents with children living at home, moms with young children ages 2–9). Or you can describe your target in psychographic terms (football fans, outdoor types, animal lovers, homemakers, working women). The target audience is the group of consumers that has the greatest potential for purchasing your product. Of course, you will nearly always find some consumers outside your target that also purchase your product. Don't include them in your definition. A target audience doesn't exclude other consumers; it merely describes your core group. You must be specific and knowledgeable about your core target to develop effective consumer communications.

For example, consider Diet Coke. Both men and women drink Diet Coke, but the brand targets the product to women ages 18–35. Why? Simply because that segment of the population consumes the most diet soft drinks. Furthermore, the smaller slices of other demographic groups who also drink diet soda (men on a diet, older women) drink it for the same reason as the core group; they want a refreshing, low-calorie beverage. By marketing to the core group, the product benefit and personality are maximized—it's youthful, healthful, sassy, sexy. These are the attributes that the core group—and a few members of other groups—value most. So despite the fact that other segments of the population also drink Diet Coke, the brand group has focused all marketing efforts on the core target group, and the noncore consumers are merely a bonus.

CONSUMER BENEFITS

The most important piece of the strategy is stating the consumer benefit—what the consumer receives in return for buying the product. This is often where the marketing breakdown occurs. The consumer benefit can be functional (cleaner, brighter, fresher, more power, lasts longer—P&G brands are the kings of functional benefits) or psychological (feel refreshed, feel sexy and beautiful, have fun, gain freedom, no hassles).

Secrets of the Game

The failure to clearly state a compelling consumer benefit is the biggest problem in marketing today. Companies spend millions of dollars to tell consumers of their product, but they don't close the sale—they don't communicate a compelling consumer benefit for buying it.

My most memorable TV commercial that falls into this trap is one that airs constantly for the prescription medication Zyban. It says something like this: "Now you have another choice. Zyban. Prescription medicine available from your doctor. Ask your doctor if Zyban is right for you."

OK, I give. What does Zyban do? What is the consumer benefit? I've seen TV spots, airport billboards, and magazine ads for this brand, but not one of them tells me what medical condition Zyban treats, only that it's a prescription medication. In my opinion, they're wasting money. If Zyban can't tell consumers what benefit they will get for buying the product, they shouldn't spend the money on advertising!

PSYCHOLOGICAL CONSUMER BENEFITS

Psychological benefits are much more touchy-feely than functional benefits. In advertising jargon, this type of approach is known as "sell the sizzle, not the steak." In other words, focus on the most appealing benefit of the product (often, how the product makes you feel), not on what the product actually is.

Disney does a brilliant job of tapping into the psychological benefits of its classic videos; instead of simply selling tapes of *Snow White* or *Cinderella,* for example, they remind us of how it felt to believe in the magic of those stories as a child. Special K cereal does a great job with advertising showing a beautiful young woman modeling sexy dresses. The ads clearly imply that if you eat Special K for breakfast each morning, you can look this good—a powerful promise—while completely ignoring the usual cereal benefits (doesn't get soggy in milk, tastes great, and so on). Pantene shampoo has a campaign that combines both functional and psychological benefits: "It's your time to shine." This clever positioning overtly celebrates the feeling of confidence and success while subtly reinforcing the product benefit (beautiful, shiny hair).

DEVELOPING A BELIEVABLE "REASON WHY"

Consumers are logical. If you say something that makes sense, they will believe you. If you say something that doesn't make sense or sounds like you're stretching the truth, they will be skeptical. It's that simple.

Secrets of the Game

The compelling "reason why" is the most critical piece of a strategic positioning statement. It must clearly tell the consumer why/how your product can deliver the benefit you are claiming, and the rationale must make sense. While it seems like a simple idea, this is another area where many marketers drop the ball.

Citibank tested the strength of the "reason why" with their Citishopper service offered with Visa and Mastercard accounts. In the first group, telemarketers called consumers and offered the Citishopper service, telling them that "Citishopper can find you the lowest prices on over 200,000 name-brand items." They explained the consumer benefit but failed to offer a plausible "reason why." Only a small percentage of consumers signed up. In the second group they added a "reason why" statement. Here, the telemarketers said "Citishopper can find you the lowest prices on over 200,000 name-brand items. That's because our computers continually monitor prices at over 50,000 retailers nationwide, ensuring that you get the lowest price available anywhere." With only that change in the script, enrollment increased significantly. Why? Because Citibank told shoppers of the benefit (finding the lowest prices nationwide), then backed it up with a plausible "reason why" (continual monitoring of pricing at over fifty thousand retailers nationwide).

THE POWER OF PASSION

The final and most powerful part of the positioning puzzle is to develop the "relevant yet unexpected" element to create meaningful differentiation in the mind of the consumer.

Secrets of the Game

To develop a successful "relevant yet unexpected" strategic positioning, you must align the consumer benefit better than any other competitor, with the most relevant consumer passion point.

A passion point is a characteristic within your product category that evokes a strong consumer reaction—in other words, a characteristic upon which consumers have a definite point of view. You must effectively communicate your understanding of the passion point to consumers and convince them that your product best delivers that benefit.

Keep in mind: *Passion points do not equal emotion.* Consumers can have a passionate opinion about something while not having an emotional reaction. Think back to the Toyota example used earlier. The consumer passion point was "a car is a grown-up's toy." That's not an emotional reaction, but it is a passionate feeling to many. For the Michelin example, "protecting the lives of your loved ones" is the passion point.

This strategic principle is the cornerstone of success. Nothing you will ever do will be as important as developing your strategic positioning, and the key to developing an effective "relevant yet unexpected" strategic positioning is to find and integrate the most relevant passion point.

WHY PASSION POINTS ARE ESSENTIAL

The biggest change in consumer purchase behavior in the past ten years is that most no longer base purchase decisions on product performance alone; instead, consumers are using criteria that combine product performance and passion points. Some of this shift can be credited to evolving technology that has enabled many different products to achieve high-quality performance. You don't have to buy a Wham-O frisbee anymore; plenty of flying discs work just as well. Without a significant difference in product quality, consumers use the passion criterion as the differentiating factor that leads to the purchase decision.

Like most matters of the heart, a passion criterion often isn't based in reality. Brand loyalty—or brand avoidance—can be triggered by overall brand equity ("this company always makes good products"), by childhood memories of Mom using the product, by a bad experience with another product in the category, or by any number of associations or experiences. Digging to find the most relevant passion point can be the most difficult and challenging task you will face in developing a strategy.

THE GOLD STANDARD

Passion points were the key to successfully repositioning the Winnie the Pooh videos at Disney Home Video. In 1992, there were fourteen Pooh video titles available in stores. Sales were dreadful. Pooh was getting stomped by Barney the dinosaur. Four of the Pooh videos were in a product line entitled "Walt Disney Mini-Classics." These were the classic Pooh videos you remember from childhood: *Winnie the Pooh and the Honey Tree, Winnie the Pooh and Tigger Too, Winnie the Pooh and a Day For Eeyore, Winnie the Pooh and a Blustery Day.* The other ten videos were in a product line entitled "The New Adventures of Winnie the Pooh." These were compilation tapes, each containing two episodes taken from the Saturday morning cartoons that aired for several years on the ABC network.

At the time, Disney used what I call the "Field of Dreams" marketing approach. They believed that if you put anything with the Disney name out on the store shelves, it would sell. They applied no marketing discipline within the video division. No strategy, no positioning. The brand groups spent all of their time designing packaging and putting out new videos, paying no attention to titles they had previously released.

A transition period began after my arrival. The Disney creative well was beginning to run dry. Disney Home Video had exhausted nearly all of the offerings in the studio vaults. Our task as a brand team was to figure out how to stimulate consumer interest in buying tapes that were already available in stores—like Winnie the Pooh.

When we began the research to try to figure out why Pooh wasn't selling, we unearthed many fascinating tidbits. First, moms still loved Pooh. We had a solid consumer base and interest in Pooh—that was the good news. The bad news was our titles and packaging—"Mini-Classics" and "The New Adventures of Winnie the Pooh"—were turning moms off. Why? To them, "Mini-Classics" meant "short in length" and "not as good as a Disney classic." The title of "The New Adventures of Winnie the Pooh" was bothering Mom, too, because she didn't think of Pooh as an adventurer. The packaging in both cases was inadvertently sending negative messages.

Further research revealed what connected moms with Pooh—the passion points. They remembered him fondly from the storybooks they loved as children and that they now read to their own kids. They loved the gentleness and innocence of Pooh and his friends Tigger, Piglet, Eeyore, and Christopher Robin. Moms believed that Pooh stories taught their children good values—sharing, trust, caring, friendship, and love. They were pleased that their children liked to play along and pretend with Pooh.

We had found the holy grail. We immediately recalled all of the Pooh videos from stores, creating a panic attack that garnered some media attention and helped drive sales to clear off the store shelves. We began a repackaging and repositioning initiative, aligning the product with the strategic passion points.

Three months later, we released Pooh under three new product positionings: "Winnie the Pooh Storybook Classics," "Pooh Learning," and "Pooh Playtime." In effect, all we had done was repackage existing product, but sales soared. In the first year after the relaunch, Pooh videos sold over thirty times what they had sold the year before. As of this writing, sales continue to increase, five years since the transition. The product didn't change, but the strategic positioning aligned to the passion points of consumers paved the road to success.

WHERE TO FIND PASSION POINTS

In the words of *Star Wars* guru Obi-Wan Kenobi, "you have the power within." Inside yourself is the best place to begin looking for passion points. What are your reactions to the product? Try to remember the first time you used it. Ask your friends what they think when they use the product, or a competitive product. Ask your mom what she thinks. Try to learn everything about what normal, everyday people think about the product and the product category. Try to find pet peeves. You don't need focus groups to do this. Look at the grocery shelf or the consumer marketplace in which you compete. Is there an unfulfilled need that no product is addressing? Is some competitive product addressing a consumer need better than yours? How can you capture a proprietary positioning within the category that is meaningful to consumers and provides a competitive edge?

To illustrate, let's look at the airline industry. As a consumer, what are the relevant and meaningful product attributes that consumers use to decide in choosing their airline? If you do standard consumer research, the list, in order of importance, will look something like this:

- Low fares
- Recognized carrier (United, Delta, American, etc.) w/good safety record
- Convenient flight schedules
- Good frequent flyer program
- Friendly service (check-in counters, boarding procedures, flight attendants)
- Adequate leg room/seat width
- Good food
- Good movies/in-flight entertainment
- Careful baggage handling
- Perks for the "best" frequent fliers

Now that you've got your basic research, you can dig for the passion points.

Assume that you are a marketing manager for a major airline. Put on your strategic analyst hat and look at the above list. What attributes are pretty much at parity between most of the major airlines? Are there any attributes about which you perceive a distinct point of difference that could be or has been carved out for one airline in particular? Do any of these attributes fall into the "pet peeves" category for you or for others that you know?

My pet peeves with airlines are seat width and leg room. Either my rump is expanding or the seats are getting smaller, and the row in front of me keeps inching its way back. On a recent flight, I literally had only two inches of breathing room between my nose and the seat back in front of me when that passenger reclined!

If I were to develop a strategic positioning statement for my own airline, it would probably be something like this: "For business flyers, Eric's Airline is offering widebody service on every flight, even if you're skinny. That's because on every Eric's Airline plane, we've installed seats wide enough for all bottoms to comfortably fit, with ample leg room, ensuring a comfortable, relaxing flight."

Relevant yet unexpected. The play on the word "widebody" gives the positioning an edge without being insulting. Now think about the current tag-line positionings of the major airlines:

United Is Rising
American: Something Special in the Air
Delta: On Top of the World
Southwest: Freedom to Fly
Eric's Airline: Widebody Service on Every Flight

Which of these positionings are consumer propositions that communicate to the consumer that the airline is different, better, and special—relevant yet unexpected? Only Eric's Airline. The big boys are so caught up in trying to craft a corporate image, they've fallen into the trap of conventionalism and sameness. Nothing about their positionings separates them from the competition.

Different, better, and *special.* Everything communicates. That's why you must create a "relevant yet unexpected" positioning statement to define how you address the consumer. It will separate you from the competition and define how your product is better.

This principle applies to every business in the world. If you are selling something, you need a positioning statement to define why consumers should buy from you instead of someone else. Even a business as small as a local deli can derive benefits from developing a positioning statement. Just think for a moment about how much more appealing it would be to eat at a deli that positioned itself in the following way:

> For lunch-time consumers, Joe's deli features "the taste of freshness."
>
> That's because Joe's deli uses only fresh meats and vegetables, and all of our sandwiches are handmade to order, guaranteeing the freshest and tastiest sandwich in town.

Such a positioning, even if it was only communicated with in-store signage, would create a distinct point of difference that is meaningful to consumers, and give them a reason to eat at Joe's deli rather than any other.

Don't ever underestimate the power of simple, clearly focused communication. No matter what business you are in, if you can clearly define what it is you are selling, and if you can craft your positioning in a relevant yet unexpected way that taps a passion point for consumers, you will have created for yourself a brand name.

Developing a positioning statement is hard work combined with a good sprinkling of insight and creativity. Slow down, take a deep breath, and commit yourself to the process. It takes time to find the right positioning for your product. Even Pooh, a bear of very little brain, would sit down at his Thoughtful Spot from time to time and say, "I think this may require some . . . thinking." Find your Thoughtful Spot, do your thinking, and watch your business develop a form, an identity, and a personality right before your eyes through the creation of a strategic positioning statement.

CHAPTER SUMMARY

- What you want to say to consumers about your product and who you are targeting it to, are accomplished through the development of a strategic positioning statement.
- This statement is the foundation of all your consumer communications, including advertising, pricing, packag-

ing, merchandising, promotions, public relations—anything that reaches the consumer about your product.

- The statement itself is as easy as ABC:
  - Audience
  - Benefit
  - Compelling reason why
- The best marketers find "relevant yet unexpected" ways to position their product that make it stand out in the marketplace.
- Product benefits are usually either psychological or functional.
- The "reason why" tells the consumer how your product can deliver the benefit you claim. Be sure it is believable.
- Finding a consumer passion point is the ultimate way to differentiate your product from the competition. It can make your product stand for something that is meaningful and compelling to the consumer.

The New Products Underworld

INCREASING YOUR CHANCES OF
NEW PRODUCT SUCCESS

W ORKING ON NEW PRODUCTS is the sexiest job in the marketing world. Here you have the opportunity to experience the exhilaration that the great inventors like Benjamin Franklin, Thomas Edison, and others must have felt, bringing new innovations to life, creating something from the vast void of nothingness, using only visionary insights to bring thought to creation.

The dream of every new product manager is to originate a great idea that can catapult business into the sales stratosphere. Unfortunately for most, this dream is about as close as they get to nirvana. It is far more likely that they will end up feeling like Dr. Frankenstein, with a mutated idea that might have seemed pretty at the start, but ultimately must be destroyed in order to save mankind (or more likely, the company's bottom line).

Academic studies claim that eight out of every ten new products introduced into the marketplace fail within the first twelve months. Despite these daunting odds, nearly every major corporation continues to invest millions of dollars each year in new product research and development, searching for the big idea that will propel their business into the next decade.

THE SECRETS OF NEW PRODUCT CONCEPT DEVELOPMENT

There are a few simple yet elegant principles that have been found over time to be critical to new product success.

Focus on Consumer Benefits, Not Product Function

The biggest learning when creating new product concepts is to push the consumer benefits and don't focus on the product functions. Consumers buy benefits. They don't care about the nuts and bolts.

To illustrate the principle, a local mother who was starting up a child performance group recently came to me to ask for marketing help. She was having a tough time attracting kids to sign up for her program. The name of the group was Sunshine Generation. In the group, children learned to sing, dance, and offer community service by performing in public at various functions.

The advertising she had been using called out "Join a Kid's Performance Group" and detailed the functions children would learn: singing, dancing, music theory, and performing in front of audiences. She was featuring all of the functions of the group, but not mentioning the benefits kids and parents would receive from participation.

I helped her develop a new strategic positioning targeted to moms, encouraging them to sign their kids up for Sunshine Generation to "Give Your Child a Chance to Shine"—the benefit mom and the child would receive. What mom doesn't want to give her child a chance to shine? The new ad copy highlighted all the benefits the child would receive from participating: he or she would develop talents (singing, dancing, performing), build self-confidence, learn to work together with others, and offer community service. Enrollment skyrocketed after the change. We sold the benefits, not the functions.

Far too often, product marketers get hung up on telling you how the product does what it does instead of telling you what benefits you'll get from using it.

Think about tire commercials that spend twenty-five seconds detailing how their innovative five-layered sidewall tires and unique tread designs channel away water to grip the road. OK, sounds good to me, but I'm no tire engineer. They could draw up just about anything and show it to me, and I'd have to agree with it. These companies have their priorities backward. They would be better off spending their time telling me up front about how their tires are the safest in the world, and that by using them on my car I'm showing my loved ones that I really care about their safety. That's the benefit I want to buy. The five-layered sidewalls and tread designs are the "reasons why" the tire can deliver the benefit. The "reason why" is important, but the benefits must come first.

The Importance of a Plausible "Reason Why"

New products must have not only a compelling consumer benefit but also a clear explanation of how the product will deliver that benefit. Consumers are skeptical about new product claims, so you have to use what I call "kitchen logic" in your reasoning. Keep it simple and understandable. Don't try to pull the wool over the consumers' eyes with fluff and hyperbole. Tell them in plain language in a way they can understand.

For example, which one of these "reasons why" sounds most plausible to you (using the rule of kitchen logic) in explaining how a liquid detergent will get your clothes clean:

1) New Clothes Clean detergent gets your clothes cleaner than any other detergent! That's because Clothes Clean has a secret patented formula that unlocks microdirt in clothes fibers, a revolution in cleaning!

2) New Clothes Clean detergent will get your clothes cleaner than any other detergent! That's because the powerful suds in Clothes Clean attack dirt, then rinse out sparkling clean, leaving your clothes their cleanest possible!

Most consumers would have a hard time believing the "secret patented formula" and "microdirt" explanations in the first concept. Mom would be more likely to respond to the more straightforward logic of the second concept—that rinsing out clean is the reason it works so well.

Good Ideas Must Be Able to Stand Alone

The third key learning is that the death of many new products comes as a result of the brand's assumption that a pretty good idea married to a great brand name can pull the new product through to success. Not true. If the new idea can't stand alone on its own without needing the umbrella of the brand name as protection, don't try it.

Recently I received a call from a friend whose father wanted to launch a new line of NASCAR-licensed soft drinks. He wanted my opinion on whether or not it was a good idea. The concept was to create the NASCAR brand with six different fruit-flavored soft drinks. Each flavor would feature a different NASCAR driver and his car on the packaging. Potential flavors would be Jeff Gordon Punch, Dale Earnhardt Black Cherry, Rusty Wallace Orange, and others.

Using this learning, my reply was simple. Take off the NASCAR name and then ask me if you should launch it. Does the world really need another bunch of fruit-flavored soft drinks? After some thought, they decided not to move ahead with the project.

You've Got to Have a Great Name

In this world of new product bombardment, a great name can make a good idea great. New products specialists spend a great deal of thought on creating product names that will stoke consumer interest. Research has proven that most successful new products have a product name that communicates the benefit of the product. Gone are the days when you could introduce a new brand of toilet paper and simply call it MD toilet tissue. You've got to use the branding as a communication vehicle!

One quick example illustrates the point beautifully. If you are in the market for the hottest hot sauce on the face of the earth, which of these would be more appealing: Taco Bell hot sauce or

Ass-Kickin' Cajun hot sauce? You don't have to read the label any further, do you?

Bringing New Products Learning to Life

The learning all comes to life when you see it put together in a new product concept. For example, let's pretend for a moment that we are inventing a new frozen food idea for potato skins—appetizers that are scooped-out potatoes covered with toppings, which you could pop into the oven or microwave to heat and eat. They would taste just like the ones you get at most sports bars and casual restaurants.

There are many ways to go about describing this product. To utilize the new products learning, we must create a great product name, clearly state the consumer benefit, have a plausible "reason why," and it must be able to stand alone, so we won't try to borrow equity from any brand name. Here's what a product concept might look like:

Introducing Spudskins

Delicious appetizers you can serve at home in just 3 minutes!

Spudskins are delicious baked potato scoops filled with scrumptious toppings just like the ones you find at casual restaurants and sports grills! Spudskins are a great snack while watching the big game or serving before dinner. They come in three fabulous flavors: CheeseHeads, topped with cheddar cheese and broccoli; Cream Kong, smothered with sour cream and chives; and Fiesta, topped with Mexican salsa and mozzarella cheese. Packed four to a box, they can be warmed in the microwave in just 3 minutes or baked in the oven for 10 minutes!

Notice the strategic positioning:

1. Targeted to "casual home meal" occasion.
2. Benefit is delicious baked potato scoops filled with scrumptious toppings, just like the ones you find at casual restaurants and sports grills.

3. "Reason why" is the three fabulous flavors: CheeseHeads, Cream Kong, and Fiesta, all smothered with favorite toppings.

NEW PRODUCTS PITFALLS

Just knowing the right way to go about developing a new product idea isn't enough. The road to new products success is lined with many perils. Recognizing these problem areas before you stumble upon them is another critical element of success.

The First Hurdle: The Trade

Researchers estimate that the grocery trade will be inundated with over twenty-five thousand new product offerings this year, in categories ranging from new foods, to beverages, to health and beauty aids, to household cleaners, to pet supplies and others. That's a rate of nearly one hundred new items foisted upon grocers each and every business day!

The failure rate of new products is largely attributable to this fact alone. Most offerings never survive their presentation meeting to the retail chains. The grocer refuses to stock the new product, and lacking distribution, it dies a slow and painful death without ever seeing the light of a grocery aisle.

Slotting allowances are required to get most new items onto store shelves (see chapter 13, "The Hush-Hush World of Trade Promotion," for a detailed explanation and discussion on slotting allowances). But retailers still may refuse to bring in the product despite the cash on the table if they think the product won't sell. The seller must demonstrate to the grocer that his product has consumer appeal and offers unique consumer benefits that other products, currently in the store, don't provide.

Even if a new product does successfully achieve distribution, it is still extremely vulnerable until it gains *sustained placement* in over 70 percent ACV (ACV stands for "All Category Volume" and is a term used to describe how much distribution an item has among the cumulative grocery trade nationwide). Why is the 70 percent threshold important? Because only with distribution at or above 70 percent ACV does national advertising make good fiscal sense. At distribution levels lower than this, advertising usually is bought on a "spot" basis (meaning you buy advertising only in specific cities or markets), which is more expensive and less efficient than national buys, increasing marketing costs and reducing profits.

Underestimating Introductory Marketing Costs

Another major reason for new product failure is low marketing budgets for the product launch. Introductions are no time to get queasy about spending. You have to tell consumers about your product to sell it, and you have to spend money to do it.

Procter & Gamble has a principle to follow on new product spending that seems to work pretty well. The marketing brand managers are permitted to spend all of the projected profits generated from the first eighteen months of sales. P&G knows that it must invest heavily to establish any new product in the marketplace. Only in month nineteen is the brand expected to have earned back the marketing investment and begin showing a profit to the corporation.

Of course, most companies shudder at the thought of an eighteen-month payback window, but that's what it takes if you're going to give your product a fighting chance for long-term survival.

Secrets of the Game

When introducing a new product, build your sales projections and financial statements based on a "slightly lower than expected" volume estimate.

Think of it this way: If you tell management your goal is to sell four eggs, and you sell four eggs, you've done what you promised. You're not a star, but you're not a goat either.

If you under-promise slightly and tell them you'll only sell three eggs and end up selling four, you're a hero, exceeding their expectations. Likewise, if you over-promise and tell management you'll sell five eggs and end up selling only four, the egg will be on your face for having failed to meet your sales objective.

In all cases you've sold four eggs, but each of the end results is *perceived* quite differently. Set yourself up for a win!

The Bass-Ackward Creative Process

Many roads to failure begin with the organizational chart. Companies establish a flawed system for creating new products. Instead of having the process driven by the marketing department, guided by consumer insight, *they put the creation process in the hands of the technical engineers and product formulation scientists*—probably the least creative minds in the company!

Let's face it, how many brilliantly creative and insightful engineers or scientists do you know? People who are trained in these areas of expertise are *disciplined*. They aren't encouraged to think outside the box; it's their job to *define* the box. They spend their days locked in technical centers, hunched over their chemical sets, not mulling over marketing sales data, competitive advertising, or consumer trends—the places where seeds for new product ideas await.

The soap and detergent division at P&G is a prime example of product initiation in the wrong hands. Its scientists and engineers continually dream up new product innovations, but most of their ideas provide corporate benefits, not consumer benefits.

The classic example was the creation of concentrated Ultra Downy, which was distributed in a small milk carton–type package that required the consumer to pour the concentrate into another container and mix with three cartons of water. P&G scientists figured "Hey, we can ship this in a small biodegradable carton and the consumer can mix in the water at home, saving us in both packaging costs and shipping costs, while making us appear environmentally friendly to the consumer!"

While they were right in their environmentally friendly stance, even loyal Downy consumers turned away from the new product. They didn't like knowing that their fabric softener was one part softener and three parts their own tap water. They didn't like mixing the product in another bottle, and the small carton in comparison to the large plastic bottles offered by competitors for the same price confused the consumers' price/value relationship. After a year of treading water, P&G returned to bottle packaging, but not before the Downy brand franchise was damaged and loyal consumers lost to the competition.

The X-Files

Another ticket to failure is *ignorance of what your predecessors have tried*. Within every company is a hidden trove of new product ideas that others have tried and tested in the past. Finding these files can keep you from avoiding the same mistakes, save time, and accelerate your learning curve.

With the high rate of employee turnover within most large corporations, old information is often buried and forgotten, leaving the current crop of marketers susceptible to retesting ideas that have already failed. Most likely, whatever you've dreamed up, somebody else has already thought of it some time ago, and the test results are sitting somewhere in a dusty cabinet.

In addition to internal snooping, another great place to learn what has been unsuccessfully tried is to buy a plane ticket to Ithaca, New York, and visit the New Products Showcase and Learning Center, run by Robert McMath. He has collected many new consumer products that have been introduced over the past three decades—about eighty thousand items in all—covering virtually every product category. It's a fascinating trip and worthwhile for understanding what roads your competition may have traveled, and where opportunities may have been missed.

Distribution Debacles

One particularly thorny path to new product purgatory is *mutating products in order to utilize your current distribution system.*

Kellogg's is in the midst of a new product meltdown from this problem as of this writing. In the summer of 1998, Kellogg's introduced Kellogg's Breakfast Mates, which has cereal and milk in one container. Just tear off the top, pour the milk over the cereal, and eat away. At first glance the product seems like a great idea, since cereal requires milk, right? Now you can buy this one package and have everything you need.

Kellogg's distribution expertise is in shipping boxes full of dry cereal to stores for stocking in the grocery aisle, a relatively simple process. Their trucks aren't set up for delivering products that require refrigeration, thus, the only way they could take advantage of their distribution system in shipping Breakfast Mates was to make the milk cartons inside the packages aseptic (meaning that it doesn't have to be refrigerated, the equivalent of canned milk). They mutated the core idea—fresh milk and cereal to canned milk and cereal—in order to utilize their current delivery system.

My guess is that when Mom discovers that the milk inside the Breakfast Mates is not fresh, she'll not buy the product. Kellogg's Breakfast Mates has been advertised as of this writing for over four months and has yet to gain distribution into any of the four major grocery chains in my vicinity. No distribution = no sales = massive losses. If you do spot Breakfast Mates in your local store, you'd better buy it, or the only place you're likely to find it will be in Ithaca at the graveyard of failed products!

Another distribution problem is associated with invading distribution channels where you don't have expertise. If you do land on a truly great idea, someone that does have the competencies and economies of scale for shipping in that channel will steal the idea. They will be able to execute it cheaper and more efficiently.

General Foods learned this lesson the hard way when it invaded the frozen dessert business. In 1979, it created Jell-O Pudding Pops and built a $100 million brand within a year of launch. With line extensions, General Foods built a $300 million business by 1984. Soon thereafter the brand was discontinued. How could this happen? Why would General Foods throw away a $300 million business? The answer was simple. Competitors had the expertise in delivering to the frozen food case that General Foods lacked, and didn't have to pay distributors for their expertise. Despite $300 million in sales, the pudding pops business was not profitable—the more pudding pops they made, the more money General Foods lost. The extra hand in the distribution chain taking its cut of the profits killed the goose that laid the golden egg.

Show Me the Difference

The sure road to new product failure *is in creating products that do not have a perceptible and meaningful point of difference versus current product offerings.*

DVD players are suffering from this shortcoming. DVD technology delivers digitally accurate sound and pictures to your TV and stereo surround sound system, recreating the "movie theater" experience at home. While the technology is wonderful, to the average consumer the sound and picture quality is not *significantly* better than what he already has. Consumers have too much invested in their current setup (VCR, purchased videotapes) to scrap them for the marginal improvement they would get with a DVD player. In my opinion, no matter how much money the electronics companies throw behind DVD, it will never become more than a technologically superior product for the niche technophile audience, because it doesn't deliver a meaningful and perceptible improvement to the VCR.

On the other hand, an example of a great new product introduction occurred when CDs annihilated the existing audio industry in a few short years. The sound quality from a CD was a clear, perceptible, and measurable improvement over audiocassettes and vinyl records. Consumers responded and shifted to CDs almost immediately, scrapping their audiocassette libraries and 33-rpm albums for the better sound quality. The product delivered a meaningful sound improvement to consumers which made it worth trashing their collections and starting over.

Me-Too Products

"Me-Tooism" is the disease that afflicts a majority of new products. The fundamental problem here is that *they aren't really "new" products—they are copies of an existing product sold by somebody else*! Store shelves are littered with Me-Too products. Go to the household cleaners and see how many knockoffs of the popular brand Pine Sol there are. The knockoffs come and go, but Pine Sol lives on. Just like in politics, Me-Too's have a tough time unseating the incumbent. To succeed with a Me-Too product, you must be prepared to spend like a drunken sailor on advertising to convince consumers that your product is different and better than the entrenched competition (even though it probably isn't). You also have to be prepared to fight protracted price wars in which profitability might dwindle to nearly nothing. Net, Me-Too's are much more trouble than they're worth.

Line Extensions

Nearly three-quarters of all new product introductions are "line extensions," new products that borrow the name and brand equity from an existing product. For years the basic cereal Cheerios has been a breakfast staple. In the early 1990s, General Mills launched its first Cheerios line extension—Honey-Nut Cheerios. The success of that product spawned two more line extensions—Multi-Grain Cheerios and Team Cheerios—giving the consumer four different variations of the popular cereal to choose from. The line extensions grew the sales of the Cheerios brand significantly.

The benefits of line extensions are many: they are much cheaper to introduce than "new" products; you can use your primary brand as a sampling vehicle; and they can expand your brand franchise significantly if done right. However, keep in mind that the Cheerios model is the exception to the rule. Most line extensions fail. They either cannibalize the sales of the mother product or merely slice up the sales pie into smaller pieces.

Often a line extension is used as a Band-Aid to cover fundamental bleeding on the core brand. Hawaiian Punch was getting slaughtered by Hi-C fruit drinks in 1991, and to try to stop the bleeding, they introduced a series of line extensions called Hawaiian Punch Colors. The flavor of each was identical to Fruit Juicy Red Hawaiian Punch—only the colors were different. Consumers bought the new offerings once and never came back. Despite success in the first couple of months of sales, Hawaiian Punch Colors soon disappeared off of grocers' shelves and were virtually extinct within nine months.

THE BETTER WAY TO INVENT NEW PRODUCTS—BUY YOUR IDEAS

Having tried and failed far too often, many of the top marketing companies have recently taken a long, hard look at their processes for inventing new products and have turned to a new resource— outside think tanks that specialize in new product invention.

Yes, this route is only for those who can afford it, but when you stop to think about it, using a new product think tank makes a lot of sense. Just as corporations turn to advertising agencies to tap into great creative minds, it seems natural to use proven creative resources that specialize in new products if you want to increase your odds of success. There is a far greater likelihood that a new products specialist who has invented thousands upon thousands of new product concepts will find the "big idea" than that a small cadre of your own employees, who may have only five or six new product success stories (if that) to their credit, will find it. The cross-pollination of ideas that the new product person brings to the party from having worked on hundreds of different product categories offers new insights that an internal group could never discover.

Secrets of the Game

Most major corporations now bring in hired guns—outside vendors that specialize in new product invention—to create new product ideas. They have abandoned in-house concept development.

The benefits of using a think tank are many. First, in the grand scheme, it's cheap. The most expensive new product specialist charges $150,000 for a three-day session to develop new product concepts. While that number sounds pricey, if you think in terms of potential rewards and manpower, it's peanuts. You could hire two full-time people to spin their wheels trying to come up with ideas, or spend the same amount and have the resources of trained new products specialists focused on your business for a few days, generating thousands of new ideas.

The biggest benefit of the think tank is the quality of the creativity behind the ideas. Hired guns can push the limits of imagination. Sure, they come up with some crazy, whacked-out stuff that will never work, but they also develop some downright brilliant ideas that will. Volume is critical to the process. The new products geniuses dream up thousands of ideas to find those few golden nuggets. The client will throw away 95 percent of the ideas generated, but the 5 percent that it keeps are winners!

Speed is another critical benefit to the process. A think tank condenses the creative process into a few concentrated days. At one popular new products company, the client comes in at 8 A.M. Tuesday morning and leaves with fifteen to twenty great new product ideas that are ready for consumer testing by Thursday at noon. No in-house creative team at any company in the world can dream up and turn around ideas that quickly.

RISK AND REWARD

When you work on new ideas, you're a bit like a trapeze artist working without a net. When you fly through the air and catch the bar, it's a beautiful thing. But if you miss, you go splat. Scary, yes, but it's still the best act in the whole show. If you prepare carefully, troubleshoot diligently, and avoid making mistakes, you can take the risk. Where you'll end up who knows. But as Ray Bradbury once said, "Jump, and find your wings on the way down."

CHAPTER SUMMARY

- Working on new products is the sexiest job in the marketing world, but it is fraught with perils.
- Eight out of every ten new product ideas fail.
- The secrets to bringing about a new product's success are:
  - Focusing on consumer benefits, not product function.
  - Using "kitchen logic" in explaining the reason why your product can deliver those benefits. Keep it simple and understandable.
  - Good ideas must be able to stand on their own. Don't try to paste a well-known brand name over a questionable product idea and expect success.
  - Your product has to have a great name.
- New products pitfalls include:
  - Getting the trade to take in your product. Most new products fail because they don't get retail distribution.
  - Underestimating introductory marketing costs.
  - Introducing new product ideas that provide corporate benefits, not consumer benefits.
  - Not doing internal research to understand all new initiatives that have been tried and tested, thus making the same mistakes.

- Distribution issues—either changing the product to fit with your distribution system or developing products that require new systems.
- Developing products that don't have a meaningful point of difference.
- Developing products that are a knockoff of an existing product.
- Developing line extensions that only cannibalize your existing product line and don't attract new users.

MARKETING
CORNERSTONES

How You Can Know that the Price Is Right

MAXIMIZING PROFITABILITY CAN BE A DIFFICULT JOURNEY

I OFTEN ATTEND MAJOR SPORTING EVENTS on the spur of the moment, showing up at the stadium with the intent of purchasing tickets from some fan or scalper wandering around the parking lot. These exercises in free-market pricing and negotiation are some of the most interesting business experiences I've ever had. If you've never tried it, you really should. Haggling over ticket prices exposes the naked underbelly of free-market economics and quickly illustrates how pricing for the same product can vary wildly, depending upon who's doing the selling.

Here's the technique I use if you want to try it. Always approach the seller by asking where their tickets are located. Then ask how much he wants for them. Now the free-market pricing game begins.

The sellers have a ticket in their hands with a price printed on it—face value—but they have no idea what I am willing to pay for that ticket. I shop around with different sellers. To my amazement, I can usually find people with virtually identical seat locations offering them anywhere from below face value to nearly double the face ticket price.

When I'm dealing with professional ticket scalpers, it's tough to negotiate them down, but I can usually get them to a price about $10 to $15 above the amount printed on the tickets. When I'm dealing with nonscalpers—regular fans or season ticket holders who have extra seats—I almost never pay above face value, and the first price offer they make to me is usually either face value or *below.* I love dealing with these people. I gleefully pay for the tickets and head to the concession stand for a hot dog, a bag of peanuts, and a Coke.

How can the ticket sellers know how to price their tickets? If they don't do some asking around, they can't. Good ticket scalpers know precisely what every person out in the parking lot is charging for their tickets, and the location of their seats. They shop around and ask others what they are selling, and when they locate naive fans significantly undervaluing their tickets, they snap them up and quickly resell them at a profit. The scalpers understand the competitive environment and the market price of the tickets.

The scalpers also know when to hold 'em and when to fold 'em. When they see an oversupply of tickets, they sell what they are holding for the best price they can get and go home. They know they can't make a profit if the market is flooded with cheap tickets.

Scalper strategy is what you must use if you are selling anything from yo-yos to yachts. You must understand what all competitive products are selling for and determine *what price is best for your product to maximize your profitability.*

MACHIAVELLIAN PRICING

When you are selling something in short supply, like rare Beanie Babies or Tickle Me Elmo during the Christmas season of 1996, you can use the Machiavellian pricing strategy. This hard-line strategic approach is intended to squeeze every last penny out of the buyer to maximize profits with no regard for the purchaser's satisfaction or feelings. It is an ideal strategy if you never intend on selling something to this person again, and it also works well for selling products with very long purchase cycles (like cars).

Most of us are in business for the long haul and would like to have repeat customers. In order to achieve success, we must price our products to maximize profitability and still satisfy the consumer that he paid fair market value for our goods.

Every monetary transaction is an exercise in balancing *value* (both intrinsic value and actual value provided through product benefits) versus price. If the value that I as a buyer attach to the product is about equal to or more than the price being asked, I'll buy it. If the price being asked is significantly higher or lower than the value I attach to the product, I won't buy. This is not an equation of absolute dollars; the same consumer who willingly shells out $35 for an attractive silk tie may balk at spending an extra $.20 for his usual brand of disposable razor. He'll switch razor brands before he'll forego the tie, not because he can't afford the razor, but because to him, the brand isn't worth an extra $.20. Figuring out just where the right price lies for your product is often a tricky proposition.

PRICE SENSITIVITY

In order to understand how much leeway you have in pricing with consumers, you must determine how sensitive they are to prices within your product category. The price elasticity analysis can answer this question nicely. If you are selling a commodity with virtually no product differentiation between you and competition—like bags of sugar—you won't have much flexibility in price before the consumer switches to your competitor's product. At the other extreme, if you are selling airline tickets, you have a great deal of latitude, since nearly every person on the plane paid a different price for his seat and nobody knows what anybody else paid.

Airlines are masters of understanding price sensitivity. They have elaborate price elasticity models built into their computer ticketing system, which continually adjust pricing based on each plane's seat occupancy. Most major airline computers automatically change over one hundred thousand fares daily! Try a little experiment for yourself. Jump onto the Internet and go to the Delta Airlines Web site: www.delta-air.com. Go into their ticketing system and get quotes for different flights from Orlando to Dallas-Ft. Worth. You'll find prices varying from $129 round-trip to over $1,500 depending upon the specific flight number and the time of day. It's the same product—transportation from point A to point B—and on the same carrier, but there's a 1000 percent change in price, based on consumer demand and seat availability. Wait a couple of days and try it again. There's a good chance the prices won't be anything like what you saw the first time you looked.

Secrets of the Game

You must perform a price elasticity analysis if your product category is highly or moderately price sensitive, because mere pennies can sometimes mean the difference between success and failure.

PRICE INSENSITIVITY

The best business to own and operate is within a category in which buyers are price insensitive, meaning they will pay just about any amount for your goods, and the sales volume doesn't change much no matter what you charge. Microsoft has lived in this world for a long time with its popular Windows platform and biannual upgrades. No competitive product can serve as an alternative to Windows, thus no market leverage exists to hold down the price Microsoft chooses to place on the product. Gates & Company continue to roll in the dough as all PC users are virtually forced to purchase the Windows upgrades in order to keep their computers current and utilize new software, all of which is designed to be run with the newest version of Windows. Monopolies like Microsoft are a wonderfully profitable machine and I highly recommend buying their stocks!

PRICE ELASTICITY

In economics classes, the fundamental technique for determining product pricing is called price elasticity. This principle follows the basic idea that the lower the price you offer, the more product you will sell; the higher the price, the fewer items you will sell. This pricing strategy makes sense for many consumer products. The goal of price elasticity is to find the right combination of price and sales volume to make the most profit. Here's an example of how it works.

Assume for a moment that we are selling baseballs to major league teams. The balls cost us $1.75 each to manufacture. As a test for the last two months, we've let our sales force sell the baseballs for whatever price they could negotiate with each team buyer. The prices have been all over the map. Some of the salesmen have sold them for as much as $8.00 per ball. Others have let them go for as little as our cost price of $1.75 each.

Once the test was over, we sat down with the sales figures and put them all onto a single list that looked like this:

BUYER	NUMBER OF BALLS	PRICE PER BALL
Phillies	200	$3.50
Dodgers	500	$2.75
Braves	200	$5.00
Reds	100	$4.75
Giants	50	$6.00
Red Sox	100	$6.50
Yankees	300	$5.50
Padres	700	$1.75
White Sox	400	$5.50
Cubs	50	$8.00
Angels	75	$7.25
Brewers	50	$6.75
Diamondbacks	200	$6.50
Devil Rays	75	$7.00

Our sales team figured out that the average price paid per ball was $3.96. The management team thinks that a price of $4.00 per ball must be the right price to go with, but you and I are still not sure if that price point will maximize our profits.

We decide to graph the sales figures to see if a picture makes any sense. The graph looks like this.

BASEBALL SALES GRAPH

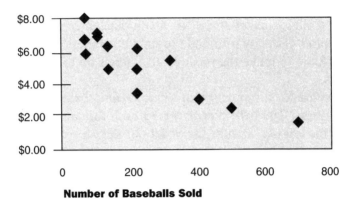

Number of Baseballs Sold

Looking at this chart, we can draw the conclusion that the right price appears to be somewhere between $4.00 and $6.00. Next, we draw a straight line between the different data points to quantify the price/sales relationship (this is called a regression analysis. The line represents what is called a price elasticity curve). It looks like this:

BASEBALL SALES GRAPH

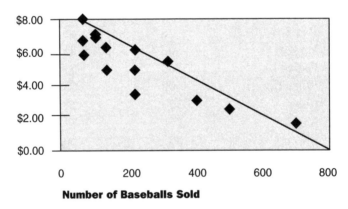

Number of Baseballs Sold

The elasticity curve represents our best guess of how many balls we'll sell to each customer as we raise or lower prices, based on the actual sales experience of our sales team over the past several months. Remember, each ball costs us $1.75 to manufacture, so now let's add profit to our scenario. The price elasticity graph converts to this financial picture:

AT THIS PRICE	# OF BALLS SOLD	REVENUE	PROFIT
$6.00	175	$1,050	$743.75
$5.00	300	$1,500	$975.00
$4.00	400	$1,600	$900.00
$3.00	550	$1,650	$687.50

The elasticity analysis shows that somewhere around the price of $5.00 per ball is where our company will make the most profit! To find the exact price, we refine the analysis:

AT THIS PRICE	# OF BALLS SOLD	REVENUE	PROFIT
$5.50	250	$1,375	$937.50
$5.25	275	$1,443.75	$962.50
$5.00	300	$1,500	*$975.00*
$4.75	325	$1543.75	*$975.00*
$4.50	350	$1575	$962.50

Notice how at both the prices of $5.00 per ball and $4.75 per ball we end up making the exact same profit! We'd naturally select the price of $5.00, because we don't want to invest the manpower in making and selling another 25 balls for no additional profit.

By performing the price elasticity analysis we found the *right* price instead of using the average of $4.00 each that the sales team wanted. If we had accepted the lower price, we would have been leaving $1.00 on the table for every ball we sold, worked harder to sell more balls, and gone home with less money in our pockets.

Secrets of the Game

Never use average pricing as a basis for setting your price. Average pricing will get you average profitability results.

Always perform a price elasticity analysis to determine the price where your overall profitability is greatest!

Work smarter, not harder!

THE SALES COMMISSION QUANDARY

Look again at the financial comparison between selling the balls at $4.00 versus $5.00:

AT THIS PRICE	# OF BALLS SOLD	REVENUE	PROFIT	MARGIN
$4.00	400	$1,600	$900.00	56.25%
$5.00	300	$1,500	$975.00	65.00%

Lurking behind those innocent numbers is a brewing conflict between sales and marketing. These two departments work off of different incentive programs, and therein lies the problem. Typically, brand marketing personnel are awarded their salary bonuses based upon how their products perform against certain overall profitability targets. Sales personnel are usually rewarded sales commissions for attaining specific sales volume figures (remember, revenue doesn't take into consideration the cost of producing the product; it only factors in price × number of units). Often, these reward systems are in direct conflict. Looking at this example, you can see that the sales team will earn bigger personal paychecks if they can sell the product for $4.00 per ball, because at that price they sell one hundred additional units. The brand team receives bigger paychecks if they set the price at $5.00 per ball to maximize overall profits. No wonder these departments have a hard time getting along!

So which is the right price? If your company has shareholders, the right price is $5.00, because you have a responsibility to the shareholders to maximize their wealth—which means maximize profitability. If you work at a privately held company, then the discussion can become a bit more lively, since mere profitability might not be the owner's primary motivation.

I can't tell you how many thousands of times I've heard sales teams whine and complain that the brand team's recommended pricing is too high, claiming they'll never be able to sell enough product to reach their sales targets. Sound familiar? Naturally, sales teams will *always* try to drive the price to the point of maximized volume without any regard to overall profitability, because that's how they are compensated. The only solution is to move sales personnel off of commissions, but that stifles their motivation and incentive. There isn't an elegant solution to the problem, and it is a very real problem within most corporations.

THE GOLD STANDARD

ONE MAN'S TRASH IS ANOTHER MAN'S TREASURE

In Park City, Utah, there is an old shop on Main Street filled with collectibles and artifacts from years gone by. I love going into this store and looking around at the antiques and their prices. You can find worthless stock certificates from defunct Park City silver mines, selling for $25.00; old 6 oz. glass bottles of Coca-Cola for $15.00 each; neon signs that don't work priced at $300.00, along with hundreds of other trinkets of the old West—horse shoes, rusty buckets, miners' lamps, and so on.

The first time you walk into this store, you look around and say "Geez, what a pile of junk." But these trinkets have made the owners wealthy. They have succeeded by transforming the consumers' price/value relationship—setting high prices on their funky goods to make consumers believe that they are buying prized collectibles, not junk. Since there is no competition or value comparison for their items, the strategy works. The old circa-1920s cash register in the store is constantly cranking up new sales as the gullible tourists snatch up pieces of what they consider to be Park City and old West history.

Now what would happen if the owners priced their goods at flea market prices and sold the stuff for what it was really worth? Let's say the stock certificate was priced at $1.00, the Coca-Cola bottle at $2.00, and the broken neon sign for $5.00. Nobody would buy any of it. Consumers would walk into the store and instead of seeing prized collectibles, they'd see a pile of junk. *The high pricing creates a perception that their products are highly valuable.*

Why do people pay $200 for a haircut at a fancy salon versus $12 at SuperCuts? Because consumers believe that the stylist at La Boutique De Bouffont is more skilled than her counterpart at SuperCuts, and the huge price differential supports that conclusion. In reality is there that much difference?

Secrets of the Game

Remember, *everything communicates* something to consumers about your product. This is especially true of pricing. The price you ask makes a statement about the value you are offering the consumer. If you are offering a low price, consumers assume you have a very modest opinion of the value of your goods. If you offer a high price, consumers infer that your product has a high value and that it truly delivers on the benefits.

I have a friend who does marketing consulting for a living. When he first went into business, he charged $50,000 for his unique services, sometimes discounting to $35,000 to get the business. He was doing fine, but not great. Finding clients was a constant struggle.

Instead of lowering the price of his services to attract new clients, he decided to raise his price to $75,000 and eliminate the discounts. Without any other significant changes to his program, he suddenly saw more business come his way. Now he charges $150,000 and his calendar is booked out eight months in advance. He didn't change what he was selling. He changed the perception of the value of his services by jacking up the price and advertising. The more he charges, the more successful and sought after he's become. Now he is considered to be the world's top guru within his specialty! Price perception *is* reality!

SUPER LOW PRICES

It doesn't take a brain surgeon or a rocket scientist to try to compete on the platform of lower prices. Many retailers have tried to establish themselves with this strategy. Most have disappeared, including such names as Woolworth's and People's Express. And let's face it, if low price were everything, we'd all be driving a Yugo. Why doesn't lowest price equal success?

Secrets of the Game

Consumers don't shop for lowest cost. They shop for highest value! Products that deliver the most value (both intrinsic value and that provided through the product benefits) are what consumers choose to bring home.

This psychological truth is why generic products didn't wipe out all name brands years ago. Consumers find intrinsic value in the name brands of many of their favorite products—Tide, Windex, Folgers, Bounty, and others. The lower price of the generic items doesn't compensate for the intrinsic value consumers place on the name brands.

Products and businesses that rely on a positioning of lowest prices are usually destined for failure. Low price is important to consumers—remember our $.20 razor example—but it can't be the sum total of the brand's positioning. Sooner or later (and usually sooner) somebody will come along with a way to either deliver the product benefit in a better or cheaper way, and at that point it's turn out the lights, the party's over.

THE PSYCHOLOGY OF "CHEAP"

Even though many consumers are poor, no one wants to think of himself that way. Poor people want to enjoy the fruits of life just as much as the country club set. Purchasing name-brand products can offer a degree of comfort and pride to consumers; they may not be able to afford a new car, but they can provide small luxuries like a favorite cereal or premium ice cream. Studies have shown families living below the poverty line purchase significantly more name-brand items for everyday use than the average consumer—soaps, beauty products, prepared foods—as well as mid-range luxury items such as watches, TVs, and stereos.

So if the poor don't want cheap generic products, what does that tell you about the middle and upper classes? Consumers want quality and are willing to pay for it. The price you set for your product translates to a value statement with consumers. Is a Rolex

Presidential watch really worth $3,999? Not in my world, but for some select buyers the brand provides intrinsic value that justifies paying the exorbitant price. Every consumer makes a value judgment based upon the benefits the product delivers and the cost associated with purchasing those benefits.

BEST-VALUE PRICING

On any given trip to the grocery store I can find a dozen or so brands with a highlighted burst on their packaging stating "Best Value," which is another way of saying "lowest price" for the volume. This promotional packaging suggests to the consumer that your brand performance is inferior to the competitive shelf set. Consumers aren't strictly looking to spend the least amount of money; they're shopping for the best performance for their dollars. They buy the product with the most compelling benefits, and that's what you should highlight!

PRICING THROUGH A PRODUCT LIFE CYCLE

The concept of product life cycle is helpful when considering pricing options. To illustrate the idea, think about the introduction of Digital Satellite receivers in the mid-1990s. In the beginning, DSS was priced everywhere at $499 for a basic system. Those media-loving consumers who were fed up with their cable companies and techies who wanted the newest TV toy happily ran to stores to gobble up this new window to the world. The DSS companies used these high profits to fund more production and lower their costs. After two years, the average price tag of a basic system was $299; four years later it fell to around $99.

Where did the companies selling the DSS systems make their profits? At the beginning. Now that competition has forced the system price down to $99, they are making virtually no profits on the receivers, but instead are raking it in from selling the programming, with over 5 million units now in homes! By pricing the product differently at various stages of the product life cycle, DirecTV was able to maximize profitability over the early stages of the life cycle.

FERENGI BUSINESS PRACTICES

In the TV series *Star Trek, Deep Space Nine,* the character who runs the bar on DS-9 is named Quark, a big-eared alien from the planet Ferengi.

Ferengi males such as Quark are taught from birth that their sole role in life is to make profit, and thus their entire schooling on the planet Ferengi is centered on mastering the rules of acquisition and the art of negotiation. Morality is not one of the tactics taught in their curriculum, and consequently, Ferengis are distrusted by the inhabitants of the rest of the solar system.

When determining the price for your products, you must have a bit of Ferengi in you, but at the same time temper the quest for profits with the understanding that you must make your consumers believe they are receiving fair value for your product. Your products must deliver a benefit to the consumer. You should always assume that each customer you sell product to will be back for more at some time in the future, and you need that consumer to want to deal with you again.

Fool me once, shame on you. You'll never get the chance to fool me twice because once you've stiffed me, I'll be dealing with your competitor next time around. Deception and greed are short-term business strategies. If you want to find long-term success, you must act with morals and conviction. It's not a sin to charge a high price for your product if the product benefits are commensurate with the consumer's definition of value. If your price is right, you'll buy business success.

CHAPTER SUMMARY

- Pricing can be tricky. It's important to find out exactly at what price you make the most profit.
- Every product category has a price sensitivity. The more commodity-like your product, the more price sensitive the marketplace will be. If you have a unique product that is unlike anything else, you can pretty much charge whatever you'd like.
- Price elasticity is an exercise that can reveal the correct price to charge to maximize profit.

- The price you charge communicates something to the consumer about your product.
- Playing the low-price game is a losing preposition.
- Consumers buy benefits. If low price were the most important criterion, we'd all be driving Yugos. Consumers will pay a premium for a product that delivers benefits.

Unfair Advantage: How to Own a Category

OFFERING THE RIGHT PRODUCT
MIX TO CONSUMERS

W HEN IT COMES TO FUNCTIONAL, no-frills products, men's underwear is about as basic as they come. But even guys whose primary interest in underwear is sitting around in it on a Sunday morning, who don't mind sagging elastic or fading, whose wives have to threaten legal action to get them to shop for new ones—even *these* guys have definite opinions about their underwear. Some of them have worn the same brand since boyhood. Others got in the habit of wearing their particular brand or style in college and never switched. A few even have lucky underwear for watching the big game.

The point is this: Even with a humble product like men's underwear, consumers have their preferences. And no matter how terrific your product may be, it probably can't satisfy the demands of millions of different people. As your research will verify, consumers have very specific, and often quite different, ideas of what they want.

Each product category has preference issues unique to that set of products. Sometimes the differences will arise from personal preference (like scented vs. unscented deodorants), or from the various ways consumers use products (I need something portable vs. I want the biggest one you make for my home). Just as often, the variety of consumer demands simply reflects the quirks of different personalities (it's the brand my Mom always buys).

Not even the craftiest marketing whiz can make his product appeal to everyone. But you can come close. The trick is in knowing your category and your consumers well enough to offer a selection of products that meets consumer needs better than anyone else's. This selection of products offered is referred to as your product mix. Finding the right product mix is a bit more complicated than simply looking at consumer research and churning out a product for every taste and occasion. If you want to own your category, you must understand how benefits motivate purchase, and whether alternative options in your line will be a strength or a weakness for your overall business. In this chapter we will look at a variety of strategies that can help you win the product mix game and dominate your product category.

SEGMENTATION ANALYSIS

Charting consumer needs is a rigorous task we call segmentation analysis. Segmentation analysis is just a fancy way of stating the consumer question "When you go to the store to buy this type of product, what product attributes are most important to you?" For example, a segmentation analysis of the beer category would likely reveal several segments such as "American" (Budweiser, Miller High Life, Coors); Imported (Beck's, Corona, Lowenbrau), Lite (Bud Lite, Miller Lite, Coors Lite), and Brewery (Rolling Rock, and a variety of microbrew brands). As a marketing manager for a brewer, you would want to make sure that you had a brand that competed in each product category in order to maximize sales. This segmentation analysis groups products into categories that suggest a rationale for a series of products that you would offer— a product mix.

Often a segmentation analysis takes form from many different perspectives. Take a look at the analgesic pain reliever category. It contains such popular brands as Bayer Aspirin, Bufferin, Excedrin, Tylenol, Advil, and Aleve. When these companies perform a segmentation analysis, they ask consumers the question "When you need a pain relief product, what product attributes are most important to you?" The answers can be summarized as follows:

- *Desired product form:* tablets, geltab, caplet, liquid
- *Desired dosages:* Infants', Children's, Junior, Adult Regular, and Extra Strength
- *Package sizes:* 2 count, 24 count, 100 count, 250 count
- *Additional effects:* no drowsiness, helps me sleep, long lasting

Tylenol, a pain reliever containing acetaminophen, is the category leader. Manufactured and marketed by McNeil Consumer Products Co., Tylenol is offered to consumers in a variety of package sizes and product forms. It is available in tablets, gel caps, and liquid forms. Its varieties include Infants', Children's, Junior Strength, Regular Strength, Extra Strength, Tylenol P.M., Extended-Relief Tylenol, and Tylenol for Arthritis. Why all the choices? Because the brand team at McNeil learned through its segmentation analysis that each of these variations is necessary to meet the numerous—and distinct—needs of consumers who are interested in purchasing pain relievers. Importantly, none of these many variations is redundant; each offers consumers a specific benefit targeted to meet a specific need.

Before we discuss the consumer benefits, let's take a look at the actual product mix, not including cold remedies:

For children
- Infants' Tylenol in liquid form (comes with convenient dosage dropper)
- Children's Tylenol in tablet (chewable) and liquid form
- Junior Tylenol, for Kids 6–12

For Adults
- Regular Tylenol Tablets and Gel Caps, various sizes
- Extra Strength Tylenol Tablets and Geltabs, various sizes

- Tylenol P.M. Tablets and Gel Caps, various sizes
- Extended Relief Tylenol Tablets and Gel Caps, various sizes
- Arthritis Tablets and Gel Caps, various sizes

You may wonder, if Tylenol were available in just one version—one that effectively controlled pain for everyone—wouldn't consumers buy it? Don't they all want the same thing—to feel better? Surprisingly, the answer is no. Consumers experience different types of discomfort, and the relief they seek is specific. The folks at Tylenol understand this dynamic and want to make sure that consumers can get precisely what they want, to deliver the exact pain relief they need. So, while the brand Tylenol has one consistent message—fast, reliable pain relief—the product mix reassures consumers that the scientists at Tylenol have developed a specialized remedy for their particular ailment, in the size, dosage, and form that most favorably delivers relief. As a powerful fringe benefit of this strategy, segmentation not only encourages the consumer to purchase Tylenol instead of a competitive brand; it may also spur the purchase of more than one Tylenol product (one for night, one for headaches, a small purse-size container . . . the list goes on).

Secrets of the Game

The adage "one size fits all" is the most untrue statement in consumer products history. "One size fits no one" is more like it. Successful marketers craft their product mix in a variety of sizes, shapes, colors, and forms in order to specifically meet consumer needs and expectations, resulting in maximized brand appeal.

THE GOLD STANDARD

Look inside any grocery store and you'll find many examples of top companies that have successfully implemented a segmented product mix to own their category. The Coca-Cola Company is the classic example. For the flagship flavor Coca-Cola Classic, it also offers Diet Coke and

Caffeine-Free varieties. Coke is available in 2-liter bottles, 20-ounce plastic bottles, 1-liter plastic bottles, 10-ounce glass bottles, and 12-ounce aluminum cans. Whatever package or flavor the consumer prefers is usually available on the store shelf. The company extends this strategy across the entire soft drink category by offering an array of brands and packages that covers virtually every flavor of soft drink. It is nearly impossible to find a successful soft drink brand for which The Coca-Cola Company doesn't produce an alternative purchase choice:

COMPETITIVE FLAVOR/BRAND	COKE'S PRODUCT
Pepsi	Coca-Cola
Diet Pepsi	Diet Coke
7-Up	Sprite (lemon-lime)
Dr. Pepper	Mr. Pibb
Mountain Dew	Surge/Mello Yellow
Cherry Pepsi	Cherry Coke
Orange Crush	Minute Maid Orange/ Fanta Orange
Root beer	Barq's Root Beer
Fruit flavors	Fanta
Snapple	Fruitopia

Through its product mix strategy, The Coca-Cola Company makes sure that every time you reach for a soft drink, one of its products is uniquely suited to quench your thirst.

DEVELOPING NEW USAGE OCCASIONS

The trick to forecasting when a segmentation strategy will work lies in careful interpretation of your research. There are many angles to consider, but at the top of the list, next to your product benefits category, should be "usage occasions." In other words, in addition to considering *what* the consumer wants, you must address *how* and *when* the consumer intends to use the product.

Usage occasion segmentation is valuable for two primary reasons. First, because it taps into key reasons the consumer makes a purchase decision (the product is easy/pleasant/convenient to use). A second powerful benefit of analyzing how consumers use your product is that the research will suggest ways to actually increase the frequency of consumer use. Naturally, if consumers use more of your product, they buy more as well.

Band-Aid provides an excellent case study of how usage occasion segmentation works. For decades the adhesive bandage category has been one of the most combative product categories in supermarkets and pharmacies. The category has two major competitors: Band-Aid, manufactured by Johnson & Johnson, and Curad, produced by Colgate-Palmolive. There are also a few smaller competitors like 3M and KidCare. Throughout the 1960s, 1970s, and 1980s, there was very little news in the category. The only significant product innovation was the development of the "Ouchless" Band-Aid (which did not fulfill the consumer promise and still hurt like heck when you pulled it off), and the licensing of cartoon characters to add a bit of fun and color for kids.

As you would expect in these static conditions, the market saw very little shift in share between Band-Aid and Curad over time. Each competitor held a strong position in the marketplace, and each seemed content to stand toe-to-toe with the other, not backing down, but not taking any real swings, either. Then in the mid-1990s, Band-Aid broke with convention and jumped out of the pack through innovation, introducing an entire array of products specifically targeted to the consumer usage occasion needs it identified through a segmentation analysis.

Suddenly, consumers could choose from Band-Aids treated with aloe vera and vitamin E, Band-Aids treated with antiseptics, special Band-Aid strips shaped for finger and knuckle cuts, sport Band-Aids, waterproof Band-Aids, clear Band-Aids, bright-color Band-Aids, and Disney cartoon character Band-Aids, featuring The Little Mermaid, Winnie the Pooh, and Mickey Mouse.

What had been a tight market share race became no contest virtually overnight. A recent trip to my local supermarket revealed Band-Aid controlling over 75 percent of the category shelf space with Curad, 3M, and KidCare splitting the remaining slots.

And here's the beautiful part of the strategy. Not only did Band-Aid address specific consumer needs, they actually created a reason to own more than one box at a time. After all, you'll need one for the kids (with cartoon characters to take the sting out of the boo-boo), one for finger and knuckle cuts (the most common kind of injury), Sport Band-Aids for the hubby or teenager's basketball games, and maybe even a vitamin E or all purpose box thrown in the first aid kit for miscellaneous cuts and scrapes. People may not need more adhesive bandages then they used to, but they now have a reason to purchase more than one box of Band-Aids for different usage occasions.

WHEN PRODUCT PROLIFERATION DOESN'T WORK

By now you may be thinking you've found the hidden treasure simply by offering more, more, more to your consumers. But many a seaworthy vessel has been sunk on those treacherous rocks. Even the biggest, savviest marketing captains have been capsized because they couldn't tell the difference between good and bad segmentation choices.

For example, look at a segmentation analysis of the toothpaste category. When consumers were asked: "When you go to the store to buy toothpaste, what product attributes are most important to you?" Consumers responded that the benefits most important to them were:

> Cleans and prevents cavities
> Freshens breath
> Whitens teeth
> Tartar control
> Prevents gum disease
> Contains baking soda
> For sensitive teeth
> For kids
> Won't damage my teeth
> Makes my mouth feel fresh and clean

Historically, Crest toothpaste held a virtual monopoly in the category through the 1960s and 1970s, thanks to its protective fluoride ingredient. Competitive brands tried to "own" other product benefits: Gleem and Ultra Brite toothpastes were for white teeth and a great smile; Aquafresh was toothpaste that cleaned, whitened teeth, and freshened breath; Sensodyne was for sensitive teeth; Rembrandt for whitening teeth; Arm & Hammer toothpaste cleaned with baking soda. Colgate toothpaste simply positioned itself as an alternative to Crest.

In the mid-1980s, the category started heating up with a vast array of new product introductions and packaging options. Top brands such as Crest and Colgate extended into consumer-friendly gels and flavors for the first time. Pump and flip-top tubes were introduced to eliminate the old squeezed-out tube complaint. The category that once had only two or three product offerings from each brand exploded to ten or more from each of its major competitors.

As the 1990s progressed, the proliferation of products continued. Virtually every major brand offered a wide selection of products targeted at each of the specific consumer needs in the segmentation analysis. Most brands developed formulas specific to fighting tartar, stopping gum disease, whitening and brightening, featuring baking soda, gentle formulas for sensitive teeth, gel and paste options, and kids' brands. Selecting a tube of toothpaste had become a major decision, with nearly eighty brand options in a typical store.

In 1998, Colgate got smart. They sensed the consumer confusion that had overtaken the category and switched direction. Instead of trying to figure out what the next hot product benefit would be, Colgate introduced Colgate Total, one product that addressed practically all of the consumer needs revealed in the segmentation analysis. It was an instant success, building a 35 percent market share within two months of introduction. Crest followed suit shortly thereafter with the introduction of a cloned product— Crest Complete— but the damage was done. Colgate had won the war, because consumers no longer saw a reason to switch. They now had everything they wanted in a single toothpaste.

Why didn't product segmentation work? Because the competing marketing teams found themselves so caught up in the new-attribute race, they forgot a basic rule of gamesmanship:

Secrets of the Game

When analyzing consumer benefits, you must determine whether any benefits are linked. *Never* separate linked benefits!

KEEP IT SIMPLE, STUPID (THE KISS STRATEGY)

Most of the toothpaste brands became casualties of the segmentation war simply because they carved up their consumer segments by unlinking product benefits. When they performed their segmentation analysis, they categorized the qualities that consumers described as important (whitens, freshens breath, etc.). But they didn't listen very carefully. Consumers didn't say they wanted whiter teeth *or* clean breath; they said they wanted both. Different consumers may have prioritized their needs differently, but chances are none of them said "I don't really care about fresh breath," or "white teeth aren't at all important to me." Similarly, consumers didn't have distinct usage needs for their toothpaste; in other words, their priorities for what the toothpaste should do for them did not change according to when or how—or even how often—they brushed.

Now, think back to Tylenol and Band-Aid. Their product segmentation strategies worked because they identified distinct consumer needs. All Tylenol products promise pain relief. But beyond that basic function, some consumers absolutely could not swallow tablets and wanted only gelcaps. Others wanted maximum strength but cared nothing about a sleep aid. For Band-Aid, while consumers all wanted clean, comfortable healing, they described very different uses for the product. Sometimes they wanted a colorful bandage for the kids. Other times they wanted a super-strong, flexible bandage that wouldn't come off during sports. They didn't want both things at the same time.

But toothpaste consumers wanted it all. They didn't need toothpaste that cleaned and whitened teeth but failed to control tartar or fight cavities. They wanted toothpaste that cleaned and whitened, prevented cavities, controlled tartar, freshened breath, *and* prevented gum disease to boot—precisely what Colgate Total promised them. In the short term, some brands were able to attract consumers who identified one particular attribute as the most important benefit on their list, but in the end, the complete package won out.

The moral of the story is that the product mix strategy for any particular product category must be determined by whether the consumer needs are *independent* or *linked*. If the consumer needs are linked, don't try to break them apart. If consumers need a soft drink that is low in calories and tastes great, don't try to sell them something that's just low in calories. Give consumers a product that specifically addresses their needs.

THE SILENT PARTNER—DEVELOPING FIGHTER BRANDS

If you truly want to create an unfair advantage over your competitors, you must learn that the public battles for shelf space and consumer attention are only a piece of the puzzle. Some of the most interesting competitive maneuvers actually occur below the consumer radar. It is fairly common for a major company to have in its stable of product a low-profile secret weapon they call a fighter brand. A fighter brand exists only to wreak havoc against the competition. They are not intended to develop consumer loyalty; they are not designed to increase volume every year. Their mission, like any good soldier, is purely to defend their sovereign: the premium brand.

To the glee of marketing strategists, fighter brands are effective, if covert, members of the product mix. Procter & Gamble used a fighter brand in the frozen concentrated orange juice category several years ago to help defend their premium brand, Citrus Hill Orange Juice. When P&G purchased a small juice company named Sundor in 1989, it acquired several small brands, among them one called Texsun. Texsun was primarily known as a shelf-stable canned juice sold in grocery stores. The brand enjoyed nearly a 10 percent share of the canned grapefruit juice market, so it had at least some name recognition among juice purchasers.

In the frozen orange juice market, unlike refrigerated juice, generic brands were dominant players. Since the product was frozen, consumers no longer valued "freshness" as the key attribute, and most found very little difference between the flavor of the generic juices and the more expensive brand names of Tropicana, Minute Maid, and Citrus Hill. When P&G introduced Texsun Frozen Orange Juice into stores nationwide, it was priced to compete with generic brands, not as competition with Citrus Hill or the other premium names.

Texsun's real purpose was not to corner the frozen juice market; it was to foil Minute Maid and Tropicana from making any profit on their major promotions. Whenever these juices were featured in a store chain's advertising circular (an expensive promotion for the brand), the P&G salesforce would offer tremendous discounts on Texsun juice as an unadvertised special. Consumers at the point of purchase would often pick up the heavily discounted Texsun product instead of Minute Maid or Tropicana frozen juices. The strategy was very effective in keeping Minute Maid and Tropicana from reaping huge volume bumps during their features.

The strategy had a number of fringe benefits as well. It allowed Citrus Hill to remain safely above the price wars, ever the premium brand, which protected both its image and its price point. At the same time, retailers became increasingly disinclined to feature the Minute Maid and Tropicana frozen juices, since these promotions never seemed to generate the expected sales volumes.

Discovering fighter brands as a consumer onlooker is sometimes quite difficult. Major consumer product companies go to great lengths to distance themselves from these products and keep their secret weapons a secret. They often use the manufacturing names of defunct companies that they purchased in the past to shield their true identities. If you see a brand name that you don't recognize, being sold at the low-generic price point, chances are it is a fighter brand, acting as a warrior for one of the major brands in the category.

PREMIUM BRANDING

Most major consumer product brands consider themselves to be "premium brands." What this means is that the consumer receives value—be it real or intangible—from using or associating with the product, and that value justifies a higher price than a product offered by competitors and generic brands.

Long distance telephone companies provide a terrific study in the power of premium brands. The market consists primarily of AT&T, MCI, Sprint, and a host of small resellers (the category equivalent of "generic brands") selling long-distance time over telephone networks. Time is a commodity. Ten minutes of time on AT&T is no different than ten minutes of time on Joe's Long

Distance service. Time is time, no matter who is selling it. So why don't consumers flock to the small resellers who offer the lowest long-distance prices? The power of premium branding is what keeps them from running away from AT&T, MCI, and Sprint.

AT&T did a very smart thing years ago, something akin to an *X-Files* conspiracy. If consumers knew the real truth, they would probably have put AT&T out of business. What did AT&T do? They created a three-tiered pricing structure that made you believe that there was a functional reason why calls placed during the day (business hours of 7 A.M. to 5 P.M.) cost more than calls made in the evening (5 P.M. to 11 P.M.). The cheapest call of all was supposedly during the late night/early morning hours (11 P.M. to 7 A.M.). Consumers were led to believe that AT&T actually incurred greater costs during business hours (because of additional staff? additional technology?) but could offer reduced rates late in the evening when call volume was lower. As a benefit to consumers, they would pass on those savings.

This strategy supported AT&T for years, building it into one of the most profitable corporations in world history. But there was a scam going on here. The truth? No matter what time a call is placed, there is no cost difference to AT&T. AT&T incurs the same cost for a phone call made at 10 A.M. as for one placed at midnight. Its premium pricing during the day was based on nothing more than the fact that they could get away with it. For years, AT&T duped the public into accepting their three-tiered pricing, and made huge profits as a result of its inflated daytime rates.

Along came MCI and Sprint, each created by former AT&T executives who understood the true cost scenario and knew that there were huge profits to be made by discounting the AT&T rates. MCI and Sprint developed brand positionings as "AT&T quality at a lower price." The battle began at 25-cents-per-minute flat rates, twenty-four hours per day, and escalated from there. The cost savings was sufficient to spur many consumers to switch to MCI and Sprint, and despite AT&T's positioning as the most reliable carrier (you get what you pay for), consumers found no difference in the quality of their phone calls placed on these alternative carriers.

Now AT&T could no longer profit solely from the strength of its image; it had entered the commodity war. Voice quality was equal, calls got through—now the only differentiating factor was price. Consumers happily jumped from one carrier to another, one low-cost promotion to the next. Many households switched long-distance carriers as often as six to eight times per year.

So how does a premium brand survive in a commodity world? The first attempts were targeted consumer promotions designed to stop the frantic switching. MCI introduced "Friends and Families," offering a discounted rate to your designated circle of friends and family if you convinced each of them to be MCI residential-long-distance customers. The tactic didn't work very well. Sprint introduced "Free Fridays" for its business customers—a more compelling offer. MCI countered with "Five-Cent Sundays" for residential customers to call relatives. Sprint offered "Dime-A-Minute" calls late at night. AT&T finally entered the fray with its "One Rate" plan, offering 15- cents-per-minute calls twenty-four hours a day, seven days a week.

Battle over? Not yet. Out of the blue a new competitor emerged and upped the ante. Internet provider America Online (with over 15 million subscribers) in partnership with a small, unbranded long-distance reseller offered its customers 9-cents-per-minute long distance, twenty-four hours a day, seven days per week. The siege began. All of the branded carriers—AT&T, MCI, and Sprint—began to lose their most technologically proficient customer base (which coincidentally was more educated, had higher-than-average income, and spent more on long distance each month than the typical consumer). The propensity to switch long-distance carriers frequently with relative ease—a tactic that the big three had nourished and perfected for so long—suddenly became their worst nightmare.

The next round of the battle began. AT&T began offering "One Rate Plus," 10 cents per minute, twenty-four hours per day, seven days per week. To lure back the Internet crowd, AT&T made an offer exclusively on their AT&T website of 9 cents per minute to customers who subscribed to AT&T Worldnet as their Internet service provider and AT&T as their long-distance provider. AT&T also provided a discount to the monthly fees of America Online. MCI and Sprint also bundled Internet Service Provider packages with their long-distance service.

The end of this contest has yet to be fought, and inevitably it will involve carnage. With the cost-per-minute rates dropping like stones, how can AT&T, MCI, and Sprint survive? The answer: Go back to Marketing 101. Perform a segmentation analysis, and start by asking the question "When you communicate with others, what product attributes are most important to you?" Notice how the question is phrased. It doesn't ask what is important about choosing a long-distance carrier—it asks what is important in *communicating with others.* This can include pagers, faxes, Internet, long distance, mail, television, satellite transmissions, radio, newspapers, sign language, and smoke signals. Figure out what besides price is important to consumers. They'll tell you. Just as Pampers needs to justify to consumers why they should choose and pay more for their brand instead of a generic diaper, AT&T, MCI, and Sprint need to justify to consumers why they should feel good about paying more for their long-distance service. Added value and added services justify premium pricing. Consumers will pay more for a well-known brand name if they feel they are receiving value commensurate to the price.

Secrets of the Game

You cannot win a price war, so don't join the battle. Instead, research and understand your consumer needs, then build added value into your brand that will clearly separate your product from competition and justify the price-value relationship to consumers.

It is possible for even the most established and sedate product categories to be overrun by a competitor with some innovative flair. The key to owning your category, today and in the competitive fray of the future, is in careful segmentation analysis and the development of a well-thought-out product mix. If you do it right and listen carefully to what consumers tell you, a mix can be developed that will provide competitive advantage.

PRODUCT MIX AND THE LITTLE GUYS

The strategy behind optimizing product mix is just as important to any retailer as it is to a consumer product manufacturer. If you own a local pharmacy for example, it is important that you understand the consumer segmentation preferences of each and every product category that you stock in your store. If you carry a product mix that covers all consumer needs, your customers will always find what they are looking for in your shop. If you don't have a mix that covers all needs, it's likely that you'll have some customers walk in and walk out without making a purchase . . . a painful thing to see. The same rules that apply to Procter & Gamble when it comes to developing an optimized product mix at retail also apply to a copy center and a fast-food restaurant. As a business operator, you must make sure that you offer a breadth of product selection that covers all consumer needs. The good news is that you have the ability to pick and choose from all of the different offerings from your suppliers to optimize your mix.

CHAPTER SUMMARY

- Know your consumers well enough to offer a selection of products that meets their needs better than anyone else.
- A segmentation analysis will help you determine the areas in which to focus.
- Often, the opportunity exists to develop new usage occasions as a rationale for your product mix.
- Product proliferation isn't the ultimate answer.
- When researching consumer benefits, be sure none are linked. Never unlink benefits to create new products.
- Fighter brands can often be used to successfully defend your premium brand and wreak havoc with competition.

Simple Steps to Powerful Packaging

CREATING DIFFERENTIATION AND
SPECIALNESS THROUGH PACKAGING
INITIATIVES

I F YOU HAVE OBSERVED any of the number of celebrity court cases grabbing headlines in the past several years, you have an idea of how much work, research, and energy—not to mention theatrics—goes into preparing the closing arguments. The jury has often been presented with a complicated collection of evidence, and only during the closing arguments does that mass of information begin to take shape. Lawyers painstakingly reiterate the key evidence, but this time they insert it into an emotional context that they hope will lead to a vote for their client. They create feelings of sympathy, rage, or confidence in the jurors that provide a medium for processing the mountains of raw information.

When a shopper steps into the retail shopping environment, she becomes a juror who decides whether your product is worthy of purchase. Her primary piece of evidence is your packaging. Like a good closing argument, strong packaging not only trumpets the functional benefits of your product, it also conveys an emotional message about whether your product is reliable, effective, friendly, prestigious, or easy to use. But unlike a lawyer who enjoys unlimited time and space to make his argument, you must do all of your communicating in three seconds and three inches of shelf space. That is why packaging is the cornerstone of product performance.

Secrets of the Game

Packaging is the *best* way to communicate to consumers the most compelling reasons to buy your product. Packaging delivers messages to consumers right up to the moment they pluck the item off the shelf. Your information must be both succinct and tantalizing to win their attention, and their purchase.

ADVERTISING REACHES ONLY SO FAR

One of the harsh realities of marketing is that advertising won't reach all your potential consumers. Even the best, most expensive campaigns only reach up to 70 percent of the target audience. Moreover, many products aren't good candidates for advertising. The *only* place where you are absolutely guaranteed the opportunity to speak to consumers about your product is at the point of purchase. Only when a shopper is standing at the store shelf ready to select an item to buy, and your product is displayed as part of the competitive set, do you have a 100 percent chance to communicate why he or she should buy your brand instead of somebody else's.

EXTRA, EXTRA—READ ALL ABOUT IT!

Consumers make purchases because they are seeking the benefit the product provides. Obvious, isn't it? So it follows that the best place to trumpet the benefits of your product is on the front of your packaging. That's where you tell the consumer that your brand delivers the desired benefit better than all those other Joe-schmo competitive products on the shelf.

More often than not, marketers overlook this apparent no-brainer. They mistakenly assume that consumers know what their product is and what it does, so they just slap the brand name on the label with the required legalese and very little fanfare. Big mistake. Sure, shoppers who have used your brand in the past know what your product does and how to use it, but unless you control 100 percent market share and have no competition, you are losing potential consumers who for one reason or another are buying your competitor's product. These are precisely the folks to whom your packaging should be talking! If a shopper is using your product and likes it, you won't have to work hard to get him or her to buy it again. Savvy marketers know that the real money lies in attracting new users and stealing competitive share.

Package copy is no time to be shy—you need to think like a hawker at a carnival. Go take a look at the products in a typical store that are category leaders. Most of them shout to the consumer what benefit the product delivers. A sampling of the front package copy from some powerhouse brands:

- Windex Glass Cleaner: More Cleaning Power! Streak-Free Shine with Ammonia D.
- Dow Disinfectant Bathroom Cleaner with Scrubbing Bubbles: Removes Soap Scum Easily!
- Drano Clog Remover: Opens Drains Fast! Safe for Pipes.
- ChapStick Lip Balm: Helps heal and prevent dry, chapped lips.
- Dove: 1/4 Moisturizing Lotion Beauty Bar.
- Lubriderm: Seriously Sensitive Lotion For Extra Sensitive Dry Skin.
- Purell Instant Hand Sanitizer: Kills 99.99% of Germs Without Water or Towels.
- Downy Ultra Care: Helps Keep Clothes Soft and Looking Like New.
- Bounty Paper Towels: The Quilted Quicker Picker-Upper.
- Kleenex Cold Care Tissues: Softest Tissue Made! Ultra Comfort.

DEVELOPING UNIQUE AND PROPRIETARY PACKAGE SHAPES

When you go to the grocery store for a gallon of milk, do you browse the aisle to consider which brand to purchase, or do you simply grab the jug that has the right fat content for you and the longest freshness date? If you're like over 90 percent of consumers, you look only at the freshness date and have no idea what brand of milk you just bought. Why? Because they all look exactly alike. Big plastic jugs, same shape, different color caps for whole, 2 percent, 1 percent, and skim milk. There is no apparent difference between dairy brands, so nobody cares to notice.

When you move over to the bottled juice aisle, same problem. All of the glass bottles offered by each of the different apple juice brands such as Mott's, Treetop, White House, Juicy Juice, Red Cheek and others look virtually alike—except one. Martinelli's bottle is in the shape of an apple! The apple-bottle not only makes the Martinelli's brand stand out from the crowd, but it makes you subconsciously believe that it contains a better quality apple juice than the others, allowing the brand to command a premium price in a commodity market.

Secrets of the Game

EVERYTHING COMMUNICATES!

You must use every available weapon in your arsenal to differentiate your products from competition. This includes development of proprietary packaging that reinforces your special uniqueness to consumers.

Coca-Cola understands the power of proprietary packaging. In 1996, the company began a shift to move all packages of Coca-Cola Classic into contour bottles, rekindling the nostalgia consumers hold for the original package shape. In the quest for differentiation and specialness, the marketing team at Coke has even attempted to develop a contour aluminum can for Coca-Cola Classic! Expensive? Yes . . . until you look at the potential profits.

CREATING PREFERENCE THROUGH IMPROVED PACKAGE PERFORMANCE

The world's best marketers are always searching for new ways to create competitive advantage through packaging innovation. Developing packaging that performs better than the competition is a great way to differentiate your brand. Patents offer protection that provides your product with a demonstrable and meaningful reason to purchase versus competition.

When liquid laundry detergent was first introduced, consumers loved the product and how easily it dissolved in their wash, but they didn't like the messy bottle caps. The caps were designed for measuring and pouring the detergent into the wash, but when consumers replaced the cap on the bottle, the liquid detergent leaked around the cap edges, causing a gooey mess. To solve this problem, the Tide brand team developed an innovative package design for no-spill tops on their liquid Tide bottles. The bottle top was designed to channel the residual liquid detergent from the cap back into the bottle, leaving the cap edges clean. The Liquid Tide bottle is protected by no fewer than thirteen patents, making it difficult for competition to mimic, and offers Tide a distinctive long-term competitive advantage.

Citrus Hill Orange Juice was another P&G brand that gained competitive advantage through packaging innovation. Citrus Hill was the first major juice brand to introduce the carton pouring spout. The development of the spout was driven by the consumer desire to shake orange juice before pouring, in order to mix up the pulp that settles to the bottom of the carton. In the old milk-type cardboard carton, the juice would often spurt out of the top when shaken. The pouring spout eliminated this problem, and gave Citrus Hill a distinctive point-of-difference versus competition. The package design became so popular with consumers that today, nearly every refrigerated orange juice carton has a spout.

Many brands outside the grocery channel have also developed proprietary packaging. Ortho Lawn Care has done a terrific job creating brand preference in this way through the innovation of a quick-attach sprayer that allows the user to stand upright and pump the stream of lawn and weed chemicals accurately and powerfully. Ortho also captured an advantage in the granular lawn food arena through the introduction of Ortho brand spreaders, with correlate settings listed on the granular Ortho lawn food packaging to help consumers understand how much food to put on their lawns. If consumers buy a lawn food brand other than Ortho, they don't know how to use the Ortho spreader settings correctly!

When you consider these examples, it's easy to see why they work. The tricky part is developing the packaging strategies in the first place. It is common to become so caught up in the process of choosing colors and fonts, developing labels, and solving manufacturing problems that you stop asking the questions, "How could it be different or better?" "How does the consumer use my product?" "How could I make her life easier or more pleasant?"

Step back from the creative process and get functional once in a while. Worry about pull tabs versus screw tops and whether your product reseals easily. These are the unglamorous steps to successful packaging.

THE GOLD STANDARD

If you are disciplined—and creative—about considering how packaging affects the ways consumers interact with your product, you may be successful not only in creating compelling packaging but perhaps even in creating new usage occasions and new product categories through packaging innovation.

Kraft Cheese is a terrific model for this notion. The brand team saw a gap in which school-age kids weren't eating a lot of cheese for lunch. Why? Because a hunk of cheese isn't a great lunch or snack food by itself—it's better when combined with crackers or lunch meat. The brand team's response to this opportunity was simply brilliant. It created Oscar Mayer Lunchables—putting crackers, lunch meat, cheese, and a candy snack together into a single box to create a convenient way for consumers to enjoy Kraft Cheese as part of a complete lunch, and an easy way for moms to pack the lunch box. By focusing on the consumer need (convenient, complete lunch) and expanding the definition to include product categories other than just cheese (luncheon meat, crackers, and candy) the brand group developed an entirely new product category. Kraft now had a sensational, proprietary means of fulfilling a consumer need and selling cheese free from competition.

Taco Bell, the leading Mexican fast-food restaurant chain in the United States, instigated a commando raid on the Mexican food aisle in grocery stores using the same proprietary packaging technique. Taco Bell leveraged its high consumer awareness and brand appeal by introducing an entire product line of Taco Bell branded Mexican foods. The most insightful of the new products was Taco Bell Taco Kits, containing corn tortilla shells with Taco Bell seasoning and Taco Bell hot sauce. Instead of competing with the established brands like Old El Paso and Rosarita on their own terms by offering only stand-alone products, Taco Bell leveraged its key difference—the restaurant experience—into a competitive benefit, by enabling consumers to make real Taco Bell Tacos at home. No one else could do that.

At Procter & Gamble, I worked on a project aimed at changing the way consumers bought cake mixes. This change was to be accomplished—you guessed it—through creative packaging. We studied the cake habits of consumers and noted that they had two basic options; buy a cake mix for 79 cents and a can of frosting for $1.59 and bake the cake yourself; or go to the in-store bakery and buy a cake that was ready to go with icing and decorations for between $15.00 and $25.00. We were sure there was an opportunity to fill a gap in the middle.

We developed a new product line called "Pantastic Party Cake Kits," which included everything you need to create a great cake in your own home in one box. The box included the cake mix, frosting, a coloring packet for the frosting, and a proprietary paper baking pan that allowed the consumer to bake great looking shaped cakes at home. The kits came in Kermit the Frog, Miss Piggy, Garfield, Major League Baseball, Sweetheart, and Party Bear varieties. In test market the product sold wildly, and we knew creative packaging had succeeded once again. Unfortunately, you haven't seen this product yet because technological problems with the paper baking pans have delayed its release.

CREATING BRAND PERSONALITY THROUGH PACKAGING

Just as Tommy Hilfiger clothes communicate a message about the person wearing them, the graphic treatment and design of your package can communicate attitude and personality. It may seem silly, but yes, a package can sport an attitude. Dark packaging connotes upscale and fashionable; pearl white is high class; multi-colors can be wild and irreverent.

Many brands have created a very specific brand personality as part of their overall positioning strategy. Dow Bathroom Cleaner with Scrubbing Bubbles is an example. The personality of the Scrubbing Bubbles gets carried through all the product's advertising as well as packaging—whimsical and fun, not at all what you would think the personality of a cleaning product would be. But it works because the brand has focused on reinforcing the brand personality in everything it does, including packaging.

Breakfast cereal brands are kings at developing and reinforcing a personality and attitude through packaging. In fact, they go so far as to develop characters that embody the product's personality: Rice Krispies—Snap, Crackle & Pop; Cap'n Crunch; Frosted Flakes w/Tony the Tiger, to name but a few. Coors Beer reinforces the brand's use of pure Rocky Mountain spring water through the graphic of a mountain waterfall on its cans. In all, brand personality and attitude can be quite powerful if considered as part of the communication objectives for packaging.

LINE EXTENSIONS AND FAMILY PACKAGING OF PRODUCTS

I was in a grocery store recently and saw a women on her hands and knees in the juice aisle, peering at different boxes of Capri-Sun juice. She was perplexed, searching for a specific fruit punch flavor. As I looked at the boxes lining the shelf, I understood her dilemma. The brand had seven rows of product, and all of the boxes looked virtually identical from a standing position in the store aisle. Only by dropping to hands and knees could I find and read the flavor listing, which was buried within the graphic elements of the design.

As I moved to the men's personal care section, I encountered a similar problem. The brand AFTA, manufactured by Mennen, makes a terrific pre-electric shave lotion that I have used for years. But every time I shop the section I have to be extremely careful to pick up the right bottle, because several different AFTA products are packaged in virtually the same gray bottle with identical graphics and colors. I have to squint at the extremely small print at the top of the label to differentiate one product from another. It's so confusing that about once in every five trips to the store I end up picking up the wrong bottle, and this after being a loyal user for over a decade!

Often brands have several different product varieties to sell to consumers, requiring that the packaging differentiate between options yet still reflect a "brand family" look. Sometimes this can be accomplished with as little as different-color stripes on the packaging, and at other times it requires more radical alterations. Creating a "line look" can often be a challenging task, but consumers must be able to identify your brand and differentiate between products to obtain the benefits they value most.

QUICK-READ PACKAGING

In the mid 1990s, Disney Home Video undertook an entire repackaging effort to make shopping for their videos easier for consumers. At the time of the initiative, the Disney video aisle was a mishmash of packaging, with no thought to how one product line looked in relation to others. Each line had been designed independently. As the Disney segment of the category had grown to include over a dozen different product lines, the brand teams wanted to ensure that consumers could quickly and easily find the Disney videos of their choice.

Packaging experts from San Francisco's Landor Associates were hired to develop the line look. The goal was simple: Blindfolded consumers were brought in and placed in front of a video aisle containing all of the different Disney videos in their new packaging—about 120 different video titles in all. The consumers would be told to find a specific video when their blindfold was removed—for example, *Ariel's Undersea Adventures*. The consumer had to be able to find that video line in three seconds or less or the packaging was deemed unacceptable.

It took several iterations, but we finally achieved our goal. How? By creating a "billboard" effect on the shelves with the packages. Each of the different Disney Video product lines had very distinct graphic designs that when stacked next to each other on the shelf created a miniature billboard, making it very easy to find the right section to look in: Masterpiece Collection; Sing-Along Songs; Favorite Stories; The Little Mermaid; Walt Disney Film Classics; Winnie the Pooh and others each were designed to pop off the shelf, while at the same time maintaining a distinctive Disney feel. When introduced into the marketplace, Disney video sales increased significantly and consumer satisfaction was high.

Minute Maid Orange Juice does a fantastic job of creating a billboard effect with packaging that reflects the familial look yet communicates effectively the different options of juices available. The brand communicates the different products through a simple colored bar across the lower third of each package's front panel. It is very easy to read and the family grouping of packages is appealing and attention getting.

PACKAGING CAN MAKE OR BREAK SALES

Procter & Gamble learned the hard way what a small mistake in packaging can do to brand sales. When Folgers Coffee Singles (an instant-coffee product in a single-serving size) were introduced into test markets, the product failed because of packaging issues.

The first problem was a disadvantageous price comparison to instant coffee because the brand group had designed the boxes to hold too many Coffee Singles packets:

AVERAGE RETAIL PRICING

FOLGERS COFFEE SINGLES	INSTANT COFFEE
20 ct. box = $2.99	8 oz. jar = $2.79
40 ct. box = $5.99	16 oz. jar = $5.59

A second issue concerned the way the product was stacked into cases when shipped to the grocery stores. The cases did not fit correctly onto a normal shipping palette, overhanging on each side by about 1.5 inches. This overlap resulted in crushed cases as forklifts moved things around in the stock room, causing abnormally high returns for damaged goods.

To fix these problems, P&G managers reduced the number of Coffee Singles in each box, lowering the package counts from twenty to eighteen and from forty to thirty-six. Now Folgers Coffee Singles had a pricing *advantage* over instant coffee while maintaining an identical profit margin to the original packages:

AVERAGE RETAIL PRICING

FOLGERS COFFEE SINGLES	INSTANT COFFEE
19 ct. box = $2.69	8 oz. jar = $2.79
38 ct. box = $5.49	16 oz. jar = $5.59

The resulting smaller shipping boxes fit perfectly onto the palettes, virtually eliminating damages. The difference? By making this seemingly insignificant change, Folgers Coffee Singles went from a disappointing .5 percent share of the instant-coffee market to over a 5 percent share. Fixing the packaging problems increased sales by a factor of 10×, turning Coffee Singles into a profitable success story for P&G.

DEVELOPING PACKAGING IN A COMPETITIVE VACUUM

A mistake commonly made is developing packaging concepts in a competitive vacuum. Many times I've seen new graphics being evaluated in someone's office, or packaging mock-ups placed alone on a desk or on a giant conference table for everyone to admire and comment on. The problem is that the packages are not viewed in the context of the environment in which they will be displayed and sold to the public. I've seen hundreds of sample packages that looked great when they were sitting alone on a conference-room table but got lost or looked horribly out of place when put into the store selling environment with competition.

Secrets of the Game

Top marketers re-create a typical store shelf setting inside their offices so that they have at hand a ready reference of the competitive environment. As new packaging options are considered, they place them onto the shelves and see what different options look like within the context of the competitive setting to ensure that their brand pops off the shelf.

Rule of Thumb: If a consumer cannot walk up to the shelf and locate your product in three seconds, your packaging is failing to communicate.

POINTS TO PONDER BEFORE DEVELOPING PACKAGING

There are several steps required and questions that you must answer before embarking on any packaging initiatives. First, look at the competitive set of products that your product will be situated next to on the store shelf. Analyze all brands carefully. What primary colors are they using? Study their unique packaging designs—both graphic designs and engineering designs of the packages. Read the words on the labels very carefully. Notice the size of each product, the shape of each product, the number of packages that fit on the store shelf. How well does each product fit in the consumer's hand? What consumer benefits are the competitive products communicating well with their packaging? Can you think of consumer benefits that the competitive packages fail to communicate, offering you an opportunity? Does your product have performance superiority versus competitors?

Consider how the package will be displayed and stacked in the store. How tall can it be to fit on the shelf at a typical store? How deep is a store shelf, and how should your product sit on the shelf? Is there an ideal number of packages that will stack on the shelf?

Most large retailers measure the success of products by how much profit a particular item will return to the store commensurate to the amount of shelf space the item requires. Retailers want to maximize their profits, and so those brands and items that return the highest profit (both in terms of gross margin and penny profit) per square inch of shelf space are the ones that receive the most room. It is important to design packages that utilize space efficiently. Along these lines, you should carefully consider the number of items packed into shipping cases so that when store personnel restock the shelves, they always put out a full case and do not have to return partial cases to the back room. This logistical allowance enables the retailer to efficiently use his money to keep products on the shelf and not incur carrying costs for product in the back room. Store managers *hate* having partial cases of products in the back room!

Even if your product is an established category leader, you should always be asking questions like: How does the consumer open the package? Is there a way of making it easier to use? Can it fit into a consumer's hand more comfortably, or function more effectively? Is the package thrown away immediately, or is product dispensed from the package over time and stored? Is there a way to make it more storable? Are there other products that are typically used with this one? Could I package them together?

TRENDY VS. CLASSIC GRAPHIC TREATMENTS

The choice of graphic treatment is critical to the success of the package. Trendy graphics commit products to long-term problems. Trends are short lived. Packages that reflect short-term thinking often have to be revised time and time again, and each change confuses consumers.

Classic packaging that will stand the test of time is what every product should strive for. The most successful brands in the world all have logos and packaging graphics that have endured decades with very little change—Coca-Cola, Tide, McDonald's, Shell Oil, Gillette, Hershey's Chocolate Bars, Heinz Ketchup, Campbell's Soup, Jell-O, and Domino's Pizza to name but a few.

PREPARING A PACKAGING BRIEF

The final step in undertaking a packaging project is the development of a document called the packaging brief. A packaging brief contains all of the information that is relevant to development of the packaging assignment. It:

1. outlines the competitive environment;
2. addresses important issues and insights;
3. specifies opportunities to create competitive advantage;
4. delineates important consumer benefits; and
5. states the positioning strategy for the product, brand personality, and attitude.

The reasoning behind developing a packaging brief is to think through all of the functions the package must perform and specify the information the package must communicate *before* you begin looking at different artistic options. Why? Because as soon as the pretty artwork and packaging ideas start streaming in, strategic thought goes out the window. It's easy to become infatuated with packaging proposals. Seeing new artwork is a little like seeing your own newborn child for the first time. Your baby is the most beautiful baby in the world. Other people might have ugly babies, but not you. The package is the personification of you. It becomes very easy to lose perspective. You need to develop the packaging brief to have strategic focus to ensure everything the package needs to accomplish is ultimately achieved.

Secrets of the Game

Packaging strategy must be driven by marketing, not by manufacturing! Let the people at the plant tell you how the machines work and try to understand the limitations as well as capabilities, but do not let that kill a great idea. Most innovations change the way things are currently done. If a new machine is required to create a kick-butt packaging idea, then buy it!

Packaging development is perhaps the most rewarding task marketing managers perform, as the fruit of their labor appears in stores all over the world. Great packaging can sustain a brand. Poor packaging can kill one very quickly. It is critically important that all initiatives are developed in line with strategic objectives and that those objectives are adhered to.

PACKAGING AND THE LITTLE GUYS

The strategic underpinnings of great packaging expand well beyond the boundaries of consumer products. Every business that advertises or has a sign hung out to attract customers should think about these same issues. Whether you own a small taco stand or a software company, the way you package your business to your consumers is just as important as how P&G develops a package for Tide. Great packaging increases consumer preference and ultimately increases sales.

A friend of mine was doing some consulting for a small family-owned furniture manufacturer in the mountains of North Carolina. They wanted to grow their business outside the confines of the state. By using sound packaging principles, they found success. They didn't change their products, but they changed the way they presented their products to consumers by crafting a new-look product brochure that captured an upscale mountain feel and offered differentiation from other furniture makers. Now the same product line commands a premium price and is on its way to becoming a solid brand name.

Another friend runs a small Allstate Insurance office in Roxboro, North Carolina. For him, his office space and outdoor sign is his packaging. He's moved his office three different times in order to upgrade his office space, and each time, his business has grown. What he has come to realize is that consumers buy insurance to feel security and safety. It's important to them that the office setting of the agent communicates that. An old, run-down building doesn't give the consumer confidence in the agent or the company. An office in a newer complex, with nice furnishings and a comfortable interior, helps consumers feel good about their choice.

When the great baseball legend Yogi Berra said "You can observe a lot by watching," he could have been talking about packaging development. You can learn a lot by studying and paying attention to what other brands and competitors are doing. Don't try to design your packaging in isolation. Here, more than anywhere else in The Marketing Game, you must force yourself to step back from the excitement and glamour of logo treatments and colors and take a long, analytical look at the job you aim to do.

CHAPTER SUMMARY

- Packaging is the best way to communicate to consumers the most compelling reasons to buy your product. Packaging can deliver messages to consumers right up to the moment when they pluck it off the shelf.
- Communicating to the consumer through your packaging is critical, as even the best advertising campaign reaches only 70 percent of target consumers. If your product is part of the competitive set in a store, you have a 100 percent chance of communicating your message to the consumer!
- Package copy is no time to be shy—you should think like a carnival hawker.
- Unique and proprietary packaging shapes can offer distinctive brand differentiation.
- Consumers love packages that perform better than the competition.
- Smart packaging can sometimes lead to the development of new product categories.
- Packaging can help reinforce brand personality.
- Packaging should be easy to read. If a consumer can't find your product on the shelf in less than three seconds, your packaging graphics are not communicating well.
- Packaging can have a direct effect upon sales (both good and bad).
- When developing packaging, don't do it in a competitive vacuum. Look at it in relation to what it will look like in stores among the sea of products.

Solving the Merchandising and Distribution Mystery

PUTTING YOUR PRODUCT IN THE
RIGHT PLACE FOR CONSUMERS

L ET'S PRETEND YOU'RE IN THE MARKET TO BUY A ROLEX Presidential watch. You've shopped around and found the watch you want at Cartier Jewelers for $3,995. You go home to think about it, and on the way stop for a bag of chips at the neighborhood 7-Eleven. There at the checkout counter, to your amazement, you see the very same watch for nearly 50 percent off, at the discounted price of only $1,999!

How would you decide where to make the purchase? Would you have a nagging suspicion that the quality of the watch at the 7-Eleven might be inferior to the one at Cartier—that maybe the 7-Eleven models had some sort of flaw? Would you worry about the credibility of the 7-Eleven salesperson, and could you trust what he said about the watch between ringing up Slurpee sales at the cash register? Would you have a concern about getting the watch serviced under warranty at 7-Eleven should something go wrong later? Would you think that the convenience-store Rolex models were illegal knockoff's imported from who knows where?

Of course you would! A Rolex display inside a 7-Eleven store is completely out of context with everything you have heard or know about the Rolex brand. You'd have a hard time believing that the watch at 7-Eleven is truly the premium Rolex quality watch that you wanted. The sales environment inside the 7-Eleven is not a match with the kind of place you would expect Rolex watches to be sold, based on the brand's premium image.

Secrets of the Game

Where your product is sold, and how it is displayed, creates a powerful message about your brand in the mind of consumers—more powerful in fact than your advertising. Everything communicates. Proper distribution and display will maximize sales and reinforce your brand positioning strategy.

DISTRIBUTION STRATEGIES

You can choose from any number of distribution strategies ranging from *ubiquity,* wanting to have your product everywhere, to *exclusivity,* selling it only in a few hand-picked locations. Each has its own merits and pitfalls, and as a marketing manager you must consider the options.

Ubiquity

The distribution strategy developed by former Coca-Cola CEO Roberto Goizueta for his flagship brand was "to have Coca-Cola products available within an arm's reach of desire." By that statement, he meant that he wanted Coca-Cola products available everywhere and anywhere a human being could possibly be: ubiquity.

The company's stunning success through the 1990s is largely tied to this simple mandate: find more and more points of distribution for Coca-Cola products. Ten years ago, who would have predicted vending machines in remote National Parks locations or inside most office buildings? Or all-you-can-drink fountain dispensers at McDonald's and other fast-food restaurants? Or Coca-Cola coolers at the checkout at Target and Blockbuster Video stores?

In pursuit of ubiquity, Coke employees work cooperatively with established retailers to find new and better ways to offer Coke products to consumers. Inside many grocery stores, for example, you can find a cooler full of single-serve Coca-Cola products, a Coca-Cola vending machine, and a Coca-Cola fountain dispenser in addition to the product available in the soft drink aisle. By focusing on finding ever more points of distribution, Coca-Cola management continues to believe double-digit annual growth is possible, even with a brand nearly 130 years old.

Exclusivity

At the opposite end of the distribution spectrum is the exclusivity strategy, which limits the product to specific selling environments or even one particular retailer. Why would a brand manager choose this strategy? Simple math would lead you to believe that the more places you sell your product, the more product you sell. But remember the Rolex example; selling your product everywhere isn't always the smartest way to go.

Secrets of the Game

When choosing a distribution strategy, match *brand image* with the consumer perception of the potential *distribution point* to find the channel that *enhances and synergizes* your product identity.

Consider for a moment the brand Polo by Ralph Lauren. The brand image for Polo is upscale and elite, targeted at households with annual incomes above $100,000 and fashion wannabes who like the well-heeled image. The brand has historically adopted an exclusivity strategy of selling primarily through dedicated Polo Shops and high-end clothiers. This strategy matches the nature and tone of the brand and has worked well for years to differentiate Polo product from other brands of apparel.

If you were the brand manager for Polo considering new distribution opportunities, think about which of these potential retailers would enhance and synergize with consumer perception of the Polo brand: Walmart (no), Kmart (no), Bloomingdales (yes), Saks Fifth Avenue (yes), Costco Warehouse Club (no), The Men's Warehouse (maybe), Discount Outlet Malls (yes).

The hot new trend in creating bargain outlets for premium brands is to create a shop in the new Discount Outdoor Malls. The success of Barney's Basement, or Nordstrom's Rack, or the Anne Taylor Loft—which all sell exclusive product at discount prices—are great models for Polo to emulate. There's a big difference between offering your product at a club store or mass merchant and selling it at one of those brand name outlet stores that are cropping up all over. Outlet stores are a terrific way to sell overstocks and out-of-season items to price-conscious consumers. Instead of devaluing the product, outlet stores actually reinforce the upscale image by making consumers believe that only in this specialized outlet can they obtain authentic product at bargain prices. The displays, merchandising and general look of the stores is all carefully crafted to support the premium image— no dump bins or bargain-basement piles here!

Disney is that rare company that manages both ubiquity and exclusivity strategies with real intelligence and flair. Disney videos, for example, are available everywhere: supermarkets, drug stores, airports. People snatch them up wherever they see them. But Disney also knows when to create consumer demand—and command higher prices—by holding back on product distribution. Some brands, like Winnie the Pooh, have actually been segmented into separate looks (and separate price points) for the different channels. The colorful, cartoonish "Disney Pooh" line is designed with bold palettes and playful graphics, and it's available everywhere, from mass merchants to groceries. However, the gentler, more abstract "Classic Pooh" products modeled on the original watercolor artwork from the Pooh storybooks are only available at upscale boutiques and Disney stores. Both brands are tremendously popular.

THE GOLD STANDARD

The classic case study of a powerful distribution strategy is the shrewd placement of Disney's "The Art of Disney" hand-painted animation cels. Through proper distribution, and little else, the marketing whizzes at Disney were able to create a highly lucrative long-term business.

Faced with huge warehouses bursting at the seams with original art cels from over sixty years of Disney animation, the Disney marketing team one day looked at the pile and figured "why not try to sell them off?" For perspective, one hour of Disney animation yields 64,800 original art cels. You can only imagine the millions upon millions of cels available inside the Disney vaults after all those years of work!

Disney considered different distribution options, and the most obvious choice was to offer the cels to Kmart, Target, and Walmart and price them between $30 and $50 each. This was an appealing and financially tempting idea and seemed a safe bet with consumers. Running the numbers, if Disney sold a million cels per year, they could net around $30 million dollars annually, since the only real cost associated with selling each cel was its frame.

But the brand team walked away from the easy money. Instead, it opted for an exclusivity distribution strategy— limiting the availability and selling only through The Disney Store, Disney Catalog, and Fine Art Galleries at a price of $250–$500 per cel.

Why did the brand team pick exclusivity over mass availability? On the surface, the decision seemed foolhardy; after all, this is Disney, the most commercialized brand on the planet! But the Disney marketers knew better. They chose to create a premium image and stoke consumer passion for original Disney art, thereby establishing a long-term business. They knew that if these one-of-a-kind artworks were available for mass consumption it would have an adverse effect upon the overriding belief in the "magic" of the Disney animated movies themselves. (After all, they are so special, you can buy them only once every seven years on video!) By selling the cels at a high price in limited quantity at upscale outlets, they accepted the fact that they would sell fewer cels each year than if they'd blown them out at the mass retailers. But with the lofty price point, they'd have to sell only a fraction of the volume—only about 100,000 units each year—to net the same profit. By choosing the exclusivity strategy, they elevated owning original Disney art cels far above the mere purchase of an upscale poster. And the Disney art business is on solid ground for decades to come.

An exclusivity distribution strategy usually works best for brands that are either high-ticket—Rolex, Mercedes-Benz, Porsche—or that have a real or perceived limited supply, for example, Coogi sweaters imported from Australia, fine art, hand-made goods, etc. This type of product must provide more than function and value; it must impart status as well.

CHANNEL STRATEGIES

One way of looking at the distribution issue is to define a channel strategy, or what kinds of retailers should carry your product. If your company sells canned green beans, would you want to sell them at your local Chief Automotive store? Of course not. But you would want to have your beans available at Costco and Sam's Club warehouse stores, in addition to traditional supermarkets and independent grocers. And what about institutional food services for schools and hospitals? Restaurant suppliers? Convenience stores? Bodegas in the many Hispanic communities? You'd definitely want them to sell your green beans.

There is no magic list of distribution channels to review in order to select the ones you'd like a la carte. The channels of distribution are numerous and ever changing, and opportunities within these channels must be searched out separately and painstakingly for each individual product. If you manufacture scoreboards, for example, your distribution channels would likely be pro sports venues, high schools, colleges and universities, and city recreation departments. For audio speakers, your channels might be electronics stores, audiophile shops, automotive retailers, and high-end electronics catalogs. Each brand must specifically define its distribution channel strategy to place product where the target audience shops and in the retail environments that support the overall brand positioning.

Thinking in terms of channels is usually the best way to develop a distribution strategy. Most top companies plan distribution this way, developing separate placement objectives within each channel. For example, the green beans brand manager may expect his channel strategy to achieve distribution in 90 percent of grocery stores, 60 percent of convenience stores, 85 percent of institutional food services, etc. By quantifying these objectives, the manager can develop annual volume projections and set the benchmarks for placement and sales within the organization.

Secrets of the Game

Until you achieve distribution in excess of 70 percent of the outlets in your primary selling channel, *do not advertise* broadly to consumers.

Consumer advertising prior to a 70 percent distribution penetration is a waste of money. Think of it this way: Even at a 70 percent penetration level, three of every ten consumers who go looking for your product can't find it!

THE WRONG DISTRIBUTION STRATEGY CAN DEVASTATE A BRAND

Levi's jeans learned the hard way that even a popular established brand can sabotage its business through a poor distribution strategy. Throughout the 1970s, the brand had a virtual lock on the jeans market. The corporate distribution strategy was to offer Genuine Levi's products exclusively at upscale department stores. This strategy had paved their road to success for several decades, and they believed it would keep them on that profitable path for decades to come.

As the 1970s ended, shopping malls became the rage, obsolescing traditional stand-alone department stores. Department stores chains were forced to move into the malls to stay where the shoppers were, but here they became vulnerable to increased competition, especially in the apparel category. At most malls, boutique shops such as GAP and Banana Republic as well as a variety of young, contemporary "teen shops" quickly became the favorite clothes shopping stop for the fashion-conscience youth crowd.

As sudden as a lightning strike, Levi's weren't cool anymore because they weren't sold in the teen clothing boutiques. Guess, Calvin Klein, and private-label jeans all became much more fashionable—primarily through the image transference from the stores *where* they were being sold. Levi's were in the department stores where "my parents buy their clothes"—yuck! Ever since this distribution strategy blunder, the Levi's brand has struggled to re-establish a fashionable image with teenagers and has watched its market share plummet from the 70 percent range in the 1970s to around 20 percent today. The damage has been so bad that in early 1999 Levis closed eleven of their twenty-two manufacturing facilities.

PRODUCT STRATEGIES BY DISTRIBUTION CHANNEL

Many manufacturers adapt their product in some way to fine tune it for placement in different distribution channels. For example, many consumer products brands that gain distribution within club stores such as Costco and Sam's Club will offer a special super-large size, or create double or triple packs of product that are not generally available in traditional retail environments such as grocery stores or pharmacies. They do this for two reasons. First, they attempt to raise the "ring" price of the sale (the amount paid for the group of product). They know consumers in these channels buy in bulk (since consumers perceive they're receiving a much lower price per unit), and they have a good chance at selling more product at one time than they could in any other channel.

Second, by selling more units, they ensure that the consumer will be using their product longer and won't be back in the store anytime soon, possibly faced with a tempting competitive offer. Some categories, like facial tissue and snack foods, know that consumers actually use more product if they have more around the house. For all of these reasons, creating customized bulk packages to sell at club stores makes good marketing sense.

As unlikely as it might seem, television manufacturers also follow this customization strategy. When you shop for a thirty-two-inch

Sony Trinitron television, you can find several different variations available, depending upon which stores you shop. At Kmart and Walmart, you'll find a somewhat "stripped down" model (just a standard TV) at an attractively low price. Inside a Best Buy or Circuit City, you'll often find two or three different models of the thirty-two-inch Sony, with a variety of add-ons such as Picture-in-Picture, S-Video connections, surround sound and various plug-ins for audio and video jacks. These sets sell for as much as $500 to $600 more than the standard thirty-two-inch Sony TVs at Kmart.

Why the variation? The same reason as there are Mercedes and Hyundais. Some consumers have caviar tastes while living in trailer parks. They want the personal gratification associated with owning a big thirty-two-inch TV but don't need the extras. A big screen is all that matters to them, and Kmart and Walmart are stores where this type of consumer is more likely to shop. Yuppies want to hook up their DVD players and surround sound, so they'll shop at the higher-end electronics stores and pay much more to get the add-ons. Sony tailors the product to fit the consumer needs of the shoppers in the different distribution channels.

CREATING AN IN-STORE PRESENCE

Once you have decided where you want your product placed, the next piece of the puzzle is how you influence the way it is displayed and sold in the retail environment. It's not enough to put the product on the shelf. Where it sits, and what it sits next to, are important as well.

Secrets of the Game

The Consumer Strike Zone—the focal range in which consumers are most likely to shop for products on a store shelf—is almost identical to the traditional baseball strike zone, the top of the shoulders to the top of the knees. You must have your product placed "in the zone" if you're going to win at The Marketing Game.

On your next trip to the supermarket, watch a few shoppers as you make your way up and down the aisles. See how their eyes scan the shelf. Notice how many of the products they purchase are "in the zone." Studies have shown that while the shelves in the Consumer Strike Zone hold only about 50 percent of the products in a typical retail environment, they produce about 85 percent to 90 percent of total sales!

CAPTURING INCREMENTAL SHELF SPACE

Often, The Marketing Game is very simply played. The basic principle is *the products with the most shelf space win!* When this is the case, the battleground for top marketers is to develop a rationale to convince store managers that your product merits more space than the competitive product.

For several years, most marketing companies used a specialized computer program to help them illustrate their placement argument with retailers. The program analyzed each individual item for sales velocity and profitability, considering how many units of the product fit onto the store's shelf, then spit out a list of the number of facings each product in the category deserved in order to maximize the retailer's profitability.

This program was a successful sales tool for years. The sales people for the top consumer products companies would perform the analysis free of charge and share the results with the stores, who were thrilled to have the data. Procter & Gamble brands used this service as a primary sales tactic for nearly a decade. Of course, the analysis was often skewed in favor of P&G's products, but that bias was to be expected. Retailers took the information with a grain of salt and acted from there.

The retail chains have consolidated and grown larger and more sophisticated over the years, and they now perform regular profitability analyses on their own and don't need manufacturers to do it for them. But any good marketer still runs the numbers to understand the competitive sales environment and profitability landscape. This knowledge gives him ammunition to approach the retailer for more shelf space.

Savvy marketers now create their own personalized versions of a profitability model with any spreadsheet program such as LOTUS or EXCEL by plugging in sales information and running the numbers. The calculations are fairly straightforward. Obtain the store's sales numbers in your product category for a month or two; then load in pricing and cost information (most large companies always have competitive sheets so that they know what prices are being offered to the trade). Multiply sales volume times profit per item. This calculation will render a "profit by SKU" and can be sorted to produce a rank order from top to bottom for each of the items the store carries in your product category, showing which are producing profit and which are not, as well as documenting the differences.

Remember, stores are most interested in maximizing profits for every square inch of shelf space. Products that aren't producing profits are vulnerable to being replaced by something that sells better. The "profit by SKU" ranking identifies the products in peril. Looking at the bottom of the list (let's hope none of your products are there), you can create a rational argument with the retailer for dropping those items, adding more of yours, and increasing your shelf space.

The advent of profitability analyses in the 1980s and 1990s caused the death of many small brands that simply could not generate the sales velocity to compete effectively with major brands. It's a shame, too, because many of these small local brands were actually better products than the national competitors.

BLOCKING STRATEGIES

If you're managing a brand with multiple products in a typical store—like Folgers Coffee with Regular, Automatic Drip, Decaffeinated, and Gourmet Supreme flavors, each offered in 13 oz., 26 oz., and 39 oz. cans—you can create an in-store advantage by developing a blocking scheme that maximizes your brand recognition and aids the consumer in finding your product.

A blocking scheme is really nothing more than designing the way you want the products to be displayed on the shelf. A good blocking scheme will increase sales and call attention to your products.

Wander by the coffee section in your store and notice how the Folgers (red cans) and Maxwell House (electric blue cans) pop off the shelf. These brands are so easy to find because they have convinced the retailers to display their products in a block section on the shelf. In the soft drink aisle, you can always find the Coca-Cola section by quickly scanning the aisle for the bright red cans and bottles. Most top brands devise a blocking strategy for their products. If you don't, you leave your product shelf placement in the hands of store clerks and even worse, your competition!

SPECIAL DISPLAYS

For some brands, proprietary special displays are the best place to spend merchandising dollars. These displays can be permanent, or temporary, displays that are discarded when the product sells out.

Permanent displays are the most desirable merchandising a marketer can ask for. They mark your territory against competitors and allow you to directly control the way your product is presented to the consumer. You'll often spot permanent branded displays for products such as sunglasses and watches in mass merchandisers, but sometimes a very important part of the display is something you can't see.

Have you ever been in a jewelry store with a display for DeBeers Diamonds? Not only will you see the diamonds displayed with highly effective branding, but what you don't see is that the lights in that store are part of the display provided by DeBeers. Lighting can have a significant effect upon the way a diamond appears to glitter, so stores carrying DeBeers diamonds are offered this special lighting by DeBeers as part of their display program in order to optimally showcase their products. Very smart, and very effective.

Temporary displays usually work only if your product is seasonal in nature or a quick hit-and-run, like a video release for a hot movie or a new CD. Most retailers are predisposed against taking in temporary displays because they think they look junky. To get yours in, you have to make it gorgeous!

When I was at Disney Home Video, the Halloween seasonal tapes were part of my domain. Sales of these videos had been sluggish for several years, and so my brand team decided to take an aggressive position by dreaming up a totally new temporary display concept that would drive retailers to want to take in these titles just to get the great-looking displays in their stores. The team in Creative Services used the inspiration of Disney's Haunted

Mansion (one of the classic rides in the Magic Kingdom) to create The Haunted Mansion Video Shoppe, a display containing forty-eight videos in a wickedly cool and spooky display. They sold like a glass of ice water in hell, and retailers loved them. These displays became the centerpieces of the seasonal section, which not only ensured our distribution but nabbed us a premium location for shoppers as well.

Music stores are effective in using temporary displays to capture the cutting-edge attitude of the music industry and feature hot, contemporary artists. Have you ever noticed that when you walk into a MusicLand store or other dedicated music shop, the mood is suddenly really cool and the lights are just a little dimmer than in the rest of the mall? It's all part of the merchandising scheme. The environment is designed to make you feel the music, to feel like you're cutting-edge, even if you go in shopping for Barry Manilow CDs and not Smashing Pumpkins.

Secrets of the Game

Top marketers try to influence everything associated with the display and sale of their product. Lighting, ambiance, and product displays in the retail environment are all powerful marketing tools that can directly increase the appeal of your product to consumers and ultimately increase sales.

Saturday Night Live comedian Kevin Nealon used to portray a character who peppered his conversations with subliminal messages to convince others to do his bidding. Distribution and merchandising strategies work in almost the same fashion. They can subtly influence consumers, effectively and proprietarily enhancing product sales; increase consumer appeal; and stay off the radar screen of competition, creating a scenario to develop competitive advantage.

CHAPTER SUMMARY

- Where your product is sold and how it is displayed create a powerful communication message about your product in the minds of consumers—more powerful in fact than your advertising.

- Distribution strategies can range from ubiquity to exclusivity.
- The most important issue to address when developing a distribution strategy is to match the brand image with the consumer perception of the potential distribution point to find channels that enhance and synergize with your product identity.
- Another way of looking at distribution is to develop channel strategies.
- A bad distribution plan can devastate a brand.
- Often you can alter the product offering by distribution channel to match the consumer needs.
- You should always strive to display your product in the consumer strike zone—from the top of the knee to the top of the shoulder.
- Often, the main factor that affects sales is shelf space. The product with the most space gets the most sales.
- Often, you can help draw the consumer to your product through smartly using a blocking strategy.
- Special displays can be effective in getting product, like video releases, in and out short term.

CONSUMER COMMUNICATION

Cracking the Code to Great Advertising

THE KEYS TO GETTING GREAT
RESULTS FROM YOUR AD AGENCY

E ARLY IN MY MARKETING CAREER I stepped into the office of a category manager at Procter & Gamble and asked him a simple question: "Since P&G does so much advertising and creates so many different campaigns over the course of a year, why don't we make the advertising ourselves? Wouldn't it be more cost effective to develop an in-house advertising agency and hire our own creative teams, saving the millions upon millions of dollars we pay to the dozen or so ad agencies in New York, Chicago, and Los Angeles that work on our different brands? And wouldn't we have more control over the finished product that way?"

His answer was simple. "We need different creative perspectives for our many products. Most creative people have a certain personal style to the way they develop their creative campaigns. If we hired our own creative people to work on all of our brands, the content would begin to look very similar over time. It's the nature of the beast. Without new blood, new visions and challenges to our ways of thinking about our brands, we would quickly land in an advertising rut. But by hiring different agencies, each brand receives its own unique creative approach and we can tap the brains of many talents, not just a few of our own, to achieve consistently great and unexpected results."

That is probably the best explanation I've ever heard of why advertising agencies exist. As my career has unfolded, I have experienced both incredibly wonderful and horrifically painful interactions with agencies. I have discovered along the way that developing a good working relationship with an agency—one that fosters a creative environment and consistently produces great work—is a learned skill. It begins with a thorough understanding of the agency business, and ends with the development of good client skills that mesh with the agency's needs.

To develop a positive working relationship with an advertising agency that results in consistently strong campaigns, you must first understand some realities of the advertising agency business.

REALITY #1: ADVERTISING AGENCIES ARE BUSINESSES WITH PROFIT MOTIVE

Advertising is the area in which most marketing people have the least amount of hands-on practical experience. Understanding fair market value for agency services is difficult to do, and costs can vary widely from agency to agency. If you don't know what you're doing, an advertising agency can fleece you faster than a three-card monte player in Central Park, and the stakes are astronomical.

So here are the basics behind the razzmatazz. Agencies make their money from three primary channels: 1) a monthly retainer fee, usually locked in for a six- to twelve-month duration; 2) a markup on all of the advertising materials they produce for you, usually in the 30 percent to 50 percent range; and 3) a commission on all advertising placements they "buy" for you.

To understand the magnitude of the dollars, let's examine an average brand's financial interaction with an agency over a one-year period:

ANNUAL AGENCY INCOME

Monthly retainer of $7,000:	$ 84,000
Materials development markup @ 40%:	
$250,000 of print materials	$100,000
Two TV spots @ $250m each:	$200,000
Four radio spots @ $10m each:	$16,000
Ad-buying agency commission @ 12%:	
$2 million campaign	$240,000
Total:	$640,000

If you assume the advertising campaign was the primary marketing effort of the year, the agency hauled in around 20 percent of the total marketing budget!

Just think what a bonanza it is for an agency to land an account like McDonald's or Coca-Cola, companies that spend hundreds of millions of dollars each year on advertising. It's no wonder so many agencies can afford huge digs on Madison Avenue.

REALITY #2: ADVERTISING AGENCIES ARE NOT YOUR PARTNERS

Advertising agencies are not your friends, and they certainly are not your partners. They are suppliers, the same as any other supplier. Unfortunately, they can have a much more dramatic impact upon your business than most suppliers, depending upon how well they do their jobs.

Agency folks will vehemently disagree with this assessment, but if they were your partners, they would share the risk of failure with you. I have yet to come across an agency with a money-back guarantee if the campaign they develop for you flops. If you ever do find one with that promise, hire them!

I remember a budget presentation for a P&G brand where the brand team was giving its annual marketing spending recommendation to senior management. The brand team had determined through a research study that Hispanics presented an opportunity for incremental volume. It recommended that a new Hispanic campaign be developed, and that an agency that specialized in Hispanic marketing be hired to develop the campaign.

Senior managers for the ad agency that worked on the account were in the room. You should have seen the blood rush to their faces when the brand team recommended that $5 million of the annual advertising budget be diverted to this new Hispanic agency. You've never seen such vigorous objections in your life. They were watching $600,000 of commissions walk out the door! If they were truly partners, they would have acknowledged the benefits of the recommended Hispanic campaign. But they were watching their piggy bank!

REALITY #3: ADVERTISING AGENCIES ARE NOT RESEARCH GROUPS

Some of the large agencies claim they are the best because they have developed proprietary intellectual models and research tools to understand consumers that give them unparalleled insights into buying behaviors. They brag that their experience is so vast and extensive that they alone truly understand the consumer.

The truth? It's all poppycock. While some of the consumer research that agencies generate is genuinely useful, data is only data until it can be transformed into action. And most creative people within the agency abhor research and statistical information, so the net result is that the insight is never exercised in the development of creative materials. The account executive will rely heavily on the insight as part of the razzle-dazzle during the pitch for your pocketbook, but nine times out of ten, the consumer learnings are not reflected in the campaign concepts.

REALITY #4: GOOD CREATIVE TEAMS ARE NOT A GUARANTEE OF SUCCESS

Many agencies will try to convince you that their creative teams are so gifted and insightful that they are virtually privy to divine revelation. Some lay it on so thick, you'd think the Dalai-Lama himself sits in their conference room!

It is true that agencies are only as good as their creative teams. Now allow me a horrible generalization: Most agency creatives are usually slightly off center, functioning on the fringes of reality. That off-kilter quality in itself is not necessarily a bad thing, but you have to understand that these folks operate in a different world than you and I. They see their work through rose-colored glasses. While the last campaign they created for a client might have been absolutely brilliant and insightful, it's no sure bet that the concepts they develop for you won't stink. Think of it this way. Steven Spielberg brought you such wonderful films as *Jurassic Park*, *Schindler's List*, and *Saving Private Ryan*. But he's also the guy who made *Howard The Duck* and *1941*. Even with talented and proven creative people, sometimes you win, and sometimes you lose.

Secrets of the Game

The most critical issue in working with an agency is knowing the creative team that's working on your campaign. Insist on seeing the *full* portfolio of the creative team's work, not just their highlight film. Agencies, just like every other business, have new hires and inexperienced rookies in their ranks. Insist that only *experienced* creatives are working for you! Let the rookies earn their stripes on somebody else's nickel.

REALITY #5: BIGGER ISN'T NECESSARILY BETTER

Most advertising agencies like to make a big deal out of how many millions of dollars of billings they do each year. As a client, why should you care? When you're buying a car, do you consider as part of the decision set that Ford has sold $10 billion worth of cars this year? In my experience with the agency world, bigger isn't necessarily better—in fact, bigger can be worse.

WHAT DRIVES AGENCIES TO SUCCEED

That said, advertising agencies can do amazing work if you manage them well and give them good direction. The work an agency produces for you is only going to be as good as the foundation you provide. If you give them a solid positioning strategy to work from, an understanding of the target consumer, and allow them the freedom to explore, often they will develop campaigns that both captivate and inspire, bringing your strategy to life in ways you'd never dreamed possible.

But you won't taste that sweet success unless you see the agency for what it is and understand the motivations that drive it. Agencies live and breathe because they want to win awards. Creativity is their primary motivation. This fuels a desire to be as innovative as possible with your brand—their industry rewards are Clios and accolades for beautiful ads. Only a few awards programs recognize agencies for campaigns that generate the most sales. Your business results are down on their priority list and are there only because good business results allow them to keep your account and stay in business.

MANAGING YOUR RELATIONSHIP WITH AN AGENCY

Managing your relationship with an agency is like walking a tight rope in many respects. Advertising agencies are loaded with people with inflated, and fragile, egos. Many of the creative folks are incredibly insecure. You need to understand how to manage your relationship with both ends of the personality spectrum and everything in between. Happy people are a critically important element to success!

You Are the Boss

That said, you must still establish right off the bat that you are the client and the agency is a hired gun. You drive the business; they don't. While this may sound aggressive, I've encountered several agency executives over the years who thought they knew more about my business than I did, and tried to ignore the strategic direction they were given. I've seen smaller consumer product companies who have let their agencies work as de facto brand teams, and when it happens, invariably strategic focus is lost in creative maelstroms. The brand gets advertising that is incredibly creative, but consumers walk away thinking, "huh?" The campaigns do nothing to communicate product benefits or convince consumers to purchase the product—but boy, are they creative!

Keep a Focus on the Positioning Strategy

Often, agencies will take the positioning strategy you've given them and rework it to fit their own frame of reference or business style. For example, they may have a specific type of language or format that they use for all of the strategies across their different clients. You should usually give them the leeway to organize themselves internally if their creative teams work better off of their own structure. Be aware, however, that reworking your strategy is a big yellow caution flag. When the agency rewrites your positioning strategy, make sure that your strategic underpinnings are still in place. Often in the translation, agencies will try to dilute the strategic direction, providing themselves with more creative latitude and offering less restrictive strategic guidelines. So even if you think you've ordered a steak, the agency may try to feed you a lamb shank.

One very famous and well-respected agency tried to pull this trick on me. When I was working with them in developing an advertising campaign, I had to keep reminding them to adhere to the strategy. They didn't like the strategy we had provided them with, and wanted to create their own—a watered-down version that would have been easier to execute. This became a loud and raucous bone of contention on more than one occasion. Fortunately, in the end they stayed with the strategy we provided them with, and the work resulted in the creation of two TV commercials that notched the highest persuasiveness scores in the history of The Coca-Cola Company, putting them into the class of the legendary "I'd Like to Teach the World to Sing" and "Mean Joe Greene" Coca-Cola ads.

Agree to Spending Before It's Spent

Caution is the watchword when it comes to protecting your marketing development budget. Agencies love to tell you that they're going to do this or that and need your verbal approval. What they pitch usually sounds great—but they don't mention the price tag until the project is completed. If this happens, you might as well just do a wire transfer of all the money in your marketing account to theirs. By not locking down a price, you've essentially given them a blank check to spend your money like a drunken sailor in Las Vegas!

I learned this lesson the hard way. When my team was developing the concept for a theme park in downtown Atlanta during the 1996 Olympic Games, to be called "Coca-Cola Olympic City," we contracted with an agency to develop conceptual ideas of what would be in the park. They were to create artist renderings for a presentation to Coke's senior management and the Board of Directors. We believed that an eight-person team from their shop was working on the project. No price tag was ever confirmed, because when we began the project we weren't sure of everything we would need from the agency. Thirty days later, we received a bill for $550,000 and I nearly had a heart attack. The itemization showed over sixty people inside their shop, working full time on our project!

> ## Secrets of the Game
> Make the agency provide written estimates of everything they are going to do before they do it, then probe every single line item to understand exactly what it entails. Question everything and every minute detail. You'll save thousands of dollars on each job by finding and shaking out the fluff!

THE GOLD STANDARD

It is wonderful and rewarding when your agency delivers a campaign that not only looks good, but works! There are several things to keep in mind when dealing with an agency that will foster an environment for developing great work.

GIVE THEM THE FREEDOM TO EXPLORE

Creative people need their space. They need to feel free to open their minds to the cosmos and make connections from wide and varied stimuli. Remember, agency creatives are not like you and me. They walk to the beat of a different drummer, and the key to their success is in making brilliant connections that you and I could never dream up in our lifetimes.

Many marketing people make the mistake of telling the agency how the finished campaign should look. Usually the comment can seem very innocent when the client is chatting with the account manager on the phone. But what happens afterward is stifling. By making a seemingly innocuous statement, you paint a vision of what the agency believes you want them to create. This is a surefire way to mess up a campaign's creative development. When the information shuffle is completed, it typically has been translated into what sounds like a dictum by the time it reaches the creative team—leaving them feeling undercut—killing motivation and curtailing independent creative thought. The creatives don't give you their best work but just crank out what they think you, the client, wants.

The better way to manage the agency is to give them a clear, succinct positioning strategy—one that has a clearly focused target audience, strong consumer benefits, and rational "reasons why"—and let them go! Encourage them to get out of the box, to do something great, and tell them nothing more than you're expecting incredible work. Give them an energy booster. This will inspire the team to give you their best. By encouraging them to be free, they will feel unrestrained, allowing their brains to function and do the job they are best at doing.

To demonstrate what I mean, I want you to pretend you are an agency creative. You're being asked to write a children's song that encourages kids to embrace everyone in the world—all ethnic persuasions—in peace, happiness, and harmony. That is your assignment. I know you can do it, and that when you're done, it will be great!

Now think about how you would begin this process. The assignment is very open-ended, so you feel like you have the room to create the song almost any way you choose. The assignment has empowered you to use creative license. It can be any kind of tune you want—bouncy, slow, happy, jazzy, simple, orchestral—as long as it turns out to be a children's song that delivers the message. You can choose any words, create any chorus. The only limitation is your own imagination.

Now try the assignment from a different perspective. I'm asking you to write a children's song that encourages kids to embrace everyone in the world—all ethnic persuasions—in peace, happiness, and harmony. I know you can do it, and that when you get it done, it will be great!

Oh, and by the way, if I had to describe to you what our goal would be, I'd say you should make it a great tune like Disney's "It's a Small World." To help you remember, it goes something like this:

It's a world of laughter and tears
It's a world of joy and fear
It's a place where we can play and be happy today,
It's a small world after all.

Now how do you feel about tackling this assignment? It's likely that right now the creative part of your brain has probably shut down. You can do nothing but play back "It's a Small World" in your head. Go ahead, try to hum a new tune!

This is the dilemma the agency creative team faces when clients, no matter how innocently, offer creative suggestions. The direction curtails creative processes and inhibits free association, forcing their minds to think in restricted channels. You can't get the best creative ideas if you work this way!

PROVIDE STIMULUS AND INSPIRATION

It's not often that great new ideas are developed by someone sitting at a desk in an office with phones ringing and distractions all around. Inspiration comes from seeing a sunset, walking on the beach, exploring, probing, watching, and hearing new things.

If you want your creative team to give you inspired work, you must provide inspiration. Take them on a tour of the manufacturing facility. Take them into the fields where crops are grown. Go stand in stores and watch consumers shop. Have some focus groups with consumers who use your product, with consumers who *don't* use your product, and especially with consumers who are using your competitor's product!

Involving your creative team in competitive research is incredibly valuable. You don't want the creatives to see just your own happy consumers. They also need to see unhappy consumers, indifferent consumers, passionately opposed consumers. You and they will learn much more by listening to people who don't use your product or don't like your product than you will from those who do. Don't hide your warts and shortcomings—let the creatives see everything, feel everything, touch everything, smell everything, and probe everything.

GIVE THE AGENCY ADEQUATE TIME TO DEVELOP CONCEPTS AND IDEAS

Rome was not built in a day, and most great ad campaigns take a while to develop into greatness. Most incredible ideas don't pop into your head fully formed and ready for execution. You begin with a seed of an idea, you let it take root and grow, you tweak it, you add to it, you subtract from it, and every once it a while it suddenly explodes into something beautiful you never expected.

Then again, sometimes you get what you think is a great idea one day, and by the next day, you've figured out that it stinks. The same holds true for the creative process within agencies. If you try to make the agency deliver on too-short timing, you increase the chance that you'll get half-baked ideas. Don't try to rush greatness. Most good campaigns take six to eight months of development.

SETTING GROUND RULES FOR CREATIVE CRITIQUE

Creative review meetings to evaluate your agency's work should be conducted with as much decorum and care as a traditional Japanese tea ceremony. Bear in mind that when the agency comes in to present the work, all of it has been reviewed within the agency several times before you get the chance to see it. The creative team has its egos attached to the effort. Be careful to offer fair, honest, and timely feedback, yet in a way that fuels idea building and not idea bashing. You as a client have several rules of behavior to follow that can help create this environment.

First, before the agency makes its presentation, you need to establish a pecking order within your review team and a clear understanding of rights when it comes to making comments. The majority of the team should be restricted exclusively to making comments of a strategic nature—is the work on or off strategy—and discussing which concepts better communicate the strategic positioning. Only the one or two most senior people in the room should have "creative critique" rights. You don't need everyone in the room trying to be an art director.

Secrets of the Game

When critiquing the agency's work, the first comment should always be a strategic evaluation of whether or not the concept delivers the consumer message outlined in the positioning strategy. This is a great training exercise for your most junior marketing people to develop their strategic evaluative skills.

I cannot overstress the importance of limiting junior people to commenting strictly on strategic evaluation. I learned this lesson the hard way in my first creative meeting at P&G, which happened to be a new TV campaign for Citrus Hill Orange Juice. I was only about four weeks into the job on the day of the meeting. My brand manager had failed to inform me of the rules of decorum, and so when the agency concluded its creative presentation and the category manager turned to me and asked what I thought, I immediately replied "It looks like a rip-off of a Tropicana commercial to me. They've got a spot on the air that looks just like it—a women in a plaid shirt walking through an orange grove." When I finished, there was a palpable gloom in the room, and if looks could kill, I would have been carried out on a stretcher. I broke the cardinal rule of a junior person—I insulted the agency's creativity—and the incident affected my relationship with that agency for the balance of my stay at P&G.

OFFER HONEST, OPEN, AND TIMELY FEEDBACK

When you have seen all of the work that the agency has presented, give them your gut reaction right there on the spot. Don't wait and let it settle. Your gut reaction is probably the right reaction. Tell them which concepts worked for you and which did not—again, strategically first, and creatively second. If there are hints of great ideas in some concepts but their execution just doesn't work, encourage the agency to take a look at it again and see if it can be revised to make it better. Developing a great campaign that really works usually requires several iterations. Often the seed of the best idea is buried in one of those early presentations, and only after several rounds of work does it blossom into the core concept.

THE RIGHT PLACE AT THE RIGHT TIME

Once you have a great advertising campaign, you have to figure out where to place it. Media planners are probably the most underappreciated, underpaid, and least understood members of the agency team. While the account supervisors and creatives are busy jetting to clients and making impressive presentations, the media planners sit in their humble cubicles crunching numbers and sending faxes. Don't make the mistake of taking them for granted.

Media planners are the whizzes who determine how, when, and where to place your brilliant advertising. A good planner will save you thousands of dollars and do a great job of reaching your core consumer. They might even recommend innovative strategies to maximize your consumer impressions, like providing editorial PR material at the same time you buy a print ad to double your exposure in a key magazine.

Beware media planners who offer you a straight formula of national consumer impressions, costs, and dayparts. Essentially, these types of planners are paying retail for off-the-rack ad placement. A talented planner will have ideas for beating the system, taking advantage of an undervalued show, or creatively tagging your spots to tap into your marketing development funds.

You may never have an opportunity to speak with your media planner if you don't specifically ask to, as many agencies simply forward their proposed schedules through their account executive. Let your account executive know how much you value the media planner, and ask to include him or her in your placement discussions. When you express interest and encouragement in the process, you'll probably be pleased and surprised at how energetically your media planner will respond.

ADVERTISING THAT WORKS

Great advertising is innovative, creative, unique, and convincing. When all of the elements come together, most campaigns become greater than they could have ever been imagined at the beginning when just a few strategic words were scribbled on a page. The work that many agencies turn out is truly inspiring, and the art of making great advertising is one that must be constantly nourished to get consistently great results.

ADVERTISING AND THE LITTLE GUYS

Many small and local businesses that advertise don't have the budget to work with major advertising agencies, and instead work with local production houses that cater to small businesses. Regardless of the size of the company you are working with to develop and produce your advertising, the same rules of business exist. You need to give them solid strategic direction, offer creative stimulation, and encourage them to get outside the box to do great work. You must give clear and timely feedback and offer critique from a strategic perspective first and a creative perspective second. This is the people part of marketing, and the people you have working on your campaigns are critical to success. It is your responsibility as a client to ensure that the process and environment are conducive to great creation.

CHAPTER SUMMARY

- Getting great advertising from your agency requires work. You need to understand the client/agency business:
  - Agencies are businesses with profit motive. A typical agency budget will chew up about 20 percent of your total marketing funds.
  - Agencies are not your partners. They are suppliers who can have a huge effect upon your business.
  - Agencies are not research groups.
  - Good creative teams are not a guarantee of success.
  - Bigger isn't necessarily better.
  - Agencies are driven by creativity. That is their primary motivation.
  - Managing your agency requires close attention to personalities. You need to be able to keep the creatives happy!
  - Be sure to keep the agency focused upon the positioning strategy.
  - Agree to spending before its spent. Probe for fluff.
- Getting great work from your creative team can be enhanced by:
  - Giving them room to explore.
  - Providing a clear positioning strategy.
  - Providing stimuli and inspiration.
  - Giving them time to develop their concepts and ideas. Most great campaigns take six to eight months to produce.
  - Setting ground rules for creative critiques. This needs to be managed as carefully as a Japanese tea ceremony.
  - Establishing a pecking order among the client group. Most junior speaks first.
  - Ensuring that junior people address strategic issues only, not creative.
  - Offering honest, timely feedback. Your gut reaction is probably the right reaction.
- Media planners can be a tremendous resource. Use them!

The Six Deadly Sins of Advertising

COMMON MISTAKES TO AVOID AT ALL COSTS

ADVERTISING EXECUTIONS CAN BE delightful, surprising, memorable, touching, and humorous . . . and *still* not sell the product. Why? Sometimes a muddled or indecisive positioning statement is at fault. Other times the creative concept and execution of the campaign fails to convince consumers of the product's benefits. Some commercials create a sensational mood and memorable image but don't connect them to the product. Regardless of the specific reason, every day I see millions of dollars wasted on advertising that doesn't work. The money may as well have been flushed down a toilet.

How can I be so sure? Because after examining hundreds of hours of TV commercials and thousands of print and billboard campaigns, and studying consumer response to this mountain of information—through a combination of purchase intent, persuasiveness feedback, sales figures, and qualitative analysis—I've found a series of common errors that consistently arise in faltering campaigns. These blunders, committed time and again, either leave the consumer cold and disinterested in the product or, at their worst, actually create a consumer aversion to the brand.

Although great advertising can be breathtaking, developing an effective campaign is not an art. It is the result of strategic discipline, rigorous research, and a clear understanding of the relevant and meaningful benefits that make your product appealing to consumers. Only upon this solid foundation does "art"—the actual creative endeavor of making the advertising—begin to take shape. Companies and their advertising agencies must be watchful that the creative executions deliver strong, clear messages that compel the consumer to action.

THE POWER OF THE RINGS

My analysis of the foils and foibles of advertising began during an extensive advertising review of all Olympic-themed ads created by major sponsors of the Olympic Games through the years. When I reviewed campaigns from dozens of companies over several decades, I was shocked to see that many of the executions appeared almost identical and could be interchanged without anyone noticing which company they were from.

The core problem was that the advertising failed to create a relevant connection between the company or brand and the Olympics. Usually the campaigns depicted athletes in beautiful action shots with stunning photography. The brand logo was layered in with some copy about effort, endurance, being the best, or going for the gold.

Does that ring a bell? Do any Olympic-themed advertising campaigns stick out in your mind as brilliant executions, offering a clear understanding of why that particular brand is associated with the Games? Chances are, even though the ten worldwide Olympic sponsors have all been using the Olympics as a primary advertising vehicle for the past twenty or so years, you can't remember more than two or three of these brands—and what does that tell you about the effective spending of their $50 million sponsorship fees? Do I hear a flushing sound?

VISA is one of the few companies that in my opinion has made good use of its sponsorship dollars, because its campaigns make a clear and logical connection between the brand and the Games. You probably remember VISA's "at the Olympic Games, you can't buy tickets with American Express" campaign. It uses the memorable tag line " VISA—we're everywhere you want us to be." The sponsorship is believable and consumer-relevant, which places it far ahead of the competitive sponsor crowd. Better still, it flaunts the cachet of Olympic sponsorship to reinforce the practical benefits of VISA over its key competition.

The Coca-Cola campaign for the 1996 Summer Games—"For The Fans"—also hit the mark with consumers. The underlying strategic premise, that Coca-Cola refreshed the fans of the Olympic Games, was believable and relevant. Athletes weren't depicted drinking Coke; fans were. All promotions, advertising, and collateral material contained the tag lines: "Cheering Is Thirsty Work" or "Refreshing The Olympic Spirit." The campaign earned the highest persuasiveness and awareness scores among Olympic sponsors and launched the brand to record sales figures during its execution.

EXPANDING THE STUDY

After reviewing the learning from the Olympics, I wondered if perhaps many of the "sins" committed by the Games sponsors were as pervasive in other types of advertising. My team conducted another study evaluating advertising campaigns from virtually every consumer category; fashion, packaged goods, restaurants, automobiles, airlines—you name it, we took a look at it. And here's what we saw: The very same blunders that had tripped up the Olympic sponsors were crippling the campaigns of brands in virtually every category we reviewed!

These errors were so consistently devastating to a campaign, and so negatively affected consumer behavior, that I dubbed them "The Six Deadly Sins of Advertising."

THE SIX DEADLY SINS OF ADVERTISING

I know what you're thinking: aren't there *seven* deadly sins? Yes, but in advertising, unlike in religion, lust is not a sin; it's a virtue.

Sex is used to sell everything from cars to chewing gum, and it does a mighty fine job of motivating consumers. So let the libidos run wild while we concentrate on the other six sins, still as lethal as ever.

Sin #1: Pride (i.e., Putting Your Logo Everywhere)

Like the tragic Greek youth Narcissus, many companies adore their own image. They like to see their name and logo in conspicuous places. Bigger is better; lights are sensational. They don't feel they need to tell consumers anything about their product; they assume that everyone knows their name and what they sell, and size matters more than message.

Well, those giant billboards *are* impressive, aren't they? But let me ask you a simple question: What is Qualcomm? What do they sell? What is 3Com? What do they sell? Most consumers have no idea, but each of these companies paid a boatload of money to put their names on ballparks so they could stand back and congratulate themselves. If you're not going to bother communicating with consumers about your products, why pay top dollar for a consumer advertising venue?

It should not come as any surprise that consumers ignore such empty advertising, because it doesn't communicate anything to them. Consumers pay attention when advertising relates to their lives, touches a cord, lets them in on the joke, offers interesting information. They pay no more attention to the giant logo signs scattered around sports arenas, or on highway billboards, than they do to the license plates in the parking lot!

To dimensionalize the problem, I conducted a study a few years ago that measured consumer recall of advertising inside sports arenas. If you have attended a pro sports event in the last several years, you've certainly seen how the arenas and ballparks are plastered with giant signs, usually just stating a company logo (Budweiser, Coca-Cola, United, AT&T, Panasonic, etc).

In this study, consumers leaving the facility were initially asked to write down the names of the advertisers with signage inside the building ("unaided recall"). The list they gave back was usually quite short. Then they were shown an extensive list of advertisers' names (including all the advertisers inside the building, and several others who were not) and asked to mark those they believed were advertising inside ("aided recall"). Even with this nudge to the memory, fewer than 10 percent of the consumers could name more than five advertisers out of the total fifty companies and brands advertising inside the test arena. Consumers were blocking the advertising out.

Secrets of the Game

Never produce advertising that only states your brand or company name. *Always* have a relevant consumer message linked with your name that reinforces your brand positioning strategy.

The cure for this sin is simple: *link* your brand name with a message. It doesn't have to be a long message. Instead of a sign that just says "Coca-Cola," it should say "Always Coca-Cola." What is the difference? The latter communicates the core brand positioning that is reinforced with the hundreds of other encounters a consumer has with the brand on a weekly basis, and probably makes you hear the advertising jingle inside your head. Instead of posting a sign that merely says "Budweiser," the brand should aim for "Budweiser, King of Beers," or add the Budweiser frogs/iguanas or other advertising icon to the logo. These simple elements don't require much space, and they help to reinforce the Budweiser brand identity.

These small differences have an enormous impact on consumer recall. In our stadium study, the few brands that carried a message with their name were much more frequently remembered than those that did not.

Sin #2: Gluttony (i.e., Using Pretty Images That Have Nothing to Do with Your Business)

Some brands gorge themselves on pretty pictures and affecting imagery without giving any consideration to whether those images provide any real sustenance for the brand. They don't bother to link those fabulous—and expensive—images to their product in a way that will connect consumers with their brand.

Delta Airlines and NationsBank are the poster children for this sin. Their 1996 Olympic campaigns featured images of athletes in striking poses with the company logos pasted over the top. You can imagine the campaign taking shape around a conference table: someone spreads out a collection of beautiful and inspirational shots of some photogenic athletes, and the marketing team leaps to its feet, cheering, "Wow, those images are brave and powerful and successful, just like us! What a great symbol for our business!" Well, boys, maybe *you* can make that connection, but your consumers won't. And besides, maybe they don't particularly need an airline that's all that; they might just want to fly to Chicago.

Unfortunately, many products in our day-to-day life continue to perpetrate this sin. It's bad enough when perfume ads feature naked people in strange settings, but that's at least defensible. Although the ads have absolutely nothing to do with the product, they do play to that mysterious consumer desire to believe that top designers, whose names are on the perfumes, are bizarre and visionary.

Automobile manufacturers are major offenders of gluttony, placing their cars in incredibly beautiful surroundings, perched high upon mountaintops, racing down wet mountain roads with no other vehicles as far as the eye can see. When was the last time *you* drove anywhere without encountering heavy traffic and gridlock?

Secrets of the Game

Never use imagery in your advertising that does not relevantly link and support your brand image or personality or its usage occasion. *Always* develop advertising in which the consumer can "insert" him- or herself into the picture. If you succeed in getting consumers to visualize themselves in your advertising, the battle is won.

Don't get me wrong—I'm not saying fantasy doesn't work. Fantasy works well as an advertising hook, particularly when it invites consumers to jump into the picture and join in the fun, like seeing yourself on a tropical island, sitting on the beach with servants rubbing suntan lotion on your back. A powerful way to convince consumers to buy your product is to make them believe that when they use it, it transports them to another place—one that is more fun and interesting than the mundane and everyday world in which they live.

Have you ever sprayed Dow Bathroom Cleaner into your sink and then visualized the Scrubbing Bubbles racing around, battling your sink scum? Fantasy is OK as long as it is grounded in the reality of what the product does or how it makes you feel. We all know that the Scrubbing Bubbles don't really exist, but they are much more fun to think about than cleaning a dirty sink.

Sin #3: Envy (i.e., Advertising That Imitates Your Competitor)

Envious brands are so consumed with a competitor's success that they imitate an existing campaign instead of carving out their own unique identity. In another chapter, I related the story of how Citrus Hill Orange Juice created a TV spot that looked suspiciously similar to advertising that Tropicana was airing. The new Citrus Hill ad featured a women with shoulder-length brown hair, wearing a plaid shirt, walking through an orange grove, and picking an orange. It concluded with her standing next to her young daughter by an old pickup truck loaded with orange crates.

Tropicana was already airing at that time a commercial featuring a women with shoulder-length brown hair, wearing a plaid shirt, walking through an orange grove, picking an orange, and then standing next to an old pickup truck. The difference is obvious, right? The Citrus Hill lady was with her daughter, not alone, and *their* truck was loaded with orange crates!

Guess what? Consumers couldn't tell the difference. While the agency and the Citrus Hill brand team had convinced themselves that their ad was nothing like the Tropicana ad, in reality, many consumers saw the Citrus Hill ad and assumed it was for Tropicana.

Beer brands are so consumed with envy, it's surprising the only green beer you see is on St. Patrick's Day. Just how many advertisements have you watched in the past month or so that show attractive young people standing around partying with a bottle of beer in their hand? Or how about an attractive guy and girl bantering over a beer at a trendy bar? I'll bet you can remember which ads are for which brands, right? Yeah, right. Maybe that's why Spuds Mackenzie and the Budweiser frogs/iguanas are such a hit; at least you could tell them apart from the suds studs and beer babes that usually populate beer commercials.

Secrets of the Game

Never produce advertising that looks anything like something that your competitor is *currently running* or *has run in the past*.

Always ensure that your campaign is *different, better,* and *special,* convincing consumers of the unique nature of your brand and communicating the benefits of purchasing your products.

Sin #4: Greed (i.e., Overstating Your Benefits)

Some marketers are so greedy for profit they'll say almost anything to sell their product, even if their product claims are so outrageous they cannot be believed.

Workout and fitness equipment are the worst offenders in this category. I'm sure you've seen the commercials for exercise equipment that promise to turn your body into an Arnold Schwarzenegger clone with just fifteen-minute-a-day workouts. You believe it, right? I'm sure Arnold was devastated when he learned that after all those years of torturous effort and training, he could have built the same body by buying one of those Bow Flex machines!

I'll bet Arnold was equally surprised to learn how beneficial a Snickers candy bar could be as part of his training routine. Imagine, all those years of steamed vegetables and fish, then one day he happens across a Snickers ad featuring world-class athletes pausing midworkout to nibble a Snickers bar—how refreshing! Do you think he would believe the scenario? Not for one minute. And consumers don't believe it, either. I have a hard time thinking that even the most loyal Snickers corporate employee, wiping chocolate from his lips as he reviewed the storyboards, saw anything true or real in this advertising campaign. The brand team probably just thought it was a nifty way to associate Snickers with big-name athletes. It wasn't a good bluff, and it didn't convince people to buy the product.

Occasionally the promise of a campaign is so tantalizing that it does persuade consumers to buy the product, only to be disappointed. Have you ever gone to a restaurant because you've seen a great advertisement for a meal (with a pretty picture of what you'll get), ordered it, and been disappointed that the food in their advertising looked a whole lot better than what was served on your plate? I know I've been duped a few times. But I never go back to restaurants that do that to me.

Consumers live by the old adage, "If it looks too good to be true, it probably is." They don't fall for the con jobs very often.

Secrets of the Game

Never oversell your product benefits by stretching the truth. *Never* develop advertising that puts your brand in a position that consumers find hard to believe.

Always communicate clear, meaningful consumer benefits, backed up with rational and believable "reasons why."

Sin #5: Sloth (i.e., Trying to Be Trendy by Borrowing from Today's News or Culture)

The sin of sloth is characterized by using world headlines or niche cultural trends as the genesis for your advertising creative.

Eggo waffles is a prime example. In 1998, the world news was fascinated by the development of the first cloned animal. Shortly thereafter, Eggo began running a TV ad that featured a mad professor who clones himself into a dozen or so versions and then fights with his many alter egos over who gets to eat the lone Eggo waffle—"leggo of my Eggo" he chirps. This commercial is on my Top 10 Loser List. The advertising isn't funny or compelling, the concept is tired, the product is incidental. Even the setting, a laboratory, is unappetizing, and the commercial contains no ancillary products like milk, juice, or cereal that help me envision the product as breakfast—or even as food.

Levi-Strauss is also a major sinner in the sloth category. In an attempt to reclaim the "coolness" of wearing Levi's among the teenage segment, they borrowed the grunge look and applied it to all of their ads. The result: a series of nonsensical spots featuring such things as a guy driving through a car wash with the windows down, and a prepubescent girl, who looks like she needs a bath, talking about how it's OK for people who work hard to have a big house (what does this have to do with Levi's?!). Each of the ads show about one second of the Levi's jeans. Levi's marketing folks didn't understand that those trendy-looking commercials would work for Calvin Klein, but not for them. They simply jumped on the trend, and fell flat on their faces.

Sin #6: Wrath (i.e., Advertising That Attacks or Is Angry in Tone)

It's easy to understand how so many companies and especially politicians get caught up in angry advertising. Either they emerge from consumer research saying, "Wow, consumers really *hate* that problem!" (whether it be potholes or school taxes), or they themselves work up such a lather about a particularly loathsome competitor, their venom spills over into their advertising.

Angry advertising doesn't work. The average consumer must hear a message approximately seven times before he or she absorbs it, and few people can tolerate an abrasive ad through more than a few repetitions. More importantly, the brand or person becomes associated with a strong negative emotion—"it's that *angry* guy"—and who wants to be affiliated with that? It's a lesson many politicians have learned the hard way during furious mudslinging campaigns that backfired when voters just got sick of the whole ugly mess.

Unfortunately, a few brands have fallen prey to this tactic as well. Quaker State Motor Oil is a sinner in this category, showcasing an ad that stars fast-talking pitchman Dennis Leary, who laments about the problems of regular motor oils in his angry New York style. The advertising turns people off.

THERE IS NO "RIGHT WAY"

There is no magic formula or right way to create good advertising. But there are thousands upon thousands of case studies to help you learn which types of advertising have worked and which haven't.

> ### Secrets of the Game
>
> It is not a sin to advertise to consumers. In fact, you have their permission to send them information! All they ask is that you make the advertising entertaining and enjoyable to watch—and that your message is clear so that they understand what you're saying to them!

The Six Deadly Sins of Advertising are just a few things that can help raise your awareness of what not to do. They can perhaps save you the anguish of developing campaigns that won't do the job. Just avoiding these mistakes is still no guarantee of success, but it can help reduce the chance of failure.

THE GOLD STANDARD

The best advertising will always push the edges of creativity, developing ways of presenting your product that captivate and inspire consumers. Pushing to the edge means that sometimes you'll go too far and fall off the cliff. That's OK, too, because a carefully considered failure provides a learning tool for next time. The saying goes, "Tis better to have loved and lost than never to have loved at all." It's also better to have pushed the edges of creativity and gone too far than to have never tried to get out of the box—miring yourself in mediocrity. Michael Eisner, the Chairman of the Board at Disney Studios, has a favorite saying: "Average is Awful." Heed his warning. Go ahead, take a chance, and do something great!

CHAPTER SUMMARY

- Advertising must be relevant to the brand. Analysis has revealed six common creative miscues that consistently cause campaigns to fail:
  - *Pride*—Displaying your company name without a relevant message
  - *Gluttony*—Using pretty pictures that don't relate to your product
  - *Envy*—Creating advertising that resembles your competitors
  - *Greed*—Overstating your product benefits
  - *Sloth*—Borrowing ideas from current events or culture
  - *Wrath*—Angry advertising
- Advertising should always have a relevant consumer message that reinforces your brand positioning strategy.
- Try to create advertising where the consumer can "insert" him- or herself into the picture.
- Always ensure that your campaign is *different, better,* and *special,* convincing consumers of the unique nature of your brand and communicating the benefits of choosing to purchase your product.
- Consumers have given you permission to advertise to them. All they ask is that you make the advertising entertaining and enjoyable to watch—and that your message is clear so that they understand what you're trying to say to them!

Solving the Public Relations Puzzle

IT'S NOT ABOUT FINDING
DANCING ELEPHANTS TO WEAR
YOUR BRAND NAME ON TV

PUBLIC RELATIONS PROFESSIONALS ARE LOBBYISTS in the truest sense, spending most of their day on the phone coaxing newspapers, TV stations, radio stations, and other members of the media and trade press to talk or write about their company. A PR pro at work is a study in helpful cheerfulness. But underneath the chatty veneer, the expensive coifs, and the designer suits, beats the heart of a warrior.

Like a modern-day cavalry, PR professionals ride to the rescue in times of trouble to defend the honor and good name of their employer. The moment unflattering news about the company hits the wires, they saddle up and wage a bloody campaign against the perpetrator, defending their company with vigor and valor. Once the emergency is passed, they lay down their weapons and shift back into promotional mode, canvassing the media world with uplifting and inspiring newsworthy data while awaiting the next corporate crisis.

ONE VOICE TO THE MEDIA

The most vital function of the PR department, in both times of war and times of peace, is to provide a single, consistent voice to the outside world. They make sure that everything the press (and ultimately consumers) hear and see about your company and brands is accurate and conforms to the corporate image and individual brand positioning strategies. The press and consumers are easily confused by too many "voices" speaking on behalf of the company. At the best companies, only PR interfaces with the media.

In the spring of 1995, I became entangled in a PR nightmare that almost cost me my job at Coca-Cola. I was asked to give a speech at a conference in Chicago to discuss Coke's preparation for the Olympics. The conference was scheduled one year before the onset of the corporate Olympic marketing rush. Many marketers and journalists looked to Coke to set the pace for all the sponsors, since the Games were in their hometown of Atlanta.

At that time, Coke's senior management were very nervous about tipping our hand and sharing our plans for the Games. We were afraid other Olympic sponsors (or, heaven forbid, Pepsi) might acquire information that could dilute or sabotage our multimillion-dollar efforts. We operated under strict "need-to-know" security clearances, even within the Coca-Cola corporate offices. In true James Bond fashion, projects were assigned secret code names to minimize the risk of leaks.

As I wrote the speech for the conference, I limited the information content to past Olympics sponsorships and small programs for the upcoming Games, which Coke had already made public. The presentation was informative, but it didn't give so much as a peek at any of our major new initiatives like the Coca-Cola Olympic City or the Olympic Torch Relay.

The address went flawlessly, and everything was fine until I tried to leave the building. As I weaved through the crowd for the exit, I was approached by a writer from the trade magazine *Adweek*. He asked me what we were planning to do for Coke's Olympic advertising campaign. I continued walking and brushed him off by saying that we were still considering many possibilities and nothing had been decided. I ducked out of the building and congratulated myself on my evasiveness. He couldn't possibly do any damage with that empty comment. *Wrong!*

Two days later, *Adweek* ran a front-page story prominently quoting me as saying "we were still considering many possibilities," followed by an extensive review of four or five creative concepts that the ad agency had presented to us in recent weeks. Somehow, the writer had learned from a source within my agency about the advertising concepts we were considering. By combining his investigative information with half of my quote, the article implied that I'd sat down and had a full and meaningful conversation with the man about our most secretive campaign elements!

Needless to say, senior management were furious. I was called into the chief marketing operator's office and dressed down for thirty minutes. He ranted and raved about how stupid I had been to open my mouth. Our PR department went into defensive overdrive to try to convince the writer and his management at the magazine that they were way off base and to back off. I thought I'd weathered the storm, but the following week a similar story appeared in *Ad Age* using quotes from my speech combined with the information from the *Adweek* article. Again, the magazine made it appear as though I'd had lunch with the writer to spill my guts—which meant another unpleasant trip to the hot seat.

Through this painful experience I learned a valuable lesson. Marketers should market, and PR people should work the press. From that moment on, I shunned all contact with the media. Every time the phone rang from a member of the press, I forwarded the call to my PR department for handling. This system worked out very well. I was able to stay focused on doing the job I was hired to do, and PR was able to keep the media in check.

Secrets of the Game

Marketing folks should never speak to the press without first being asked by the PR department to do so, and then coached on what to say. PR professionals are accustomed to daily dealings with the media. A good PR person can protect marketers from making gaffes that will come back to haunt them.

Coke senior management takes their media dealings *very* seriously. Every employee who *may be* approached by the media to act as a spokesperson for the Company is required to attend a full-day "media training" seminar to acquire the proper media interviewing skills. The training is a small bit of insurance to help protect Coke's pristine corporate image.

THE ONE-MAN PR DEPARTMENT

Obviously, if you're a small shop or entrepreneur, you may need to assume the PR functions yourself. How defensive do you need to be when dealing with the press? Not very. The media is unlikely to invest time and effort in researching your company, or writing a negative article, unless you are already an established player with high name recognition. If they grant you any notice at all, they'll probably use exactly what you give them, so write that press release carefully!

The actual mechanics of public relations are complicated and can be tedious, from compiling extensive contact lists for the daily, weekly, and monthly publications (backing out each press release date to correspond with their lead times) to tracking stories and planning future placements. We won't discuss the details here, but the following strategies will work for you whether you're the biggest fish in the pond with a bustling department of PR professionals, or a free-swimming guppy making your first foray into PR waters.

THE THREE INCARNATIONS OF PUBLIC RELATIONS

Corporate promotion and crisis management are perhaps the most visible tasks handled by a PR department, but there is actually much more to their jobs. There are three different and distinct types of public relations efforts, each with different goals, objectives, and tactics employed to accomplish their respective chores. I call these different PR functions the *Three Incarnations of Public Relations.*

Corporate PR

Corporate public relations handles the day-to-day operations of the company: corporate announcements and company news, executive appointments and promotions, earnings reports, development of the annual shareholders reports, organizing corporate meetings, publishing company newsletters, and other official communications. Corporate PR people are experts at making everyone feel warm, fuzzy, uplifted, and motivated about the direction of the company and the caliber of its employees.

Defensive PR

Defensive PR focuses on defending the company against attack. It springs into action at the first sign of trouble or when a negative story concerning the company hits the wires. These pros are experts in crisis management and in diffusing tough situations.

Marketing PR

Marketing PR people proactively develop programs and initiatives to support brand marketing efforts. This is an integral part of the annual business plan for each brand. These efforts are vital to gaining "free publicity" about the company's products.

Most PR people handle the tasks of defensive and corporate PR flawlessly, because this is where they get the sharpest corporate focus and, therefore, the most training. But if you use your PR department only for troubleshooting and overlook its potential as a marketing tool, you've just squandered millions of dollars of marketing value.

Secrets of the Game

A great marketing PR initiative can add millions of dollars of value in free publicity to the brand arsenal to augment marketing support spending. Top companies have dedicated individuals within their PR department who do nothing but develop and provide marketing PR efforts in support of their brands.

MARKETING DISGUISED AS PR

Public relations departments typically use two traditional methods to spread their gospel: the press release and the press conference.

The first weapon of choice for most pros is the press release. Each week, the corporate PR department writes pages filled with fantastic newsy tidbits and distributes this merrily positioned and carefully worded information to employees, the press, and key influentials. If you read enough press releases and newsletters from the same company, you start to believe that perhaps this enterprise is the most well-run business ever conceived. Many PR professionals are so gifted at writing copy, they can make the announcement of a mere building addition sound like an effort that will generate hundreds of thousands of jobs, inject millions of dollars into the local economy, and return Keiko the whale to his heartbroken Orca family.

The second implement of war used to advance the corporate agenda is the press conference. Since press conferences require members of the press to actually leave their place of business to attend the event, this tactic is usually reserved for really big news. If a company doesn't have a newsworthy story, no one will attend.

Frequently, corporations spend big money to host a press conference that is really a marketing event in disguise. The most extravagant I've participated in was the announcement of Coca-Cola's sponsorship of the Sydney, Australia, 2000 Summer Olympic Games. The event was held inside the famous Opera House, overlooking the breathtaking Sydney Harbor, in the spring of 1996.

To create the mood and ambiance, Coke shipped a $100,000 Corporate Olympic Sponsorship display from its headquarters in Atlanta and reconstructed it inside the Opera House for the two-hour session, which was attended by approximately forty members of the press and five television crews. The event began with a skydiver leaping from a plane high above Sydney Harbor, unfurling a giant Coca-Cola/Sydney 2000 flag, which fluttered magnificently over the water as the skydiver descended to land on the mooring surrounding the Opera House. He then stepped into the crow's nest of a giant crane, which lifted him six stories and allowed him to jump out onto the balcony of the Opera House, delivering the flag into the hands of the prime minister of Australia.

After the traditional speeches featuring the prime minister, the head of the Sydney Olympic Organizing Committee, the mayor of Sydney, and Coke's Vice President of Worldwide Sports, a special pen appeared that had a miniature secret-agent-like camera mounted in the tip. A projection screen descended from the ceiling, and as the contracts were signed with the special pen, the press watched the signatures forming on the big screen. *Oooh!* Once the final contract was signed, fireworks were launched over the harbor, four F-16 fighter planes from the Australian Royal Air Force buzzed the Opera House, and two thousand red-and-white Coca-Cola helium-filled balloons were released into the sky. It was quite a show, and it worked. The press event was the lead story on all newscasts and the front-page headline story in all newspapers the following day—and it made Coke look terrific!

Disney staged the largest PR/marketing event in history during the summer of 1995, with its premiere of *Pocahontas* in New York's Central Park. More than half a million people filled the park to watch the movie opening. Before the event, "exclusive" stories and sneak previews were featured on programs such as *Entertainment Tonight, Access Hollywood,* and *Inside Edition.* Coverage of the opening made newscasts nationwide that night, and even though the cost to Disney was rumored to be well over $2 million to stage the event, the value of the free media coverage Disney obtained exceeded that amount ten-fold.

THE MARKETING PR MODEL

Most corporate PR efforts fail at the starting block. Many companies mistakenly assume that PR is no more than an application of the "Three P's": keep *plugging* away, *pestering* and *plastering* the media with information, and sooner or later you'll see your name in print. Wrong. Unlike Imelda Marcos, the media doesn't want quantity, they want quality. Give them something that they can get excited about and they will use it. It's that simple really. If you offer nothing more than a standard press release with the same boring information that everyone else puts out, ninety-nine times out of one hundred it will find its way to the garbage can without being read. City desk editors are bombarded with press releases. They want to see something interesting and different—they want news!

Secrets of the Game

PR is driven by the power of the great idea. Develop a PR plan that is innovative and interesting to the media, then *package* it well.

Instead of churning out sound-alike press releases, spend your time and energy dreaming up ideas that are different, better, and special and develop a tantalizing hook for the press to latch on to.

PR HOLLYWOOD STYLE

Movie studios are the masters of the PR domain. Granted, their product category is unique, but they know how to work the press like a bunch of trained poodles, and regular everyday products can take a lesson from studying how they do it.

The PR campaign for any major movie begins before the film is in the can—sometimes, before a single frame is shot. Every step along the way is trumpeted as a major news event, from purchasing the rights to a hot novel to signing the first major star. As production begins, the studio will often hire its own crew to shoot a behind-the-scenes "making of" documentary, to air on a major network or cable station several weeks before the movie's release. They scan dailies to find enough action, excitement, and star close-ups to produce a trailer some six months before the movie's scheduled release. These are the "Coming This Summer" teasers that often run in theaters while editors are still madly working on the movie. Finally, they'll invite entertainment press to the set for "exclusive" interviews with the stars and sneak peeks at spectacular costumes or special effects. All of this PR for a film that hasn't even wrapped!

Two or three months before the movie's opening, the studio will host a press junket with its major stars. This is a national tour, often including satellite interviews, designed to give the most important members of the media personal access to the actors. Sometimes, they'll only be allotted fifteen minutes apiece with the stars, but it's enough to allow the journalist to report, "When I spoke with Demi, she seemed . . ." In between screenings and interviews, the media is wined, dined, courted, and invited to elaborate (and expensive) Hollywood-style parties to impress upon them both the scale of the movie and their indebtedness to the studio. Often, these press junkets will overlap with a major film festival, like Cannes, where all the big players march out their upcoming movies and big stars in a furious competition for attention and ink.

Next come the private screenings for the press, which in addition to the expected film-critic crowd, include invitations to virtually anyone in the media who might have something positive to say about the film. Conversely, if the studio thinks the film's final version is weaker than expected, they'll refuse to provide advance screenings to avoid negative reviews. Today, simply omitting the screenings becomes its own news and cause for tremendous negative PR. The remake of *The Avengers,* which enjoyed tremendous prerelease publicity centered on its hot stars and showy costumes, died before it ever opened when national press speculated that the movie was a dud since the studio had canceled its screenings.

Finally, the opening week PR blitz hits. By now, consumers have seen all the advertising and are wondering, when the heck does this movie open, anyway? On opening week, they'll know. For example, take a look at the premiere-week PR for *Lethal Weapon 4.* Mel Gibson made the rounds to a flurry of talk shows, including *Rosie O'Donnell, The Tonight Show, Regis & Kathy Lee,* and *Oprah;* and morning shows, including *The Today Show* and *Good Morning America.* He granted live interviews on local radio stations in every major market. He also taped several segments for *Entertainment Tonight* and *Access Hollywood,* which would run as a series throughout the week.

Sound like a lot of press? That was only Mel's part of the effort. While Mel was making the "first tier" rounds of media, costars Danny Glover, Chris Rock, and Renee Russo were traveling similar circuits to quadruple the exposure on programs like *Late Show with David Letterman* and *Late Night with Conan O'Brien.*

Why all this frantic activity just for opening week? If the movie is good, won't the news spread over the course of its run? Yes, but opening weekend can often ring up 50 percent of the film's total national gross, and announcing the film's performance at the box office ("#1 this weekend!") generates momentum for the weeks that follow. If a film is a real gem or wildly popular, like *Titanic,* box-office performance will remain strong for weeks and months to come. But most movies have a short shelf life and need to make their money up front, and like any other new product introduction, it helps to make a bang from the start. Distributors will be more likely to commit to a longer run if the film performs well at opening.

Publicity promotion is part of the stars' contracts when they agree to be in the film, but the PR department at the studio is responsible to make sure it happens and to plan how. Actors understand that as exhausting as promoting a movie can be, it's essential to create consumer excitement and "sell" the film. That's why even actors who think of themselves as *artists,* and who no longer need to sell their box-office appeal, will still make the rounds for a project they care about. Even Warren Beatty, who refused interviews for over a decade, pounded the pavement for his pet project, *Bulworth.*

Chances are, you don't have Matt Damon or Gwyneth Paltrow lobbying for your product. So how can a normal everyday business learn from the movies? Easy. Take a look at what the studios do effectively and draw parallels:

MOVIE STUDIOS	REGULAR PRODUCTS
Create up-front excitement before the film wraps	Entice the trade with "news" before your product introduction
Use stars as spokesmen	Create identity using a spokesperson
Give personal attention and exclusives	Develop exclusive angles for your press and trade
Court different audiences over the course of the campaign	Address your PR to trade first, then to consumers
Create hype over the opening	Create hype over an event or story
Climax in a one-week media blitz	Create your own blitz week

Secrets of the Game

PR campaigns should develop momentum, with a beginning, a middle, and a blitz climax. Overlap your efforts so consumers receive new, and slightly different, news about your product from many different media sources.

THE FOLGERS COFFEE PR CAMPAIGN AT MIAMI (OHIO) UNIVERSITY

In the spring of 1991, the people at Folgers were spending a lot of time worrying about the future of coffee. Coffeehouses were in their infancy, and the beverage had fallen out of fashion with young consumers. At the age when people traditionally begin a lifelong coffee love affair—sometime during the college years— people were instead choosing soft drinks, even for a morning pick-me-up. The coffee consumer base was aging and no new drinkers were emerging to take its place, leaving management faced with a declining category that was projected to atrophy to 40 percent of its 1991 size in just a little more than twenty years.

Desperate times call for desperate measures, so the company sent me directly to the heart of the matter. I found myself back in school, on the campus of Miami (Ohio) University to determine whether we could change the way students felt about coffee. We wanted to test whether the right PR plan, combined with advertising, could affect their attitudes and entice them to begin drinking coffee.

The campaign was entitled "Jump Start Your Brain" with Folgers. Phase one offered free coffee to students as they lugged their books past forty-five different "coffee stations" on campus. The stations were restocked twice each day with a freshly brewed five-gallon container of Folgers.

Next, we infiltrated campus activities. The immediate impact was impressive. Wherever the students went, or whatever extracurricular activity they participated in, Folgers was there.

At hockey and basketball games, we gave all fans a piece of paper to fold into a paper airplane for the Folgers Coffee "Miami to Miami for Spring Break" Paper Airplane Toss between periods and at basketball's half time. All students got the chance to fly their planes at targets on the ice and playing floor to win free airline tickets to Miami Beach for the upcoming Spring Break.

The piece of paper the students were given to make into a plane was filled with coffee "fun facts," strategic messages that the students read while they held onto their planes for the hour or so from the time they arrived until the airplane toss was held. The vehicle was an incredibly effective communication tool. In follow-up research we found that nearly 60 percent of the students on campus knew the "Folgers fun facts." Great, the first hurdle was behind us; we'd communicated our brand strategy and equated the product with on-campus fun.

Now, to get the students to really drink the stuff. To do that, we hosted the "Folgers Coffee Free Midnight Movie" on Saturday nights at a local theater. Admission was free by drinking a cup of Folgers at the door of the theater. If a student didn't want to drink the coffee, he could pay $4.00 for admission. The theater was packed with students every Saturday and hundreds more had to be turned away. We never collected a single dollar at the door; everyone drank coffee! Even the students who were turned away from a sellout were happy; they milled around outside drinking coffee and chatting with friends for a few hours.

Notice the elements of the PR plan. They were *fun* yet *relevant* to the Folgers brand. The paper airplane toss communicated strategic messages about Folgers coffee; the movie theater promotion accomplished product sampling in a unique way. Best of all, the PR stunts were cheap! We cut a deal with TWA to provide for free the "Miami to Miami" airplane tickets in exchange for advertising exposure on the airplanes. This was a great promotion for TWA, too, as the medium was relevant to their brand, and the movie theater buyout cost us a grand total of $250.00!

DEVELOPING A PR PLAN

There are only two steps required to create a great PR plan. The first step is *deciding what it is you strategically want to communicate*. To illustrate, I'll walk you through an example. Lisa Clements, a friend of mine who used to be the marketing director of the San Francisco Zoo, created a PR plan in which she developed four key strategic messages to communicate to the media, and ultimately consumers, through the year. Each message would be communicated via an event, one each quarter. Her spring strategy was "to communicate that the Zoo is deeply involved with captive breeding programs for endangered species."

The second step in the process is *developing a fun and interesting way of positioning the strategy to the media, giving them a unique, newsworthy hook*. While the strategic message "communicate that the Zoo is deeply involved with captive breeding programs for endangered species" seems boring, Lisa put an incredibly interesting twist on the way she presented the program to the media. She worked with the zookeepers and created San Francisco Zoo's "Sex Tour." It was a zoo tour held on Valentine's Day for adults only, showcasing the different sexual strategies and unusual appendages of various species, from bears and giraffes to insects and snakes. The program was incredibly successful, attracting huge amounts of national media coverage and sellout tours! Look in any newspaper around Valentine's Day and you'll see several zoos throughout the country who have adopted this promotion.

> ### Secrets of the Game
>
> A great PR plan reinforces some aspect of the brand positioning strategy—the benefits, the "reason why," or the brand personality—in a unique and interesting way.

FUN IS THE MAGIC INGREDIENT

Life for most adults is very dull and routine. They get up and read the paper over breakfast, go to work, eat lunch, come home from work, eat dinner, play with the kids, watch the same TV shows regularly, then go to bed.

Everyone is looking for a little excitement, something that looks fun and interesting to offer a break from the everyday routine. That's the opportunity PR offers to marketers. Give the media and consumers some fun! Figure out a way to offer up something that is unique and interesting to get the media excited—if you do, you'll get all the coverage you want and more. *Great ideas* are all that drive PR.

When we were developing the PR plan for the rerelease of Winnie the Pooh videos, we wanted to send our press kit in some sort of package that differentiated us from everyone else and would remind the recipient of how adorable and irresistible Pooh really is. We decided to pack our materials inside a Pooh cookie jar. The press loved it. They cranked out literally hundreds of articles in magazines and newspapers about our Pooh videos and the appeal of the Pooh character. The *Today Show* proudly displayed its Pooh cookie jar on TV while the hosts talked about the new video releases. This simple and fun idea generated millions of dollars' worth of free media exposure.

Like the Sheryl Crow song says, "All I want to do is have some fun. I've got a feelin' I'm not the only one." Have some fun—develop a *great* PR plan for your product by dreaming up some great kick-butt creative ideas! Just remember three words: *different, better,* and *special.*

CHAPTER SUMMARY

- The PR department can be an incredible resource for getting news about your company placed in the media.
- It is important that *all* media communication be channeled through PR. This ensures a single voice and a singular message to consumers.
- There are three distinct types of public relations efforts:
  - Corporate PR, handling the day-to-day operations of the company
  - Defensive PR, defending the company against attack
  - Marketing PR, proactively developing programs to support marketing efforts
- A well-executed marketing PR campaign can add millions of dollars of value in free publicity.

- A great PR plan reinforces some aspect of the brand positioning strategy—the benefits, the "reason why" or the brand personality—in a unique and interesting way.
- Sometimes you can disguise marketing initiatives as PR events to avoid having to pay to advertise.
- Many companies mistakenly think that PR is no more than an application of the "Three P's": keep *plugging* away, *pestering* and *plastering* the media with information. The media doesn't want quantity, they want quality!
- PR is driven by the power of the great idea. Develop a PR plan that is innovative and interesting to the media, then package it well and make it *fun!*
- Movie marketing is a terrific model of how to do PR right.
- PR campaigns should develop momentum. Overlap your efforts so consumers receive new and slightly different news about your product from many different sources.

PROMOTE, PROMOTE AND PROMOTE

The Hush-Hush World of Trade Promotions

WHAT YOU CAN DO BESIDES PAYING FEATURE, DISPLAY AND SLOTTING ALLOWANCES

TWENTY YEARS AGO, the rules at retail were pretty simple. All you had to do to earn a feature and display was to pull together some sort of generic promotion or price reduction. Retailers appreciated the investment you were making in your business and were happy to reciprocate. The brand sales team could usually walk into a store, show the manager a copy of the coupon insert scheduled for Sunday's paper, and voila, walk out with a commitment for a display.

Of course, it didn't hurt to be friendly with the store manager. And what could be friendlier than to swap a few jokes, and then slip him some tickets to a ballgame or a free cd player you just happened to have along. In return, he'd place a sizable order for your product and build a conspicuous display on a front aisle endcap. It didn't cost the salesperson anything—those tickets or cd player were on the corporate account—and the store manager had to come up with several displays every week anyway. The good-ol'-boy system worked this way for many, many years.

Today, you have about the same chance of finding a store where these arcane tactics will work as you do of having a Good Humor Ice Cream truck parked in your neighborhood on a hot summer afternoon. The rules have changed, and marketers are struggling to understand exactly how.

BLAME IT ON THE ACCOUNTING MBA'S

Those darned accountants are at the heart of the confusion. After decades of looking the other way, the bean counters at corporate headquarters for the large retail chains finally took notice of just how much money some companies where willing to throw around at the store level to buy shelf space and end-aisle displays. Legend has it that the store manager at the largest-volume grocery store in Los Angeles owned a twenty-four-foot boat, backyard swimming pool, a Jeep Cherokee, a Porsche 924, vacationed twice a year in Hawaii, and sat courtside at Lakers games—all courtesy of corporate salespeople in exchange for the in-store marketing favors he'd granted.

Like all good business-school grads chanting the mantra "maximize shareholder value," the number crunchers changed the system to channel cash to the corporate bottom line instead of allowing it to be lavished on store and department managers. A smart move on their part, but boy, did it mess up the selling tactics of the corporate sales teams and *really* put a damper on the rich and famous lifestyles that many store managers were living. Many brands were so accustomed to the old wild, wild West atmosphere at retail, they completely lost their footing when corporate standardization set in.

THE ROBISON-PATTMAN ACT

Congress also had something to do with the way trade marketing evolved, by passing the Robison-Pattman Act, which states that manufacturers must treat all retailers equally. This law was created because corporate sales teams were taking advantage of the 80/20 rule, which means investing 80 percent of your resources against the 20 percent of accounts that provides the most volume. Virtually all spending at retail—from displays and contests to those tantalizing freebies—was focused on the few largest accounts, with little or no attention given to smaller chains and independent stores. The smaller stores complained that they could not compete in this biased environment, and they were right.

Today, the Robison-Pattman Act ensures that no account can claim favored status. Consumer product companies must provide the same rewards, incentives, and displays to every retailer. The little guys still have a tough time, since "the same" rewards are offered in proportion to the number of cases a retailer orders. In other words, although the marketing company offers a promotion or display to everyone who orders twenty-five cases of product during the promotional period, they know full well the small retailers may never be able to satisfy the case requirement. But these promotions follow the letter, if not the spirit, of the Robison-Pattman Act.

MARKETING DEVELOPMENT FUNDS

Nothing captures people's attention like cold hard cash, and no tiered incentive program is more alluring than money. Marketing development funds (MDFs) are cash rewards given in return for retailer orders. These funds accrue for *each* brand independently. For example, if Von's in Southern California sells 15,000 cases of Heinz Ketchup and the MDF is $.35 per case, Von's would accrue an MDF fund of $5,250 on Heinz Ketchup (15,000 cases × $.35/case = $5,250). In addition, if Von's sold 4,000 cases of Heinz 57 Sauce and the MDF is $.50 per case, it would accrue an MDF of $2,000 (4,000 cases × $.50/case = $2,000) for Heinz 57 Sauce. Keep in mind, these MDF funds are in addition to the profit margin the retailer already receives on each sale.

MDF dollars do have strings attached. Various consumer products companies have different rules about how the money can be used, but it is usually connected to funding marketing activities within the chain for the *specific brand* on which they were earned. For example, with its $5,250 MDF fund on Heinz Ketchup, Von's might choose to fund a Heinz Ketchup coupon in its mailer, pay for an ad feature in the chain's weekly specials circular, fund a price reduction, buy an end-aisle display for a week, or participate in a proprietary marketing program offered by the retailer (like a summer barbecue promotion or sampling program). MDF typically cannot be combined between brands without the company's approval.

How often are MDF incentives used? Generally, each and every price reduction, end-aisle display, or ad in the weekly specials circular you see is paid for by the brand out of the MDF funds. There are no free rides given by retailers anymore. If you see marketing activity, the brand has paid for it.

DISPLAYS, PRICE REDUCTIONS, AND FEATURE ADS

Why would a brand pay so much money to get a little bit of marketing activity in the store, like an ad or a display? Why not save the money and just sell the product off the shelf? Because despite their high cost, marketing programs are ultimately quite profitable. Every year companies evaluate the effectiveness of in-store displays, price reductions, and ad features in moving product. The results are impressive. Display and feature activity can increase a brand's weekly sales by four to thirteen times the average volume.

AVERAGE IMPACT ON SALES (GROCERY STORE CHANNEL)

NORMAL EVERYDAY DISPLAY	DISPLAY ONLY	FEATURE ONLY*	FEATURE* & SHELF
1×	4×	7×	13×

* Assumes a meaningful advertised price reduction.

THE RESULTS OF IN-STORE MARKETING

To understand the ramifications of in-store marketing activity, let's run the numbers for a typical brand so you can see how it works. Suppose that you are a sales rep for Franco-American spaghetti. Assume the following pricing:

FRANCO-AMERICAN SPAGHETTI (12 CANS PER CASE)

COST TO PRODUCE	PRICE SOLD TO RETAILER	PRICE SOLD TO CONSUMER
Per Case: $3.12	$6.60	$9.48 ($.79 ea.)

You decide to create a program with Safeway in the Northern Virginia area, which has seventy stores in the advertising region. In a typical week with normal placement in the canned goods aisle, Safeway sells around ten cases of Franco-American spaghetti per store, at the everyday price of $.79 per can.

You'd like to explore the options of buying a display only, a feature only, and a display/feature combo. For the feature, you'd like to reduce the retail price down to $.59 to the consumer.

The price for a week of marketing activities within the seventy Safeway stores in this region are as follows:

Endcap display:	$7,000
Feature in weekly circular:	$5,000
Feature & display:	$12,000
Price reductions:	Negotiable

To persuade Safeway to agree to run the feature price for $.59 in their ad, you've agreed to offer a $1.00 per case price allowance financed through your MDF funds. Display and feature activity is paid out of the MDF as well.

Let's look at the hypothetical financials to understand the impact of marketing activity from the brand point of view.

BRAND FINANCIALS
FRANCO-AMERICAN SPAGHETTI IMPACT ON SALES—
70 SAFEWAY STORES

	NORMAL EVERYDAY SHELF	DISPLAY ONLY	FEATURE ONLY*	FEATURE* & DISPLAY
	1×	4×	7×	13×
Case sales:	700	2,800	4,900	9,100
Gross dollars:	$4,620	$18,480	$32,340	$60,060
Less cost:	$2,184	$8,736	$15,288	$28,392
Less MDF:	$0	$7,000	$5,000	$12,000
Less price MDF:	$0	$0	$ 4,900 ($1.00 per case)	$ 9,100
Net brand profit:	$ 2,436	$ 2,744	$7,152	$ 10,568
Profit margin:	52.72%	14.84%	22.11%	17.59%

* Assumes meaningful price discount

If the brand does nothing and continues selling on average ten cases per store, the brand profit for the week is $2,436. You can see that just purchasing a display will not improve bottom-line profitability. Despite moving four times the number of cases, it will only produce $308 more profit. Both feature only ($7,152) and feature/display ($10,568) significantly improve the brand profitability and sales volume for the week. A feature improves profitability by 293 percent, and a feature display combo provides a 433 percent profit lift!

Secrets of the Game

Never buy a product display without funding a meaningful price reduction to consumers. A display at regular price won't generate enough incremental sales activity to pay out!

Now look at the same scenario from the financial perspective of Safeway:

SAFEWAY FINANCIALS
FRANCO-AMERICAN SPAGHETTI IMPACT ON SALES—70 STORES

	NORMAL EVERYDAY SHELF	DISPLAY ONLY	FEATURE ONLY*	FEATURE* & DISPLAY
	1×	4×	7×	13×
Case sales:	700	2,800	4,900	9,100
Gross dollars:	$6,636	$26,544	$34,692	$64,428
Less cost:	$4,620	$18,480	$32,340	$60,060
Plus MDF:	$0	$7,000	$5,000	$12,000
Plus price MDF:	$0	$0	$ 4,900 ($1.00 per case)	$ 9,100
Net Safeway profit:	$ 2,016	$ 15.604	$12,252	$ 25,468
Profit margin:	30.37%	44.90%	27.47%	29.77%

* Assume meaningful price discount

Notice how Safeway protects its net margin regardless of what the brand does by charging for the display and feature activities.

Even though the consumer thinks Safeway is a swell store for offering a great deal on Franco-American spaghetti, the brand is actually paying for the price reduction and other marketing activities through its MDF accrual.

When brands perform in-store marketing, everybody wins! The consumer gets a great low price, the brand gets a significant boost in its weekly profits, and Safeway gets a healthy addition to its bottom line as well.

PROPRIETARY RETAILER PROGRAMS

The retail business is becoming increasingly competitive, and retailers are acutely interested in building their own consumer base. That's why you see so much advertising for grocery, mass, and convenience stores these days. Retailers have also learned their lesson from the consumer products companies; they know how well consumer promotions can work to generate sales and consumer loyalty. Most major retailers execute several storewide promotions each year, which they hope will entice consumers to shop. These are often holiday-oriented sales, checkout coupons, on-shelf instant coupons, "club card" continuity programs, case sales, proprietary signage, and shopping cart ads.

Retailers are eager for their vendors to support these promotions, not only to create a bigger splash at the store level, but also to fund their very execution. Let's take a look at a few of the retailer promotions and analyze how they might, or might not, work for you.

Checkout Coupons

Checkout coupons are often offered through a company called Catalina Marketing or directly through the retailer. The attractiveness of these coupons is that they are "smart" coupons that are generated depending upon what the consumer buys in the grocery store, printed at the checkout stand, and handed to consumers with their change and receipt.

Most of the time brands use this tactic as a competitive counterattack. For example, Pampers might fund a checkout coupon to give to every consumer who makes a Huggies purchase. Smart couponing seems like a clever way of targeting your couponing at the competitor's consumer, instead of funding a general coupon that will probably by redeemed primarily by consumers who already use your product.

Unfortunately, smart coupons at checkout are usually pretty dumb investments. Think of it this way: Every time a consumer buys a product, it takes him or her out of the market to buy from that product category until the item just purchased is used up. This is what's often referred to as purchase cycle.

Secrets of the Game

Checkout coupons are a lousy marketing investment. It puts a coupon in the consumer's hand at precisely the moment when the buyer is farthest away from another purchase. Don't do it!

As a marketer, your job is to try to figure out when consumers are most likely to make a purchase in your product category, and then hit them with your marketing efforts just *before* they buy. Good timing will dramatically increase your chances of making a sale. Checkout coupons hit consumers with a purchase incentive immediately after they've just bought the product, at the furthest possible point from another product purchase!

Direct Mail Smart Coupons

A much more effective means of targeting consumers with smart coupons is to tie them in with the club cards that many large retailers now offer. These cards are ingenious. Every time a consumer goes to the store and the clerk swipes his or her card, it stores that consumer's entire history of purchases in their store's mainframe computer. The store now knows exactly what products a specific consumer buys—the brands, the sizes, the flavors—and knows precisely when he or she bought them!

Now you have an incredible opportunity to target consumers with coupons at just about the right time in their purchase cycle. For example, if you are the brand manager for Tide, and you know that the typical box of detergent lasts twenty-seven days in a household, you can send a Tide smart coupon through direct mail to all consumers who bought a competitive laundry detergent twenty to twenty-four days ago. The loyal Tide consumers are none the wiser (they don't get anything in their mail), and you've got the targeted opportunity to steal away competitor's customers at the point where they will be going to the store to get more detergent. This is by far a smarter way to use smart coupons!

In-Store Instant Coupons

In-store instant coupons are always displayed right next to your product on the store shelf. The coupon dispenser is usually bright red with an LED flashing light to draw attention to it. These coupons often do work to stimulate product sales and steal business away from your competitors, particularly in a price-sensitive category.

So why don't you see thousands of these coupon dispensers in stores? The primary reason isn't effectiveness, but rather the expense of coupon redemptions and where the cost is borne within the corporation.

Coupon redemptions are paid by the brand marketing budget at corporate headquarters, not out of the retailer's MDF. So while the corporate sales force and the retailer *love* instant coupons because they generate sales, brand teams at headquarters *hate* instant coupons because they chew away at the national marketing budget, leaving the retailer MDF fund intact and in fact helping to build that war chest with every product sold (and that money is managed by the sales team and the retailer, not by the brand marketing team).

Why do the brand teams hate in-store instant coupons with such a passion? Because in-store instant coupons often have a 98 percent redemption rate! The feeling within the brand groups is that these coupons steal away profits by landing in the hands of loyal consumers who would have been happy to pay full price, in addition to those new users whom you may be converting from competition. This risk of couponing your loyal customer is especially steep if you are already a category leader.

For perspective, look at it this way. When a corporate brand team drops a coupon in the Sunday newspaper, the redemption rate is usually around 2 percent. So a brand team can print up 40 million coupons for the newspaper, and only around 800,000 of them actually get used. If you do the math on a $.20 coupon, that means the brand team pays about $160,000 for this national activity.

Now look at what happens when you do in-store couponing. Think of our Franco-American spaghetti example again, and let's say the brand team wants to generate the same amount of volume as it would with a feature/display combo in those Safeway stores, which means selling about 130 cases each. The coupons will offer the same discount as the feature—$.20 off. To generate the required sales means that about 1,600 coupons must be placed in each of the Safeway stores. Over the 70 stores, this would amount to 112,000 coupons. At a 98 percent redemption rate, the cost of the coupons would be about $22,000.

Compare this to the national coupon that covered the whole country for a cost of $160,000. This in-store coupon only covered 70 stores at about one-eighth the cost of the national effort. There are about 5,000 large grocery stores in the United States. If you tried to execute an in-store couponing promotion in all of them, the cost would be an astronomical $1.57 million on the redeemed coupons!

If you compare the cost of the coupon redemption ($22,000) with the cost of the feature/display activity calculated in the earlier example ($21,100) it's pretty much a wash, but the critical issue is knowing out of which bucket of money the funds are coming. Feature/display promotions are paid out of the retailer's MDF accrual. Coupons are paid at corporate headquarters. Since the corporate brand team has the yea/nay vote over how their brand marketing dollars are spent, it's a battle to get the OK to move ahead with in-store coupon activity. That's why you don't see more in-store instant coupons!

Secrets of the Game

Only use in-store instant coupons if you are the #3 brand or lower in the competitive market share race. Only then will it be likely that more nonusers than regular purchasers will be reaching for the coupons.

Shopping Carts and Proprietary Signage

Just about every retailer who has shopping carts will offer you the chance to buy advertising on them. Unfortunately, while this seems like it would be a great way to get your message delivered to the consumer at the right time, it usually doesn't work very well. Most consumers don't pay attention to cart ads. As soon as they step inside the store, their eyes are bombarded with stimulation from the thousands of products displayed on the shelves. Consumers are looking everywhere but at their cart.

Another in-store tactic you might see is scrolling electronic message boards. Brands usually buy this program to coincide with features to draw consumer attention to the special price. These electronic billboards can be very effective if they are located in the aisle in which the product is sold. The same goes for tiled floor signs. They are usually placed in close proximity to the product on the shelf. If the tiles carry a relevant brand message or highlight feature activity, they, too, can positively influence consumer purchase.

> **Secrets of the Game**
>
> Use in-store signage *only* in support of feature activity and consumer promotions. *Do not* just put your brand logo on the sign! That would commit the sin of Pride, one of the Six Deadly Sins of Advertising!

BEATING THE SYSTEM

With the Robison-Pattman Act restricting what you can offer retailers, and retailers themselves ever more focused on sending cash to the bottom line, it is getting tough for brands to execute retail promotions that stand out from the crowd. But there are ways of beating the system and developing unique, volume-driving promotions that can separate your in-store marketing efforts from the sea of sameness. You just have to be creative and think a little differently than everyone else.

Brands that execute national consumer promotions do not receive much assistance from retailers in showcasing their offers. That's because national promotions are offered to every retailer, so the consumer offer is the same in each retail outlet. Retail chains are competitive, and want to differentiate themselves from one another. They are most interested in providing the consumer with reasons to shop at their store, instead of at the market down the street. As a result, you probably won't get much support for your big national promotions—what they really want are account-specific promotions.

THE GOLD STANDARD

Account-Specific Promotions

But what if you are a little guy who doesn't have the budget of a Coca-Cola? Can a brand like Uncle Joe's spaghetti sauce still compete? The answer is yes. You can beat the system with proprietary, account-specific promotions that can be executed within the parameters of Robison-Pattman.

The sales manager at Disney Home Video who managed the relationship with Target stores was a genius in account-specific promotions. Faced with the challenge of stimulating sales after a record-breaking year at the chain, he was hungry for a big idea to drive consumer purchases to even higher levels.

Consumer research indicated that when retail stores played Disney's children's videos on in-store TV monitors, sales rocketed, even when the videos were offered at full price. Moms walking by the TV playing the video would grab one from the nearby display as an impulse purchase for their kids.

That gave the manager his big idea—to create a portable cart with a TV/VCR combo on top and a display of Disney videos below! He had the Disney creative services team put together a prototype cart, took it to Minneapolis for a presentation, and Target management loved it. The video cart was attractive and entertaining and made Target seem special for having it. They used Target's accrued MDF funds to manufacture a video cart for every store, giving

Disney a proprietary in-store promotion to stimulate consumer purchase of their videos. Walk into any Target store and you'll see this cart playing Disney videos, usually in close proximity to the front door or checkout stands.

Tagged Media

Retailers love for brands to run advertising that directs consumers to their stores. Often, as part of account-specific promotions, the brand will agree to purchase local TV and radio commercials that include mention of the retailer. This mention is technically called tagged media. For a typical TV spot, the brand will communicate its message in twenty seconds and leave the last ten seconds for a "tag"—a commercial for the retailer. For sixty-second radio spots, it is usually a forty-second brand/twenty-second retailer split or a thirty-second brand/thirty-second retailer division. Again, this is legal if accrued MDF funds are used to pay for the activity.

Offering Unique Point-of-Sale Materials

Another way to beat the system and get the retail trade to execute an in-store marketing activity for you is to produce kick-butt point-of-sale material that the retailer wants badly.

Again, Disney is the king of this tactic. They leverage the imagery of their classics characters to develop beautiful pieces of in-store display material that are often too incredible to pass on. The retailers use accrued MDF funds to purchase the point-of-sale display pieces, and Disney ends up "owning" the look of the store, with imagery from *The Lion King* or *Aristocats* or *Pocahontas* everywhere. This is a very effective tactic for the big "classic" video releases. You'll see the same strategy from Budweiser around Super Bowl time, and from Coors and Pepsi at Halloween.

Carving Out Proprietary Shelf Space

One of the fears facing all brand marketers is losing shelf space to a competitor. Just like in war, if you lose the battle, it's tough to reclaim your territory anytime soon.

As a means of "owning" shelf space, some brands have developed proprietary shelf units that they sell to the stores using accrued MDF dollars. When the shelf units are installed, they effectively eliminate the threat of competitive shelf infiltration. Most retailers won't mix and match competitive product in another brand's display unit, since it ruins the look of the shelf and generally appears messy.

McCormick's Spice is a master of this tactic. Go into any store and you'll see a rack fully stocked with the brand's offerings. They effectively own their shelf space and are impervious to competitive attack!

Coca-Cola also understands the critical value of real estate. Coke controls space by offering coolers, vending machines, and fountain dispensers to retailers that are designed to house only Coca-Cola product and keep "The Blue Devil," Pepsi, at bay.

Third-Party Promotions

Many brands beat the system by developing third-party promotions that "just happen" to also include a retail partner. This is the perfect way for a small brand to compete.

The way it works is simple. A promotion company approaches your brand with an idea for sponsoring a promotion. They tell you that they've got a major retailer involved as the title sponsor, and that if you participate as a subsponsor, the retailer will give you in-store marketing activity, typically display or features. Your brand signs the contract with the promotion company, the retailer signs the contract with the promotion company, and you've effectively circumvented Robison-Pattman!

I witnessed firsthand how third-party promotions work when I was in Cincinnati, working for Procter & Gamble. The Utah Jazz and Boston Celtics were coming to town to play an NBA exhibition game. A promotion company affiliated with the Utah Jazz cut a deal with the local Kroger supermarket chain to be the title sponsor of the event. Kroger received the sponsorship for free from the promotion company, in exchange for agreeing to allow the promoters to sign on six consumer product brands as cosponsors and committing feature/display activity for each of the cosponsoring brands at Kroger.

The brands each paid the promoter a participation fee, and Kroger ran a full-page newspaper ad for the brands in addition to large in-store displays featuring all six products. Because no money was exchanged between the brand and Kroger, the promotion was immune from Robison-Pattman.

Secrets of the Game

TV stations and radio stations are great at developing third-party promotions. When you have the triumvirate of a media partner, retail outlet, and brands, you have an extremely powerful combination!

Remember how I cautioned you against using promotion agencies to develop your consumer promotions? The rule doesn't always apply to the retail side. You don't necessarily need to offer the trade something unique, different, and special as you do with the consumer; you simply have to give them what they want, which is often funding for their own promotional programs. If you are managing a small or medium-size brand that rarely gets attention from retailers for executing in-store marketing activity, by all means pursue third-party promotions. They can often slip you in the back door. Third-party activity is also very effective for small brands that don't have enough sales clout or dollars to play in the regular feature/display game at retail. Often, this is the only vehicle available to get marketing activity at major retailers.

NEW PRODUCTS—SLOTTING ALLOWANCES

Since new products have no accrued MDF from case sales, the retail chain's corporate offices charge manufacturers a fee, called a slotting allowance, to place the product in stores on a trial basis. These fees are usually quite high, in the $10,000 to $25,000 range *per item,* depending upon the store chain. Most companies struggle with the expense of placing a new product, which is one reason why new items are often introduced gradually, market by market, as their sales show promise. For perspective, if each of the top 50 grocery chains in the United

States charged on average a $20,000 slotting fee, that's $1 million dollars to get just one new product on store shelves! That's a tremendous gamble for an unproven product.

Why are the stores so greedy? There's more to it than making a quick buck. Remember, stores are primarily interested in how much profit they can produce per square inch of shelf space. In order to put a new product in, something else has to come out, and the new product must quickly prove that it can generate the kind of sales that justify its place on the shelf. Stores charge these slotting allowances to make sure that their profits for that shelf space are covered in the event that the new product fails to sell.

Retailers have no choice but to be this persnickety about letting new products into their stores. They've been burned before. In the past 10 years, manufacturers have bombarded them with new offerings at an alarming rate. Between 1989 and 1996, manufacturers introduced 145,203 new products to the grocery trade. If the stores accepted every new product produced, they would have no room for your favorite brands.

NEW PRODUCT INTRODUCTIONS—

GROCERY TRADE—1989 THROUGH 1996

CATEGORY	1989	1990	1991	1992	1993	1994	1995	1996	TOTALS
Foods	7,019	9,020	8,061	8,159	8,077	10,854	10,816	11,072	73,078
Beverages	1,402	1,621	1,805	1,611	2,243	2,597	2,581	3,524	17,384
Heath & beauty	3,434	3,530	4,035	4,625	5,327	7,161	5,861	8,204	42,177
Household	557	921	829	786	790	704	829	785	6,201
Pet products	480	381	443	451	464	377	315	467	3,378
Other	492	406	228	254	462	293	406	444	2,985
TOTALS	13,384	15,879	15,401	15,886	17,363	21,986	20,808	24,496	145,203

Source: Marketing Intelligence Service—ProductScan

When retailers take in a new product, they usually give it forty-five days to prove itself, or out it goes. If the new product loses its distribution, there is no refund of the slotting fees; and if the manufacturer wants to get the product back into stores to give it another try, they must again pay the slotting fee.

Considering that eight out of every ten new products fail, slotting allowances are the only means retailers have of protecting their bottom line. The hefty fee also forces the manufacturers to take a long, hard look at their new products to make sure that they are worth the investment, with meaningful consumer appeal that will produce sufficient sales to sustain distribution.

Circumventing Slotting Fees

So you're stuck with paying slotting fees . . . that is, unless you know how to play The Marketing Game. Developing unique and proprietary marketing initiatives to offer the retailer can sometimes entice him to reduce the slotting allowance to about $200—the actual cost for setting up the new UPC in the computer checkout system. All of the examples in the "Beating the System" section are applicable here. The trick is you've got to offer them something they can get *only* through you!

Many Coca-Cola bottlers effectively used the inducement of "Torchbearers" in the 1996 Olympic Torch Relay as a means of leveraging retailers. They gave certain retailers the opportunity to select one of their customers to carry the Olympic Flame, in return for waiving slotting allowances on new soft drink flavors. It worked like a charm. Other ways to use this tactic are to offer unique prizes for in-store raffles. Retailers love these proprietary in-store activities!

> ## Secrets of the Game
>
> To win The Marketing Game, you must create ways for your product to gain more in-store marketing activities than your competitors on a calendar basis. It's all a numbers game. If you can get more frequent in-store activity than they do, you'll win!

If you can effectively master the art of working with the trade, you'll be ahead in the game. Take a bold approach to wooing your trade partners. Make your company the most original, interesting, and just plain fun organization that your buyer deals with in his busy week. Take some risks, and offer him opportunities he's never heard before, even if he hates the first five or ten you try.

Remember, you always miss 100 percent of the shots you don't take. Trade relationships are too valuable not to make the effort.

CHAPTER SUMMARY:

- The rules have changed in how companies can interact with retailers. The Robison-Pattman Act specifies that all retailers must be given equal opportunities to participate in manufacturers' marketing programs.
- Most manufacturers offer cash awards to retailers based on the number of cases they purchase of each product. These funds, call marketing development funds (MDF) can be used only to finance promotional activity for that particular product within the retail chain.
- In-store marketing—display's, price reductions, and feature ad activity—can dramatically increase sales and profitability for both the manufacturer and the retailer.
- Many retailers offer proprietary marketing programs. They include:
  - Checkout coupons
  - Direct mail "smart" coupons
  - In-store instant coupons
  - Shopping carts and proprietary signage
- Most retailers now prefer that manufacturers bring them account-specific promotions. There are very few national promotions executed anymore. Account-specific promotions are usually funded out of the MDF funds.
- Third-party promotions are a great way to dance around the restrictions of Robison-Pattman. Many small brands have found success in these types of programs.
- TV stations and radio stations are great at developing third-party promotions.
- New products are charged slotting allowances in order to get distribution. These can range as high as $20,000 *per* retail chain.
- Taking the retailer a great account-specific promotion can sometimes get him or her to wave the slotting allowance.
- Usually, the brands that generate the most in-store marketing activities are the most successful.

What You Don't Know about Consumer Promotions

CREATE BRAND PERSONALITY,
COMPETITIVE ADVANTAGE *AND*
BOOST SALES!

W ALK INTO ANY SUPERMARKET, DRUGSTORE, MASS MER-
CHANT, CONVENIENCE STORE, OR LOCAL CAR WASH
and you'll soon be dizzy from the onslaught of consumer promotions. Enter here to win a cruise, redeem an instant
coupon, buy one and get one free! Chances are, you're so accustomed to the promotional hoopla where you shop, you hardly
notice anymore. You're not alone. Although virtually every brand
in the market executes consumer promotions, presumably with
the intention of boosting sales and attracting consumers, very few
do anything that consumers notice. And fewer still create promotions that are truly great.

There is a good reason why so many consumer promotions
fall flat. The primary culprit is short-term thinking by the brand

team. Most generally view consumer promotions as a way to get a quick volume bump, and never consider the possible long-term implications. In fact, promotions are often so underappreciated that promotion planning, development, and execution are delegated to the most junior marketing-staff members. After all, how much expertise does it require to drop a coupon, organize a sweepstakes, or coordinate a mailing? Anyone could do it, right? Right. That's why everyone does, and also why these promotions usually don't work. But a well-executed consumer promotion, one that has been developed with care and thought, can serve as a catapult for your business. Sure, it'll create a bump in sales, but its impact won't stop there. A great promotion creates brand personality, carves out competitive advantage, *and* drives sales, with results that endure long past the promotional window.

CREATING PROMOTIONS ON STRATEGY

Like every other piece of the marketing mix, consumer promotions must be grounded on sound strategic positioning. This means using the ABCs of Strategic Positioning—addressing a target *A*udience, strongly stating the consumer *B*enefit of the brand, and calling out the *C*ompelling reasons why your brand delivers this benefit better than anyone else. These are the cornerstones upon which the idea must be built (refer to chapter 4 for more on positioning).

Let's assume, for example, you are selling bubble bath to an audience of women ages twenty-five to forty. Your benefit is providing a relaxing oasis in her busy day, and your compelling "reasons why" are tingling bubbles and unique relaxing scents. Before you start to wonder, "Should I drop a coupon, or should I build a display?" you should be thinking, "How do I communicate my core benefit—a relaxing oasis—in a promotion?" Next you ask, "What are the best channels to reach my audience?" and finally, "Is there a way to reinforce my reasons why—tingle and fragrance?"

Once you've focused on your strategy, the next step is to take a good analytical look at your competition. Catalog the consumer promotions that have been executed by your brand and by competitors to search for strategies that have worked and identify patterns for success. Along the way, you'll also begin to recognize the trappings of failure.

THE FOUR PLAGUES OF CONSUMER PROMOTION

One way to learn to do things right is simply to avoid doing them wrong. The Four Plagues of Consumer Promotion are guarantees of mediocrity, if not disaster. Avoid them at all cost.

Been There, Done That

Many brands have an overwhelming compulsion to "do what we did last year." After all, it's safe, it's familiar, and it doesn't require much mental energy. If your business improved by 2 percent last year with promotion "X," you can predict that if you do it again this year, you'll see a 1.5 percent to 2 percent lift. You won't earn any medals for valor, but you don't risk total failure either.

This is the worst virus any marketing person can become infected with—and it's contagious. At Coca-Cola, the entire USA brand promotion team was contaminated for quite some time. Their summer promotion in 1994 was entitled "Red Hot Summer." In 1995, it was called "Red Hot Summer II." In 1996, they really went out on a limb and executed "Red Hot OLYMPIC Summer." The prize pools in each execution were virtually identical. After the first round, consumers stopped paying attention— as well they should.

Many Procter & Gamble brand teams and those at other consumer products companies are also infected with this disease. The promotion plans of P&G brands are numbingly predictable. Drop a Sunday newspaper coupon on the same week as last year, drop another in the Publisher's Clearing House envelopes during January and July. For the big excitement, throw in an on-pack promotion or sweepstakes once a year.

Been There, Done That doesn't set in each time a promotion is repeated. Every once in a while a promotion is so compelling, unusual, or otherwise remarkable it bears repeating. The McDonald's "Monopoly" promotion was successful twice for that reason; the third time, it flopped. The McDonald's Beanie Baby promotion also worked great—twice. Budweiser has been successful in executing multiple "Bud Bowl" consumer promotions, but the effectiveness diminishes each year. Sometimes you *can* get away with a repeat promotion and be effective, but you can bet it won't be as successful the second or third time around.

Sleeping Sickness

The second affliction that besets many consumer promotions is the dreaded Sleeping Sickness. This ailment is characterized by brand promotions that are lame or so tiresome they put consumers to sleep.

Couponing is a prime carrier of Sleeping Sickness. Very few consumers look through newspaper coupons anymore, and redemption percentages are at an all-time low; yet companies persist in placing them. They also can't seem to resist copycat consumer sweepstakes, despite the deafening sound of snoring that accompanies them. How many hundreds of brands have offered grand-prize trips to Walt Disney World in the past twenty years? Not only is the trip an overused prize, the promotion almost always fails to support the brand's positioning statement and core consumer benefit. Ditto for the hundreds of brands who have given away a car, TV, VCR, or other electronics equipment. Yawn. Consumers are sleepy and so are sales.

Trinkets & Trashitis

The most prevalent promotional ailment is Trinkets & Trashitis. This malady offers some piece of merchandise (often referred to as a premium) to the consumer in return for purchasing the product. Usually the premium is a cheaply made imported plastic doodad, which might be exciting if you're a seven-year-old but probably won't impress anyone else. Brand teams love premiums because they misguidedly think they can "self-liquidate" the items—sell them to the consumer at a small price, usually the price the brand paid—to recoup dollars and balance the promotion budget. That way the promotion in theory costs them nothing, which looks great on paper for senior management. This type of promotion is usually presented as

"Buy 3 boxes of product X and send in $1.99 (plus shipping and handling) to get this wonderful trinket of trash, overstated as a $10.00 value."

Folgers suffered a doozie of a Trinkets & Trashitis promotion shortly after I arrived at P&G. A relatively new hire in the brand team had the bright idea of offering sets of napkin rings to consumers to stimulate multiple purchases of Folgers Coffee. His thinking must have been: "you drink coffee with meals, and meals require napkins . . ." He somehow convinced management that millions of women were simply chafing for new napkin rings and would be willing to purchase six jars of instant coffee to acquire a matching set. Then he placed his order for the premiums, nearly doubling the U.S. annual production of napkin rings. Consumers ignored the promotion in droves, and the brand team was left sitting on nearly a million rings when it was over.

Unfortunately, one of the brands on my watch contracted this illness as well. In an attempt to stimulate sales of Disney's Sing-Along Songs videos, my team developed two cute little Sing-Along microphones featuring Mickey Mouse and Ariel, The Little Mermaid. The brand team's plan was to create a box that contained both a Sing-Along Songs video and a plastic microphone, charging about $2.00 more than the cost for the video alone—a $14.99 suggested retail price (versus $12.99 for the video alone). Senior management fell in love with our adorable microphones just as we had hoped, but then they arbitrarily raised the suggested price to $17.99—over protests of the brand team, I might add. Consumers didn't bite. They knew the cheap plastic microphone wasn't worth $5.00, no matter how cute it was. Right now, approximately 1.5 million of those darling little gems are stashed somewhere in Disney's warehouse, if anyone is interested!

But don't feel too sorry for our microphones; they certainly aren't lonely. If you checked the warehouses at most major companies, you'd find millions upon millions of dollars' worth of trinkets and trash produced for unsuccessful promotions, just sitting around collecting dust until somebody can figure out what to do with them. Nobody ever will. Who wants to dig up stuff that didn't work before and have his or her name attached to a second failed attempt? It's better forgotten and buried in a warehouse. Hear no evil, see no evil, speak no evil.

Oddsitis

Las Vegas bookies are the inspiration of the final infirmity in the Four Plagues of Consumer Promotion. The disease Oddsitis is one that marketers manifest when they misguidedly believe that if they offer high odds of winning some kind of prize in their sweepstakes, consumers will automatically respond positively.

Soft drink brands are common victims of this disorder. You can almost always find a brand on the store shelf touting "1 in 12 Wins" or "1 in 6 Wins" with an under-the-cap promotion.

Unfortunately, offering what consumers perceive to be "high" odds of winning creates an expectation of winning every time. When the consumer loses, he thinks, "Hey, why didn't I win?" But high odds also work against the brand even when the consumer wins. Since he is already expecting to win, a low-level prize is a fizzle instead of a bang.

Secrets of the Game

The Four Plagues of Consumer Promotion

The afflictions of Been There Done That, Sleeping Sickness, Trinkets & Trashitis, and Oddsitis are sure-fire bombs that neither captivate consumers nor drive sales.

Avoid them like the plagues they are!

ELEMENTS OF PROMOTIONS THAT WORK

Just as we have discovered patterns of promotional strategies that consistently don't seem to work very well, we also saw a distinct set of core ideas that seems to invariably be associated with all great promotions.

Publisher's Clearing House Prize Patrol Giveaway is a promotion that illustrates all the elements of success. Although I will admit that PCH mails so many packages it's downright annoying, you've got to hand it to them; the uniqueness of their offering—giving away millions of dollars live on TV from your front door—is an intriguing consumer hook that never gets old. Everybody wants to win $31 million on TV in front of his or her neighbors and the whole wide world. I know I keep a lookout in my driveway for Dave Sayer and the Prize Patrol van every time they go on the air to give away the money on Super Bowl Sunday—and I bet you do, too!

What is it about this promotion that keeps me glued to my window—and my mailbox? If you break it down to its elemental features, you'll find a terrific blueprint for success. First and foremost, the Prize Patrol is successful because it allows the consumer to fantasize about seeing himself win. The prize is compelling and the spokespeople are credible; nobody doubts that there actually is a big winner. And with every mailing, each more personalized and tantalizing than the last, the consumer is strongly led down the rosy path to believe that the big winner has every likelihood of being him.

The promotion also has incredible momentum. Consumers receive early mailings for registration (registration occurs automatically with a purchase), then continually advance through stages over several months. Naturally, each of these progressive stages includes a strong incentive to make yet another purchase. Sure, by law you can enter the sweepstakes without buying anything, but nonpurchase entries must be mailed in a plain white envelope with a measly 3" × 5" card inside, instead of being rushed to Clearinghouse Headquarters in an exciting "Winning Number Enclosed!" envelope with colorful bonus prize stickers. No one with any secret hope of winning would trust his entry to the plain white envelope!

As the giveaway date draws near, TV advertising announces the time of the next live giveaway. Concurrently, the consumer receives in the mail a finalist package, telling him that he is so close to winning, PCH must have his permission to televise the award moment from his front door. The mailing requests an alternate address where the consumer might be if he knows he won't be home at the time of the giveaway. They ask him to select the form of payment in which he'd like to receive his award. He signs publicity release forms (and probably makes another purchase; what's $4.99 when you're a shoe-in for millions?). The package includes a photograph of Dave Sayer and the Prize Patrol team holding a copy of the winning $31 million check—with the consumer's name on it! The finalist package is a stroke of pure genius. After all that paperwork, it seems a sure bet Dave is on the way!

Although the contest has only a single prize—the Grand Prize—it is extremely successful. The reason is clear: Publishers Clearing House knows the Secrets of the Game.

Secrets of the Game

All successful consumer promotions have the Three Ingredients of Greatness:

1. They have a unique premise, different from everything else that others have executed or are currently executing, with a highly desirable prize (or prizes).

2. They make you believe you have a good chance (or at least a fair chance) of winning.

3. They are simple to enter.

You don't have to give away a million dollars in order to create an effective consumer promotion that includes the Three Ingredients of Greatness. Miller Beer executed a terrific promotion that drove sales during the summer of 1998 with a unique and memorable scratch 'n sniff promotion. While the vehicle of scratch 'n sniff has been around forever, the way Miller executed the promotion was brilliant. The scents were all strange smells, not the usual perfume and cologne. For example, if you were to smell "beef," you'd win a half-side of frozen beef; if you smelled "suntan lotion" you'd win a trip to go hang out at the next *Sports Illustrated Swimsuit Edition* photo shoot.

This promotion was perfect. It hit a bulls-eye with males ages eighteen to thirty-four and supported Miller Beer's strategic positioning benefit of "unexpected fun" (as characterized in the long-running series of "Dick" commercials). The promotion was unique and different, unlike anything ever executed before. It was easy to play, and everyone got a weird scratch scent with purchase, so each consumer believed he had a good chance to win.

CREATING BRAND PERSONALITY WITH PROMOTIONS

Most consumer products do not have a brand personality, although they certainly should. Those that do can create tremendous competitive advantage for themselves through consumer promotions.

What exactly is a brand personality? Just as every individual has a unique personality, it is possible to create a unique personality for a brand. Budweiser has a personality crafted through the frogs/iguanas it uses in commercials; Ronald McDonald and the HamBurgler gang give McDonald's a unique and fun personality for kids. Personality can also be obtained by packaging—wild colors communicate that the brand is wild and crazy; black means cool and upscale. Most market-leading brands have a personality as part of their strategy. Nike has a "serious athlete" personality—no wanna-bes or couch potatoes allowed.

Like any relationship, the key to winning consumer friendships is to develop an engaging personality. Associating with your brand should make people feel good about themselves and their choices.

Oscar Mayer is one brand that has developed a winning brand personality using an imaginative promotional vehicle, the Oscar Mayer Wienermobile. This giant traveling hot dog on wheels is a sight to behold when it comes to your neighborhood grocery store. Just looking at it makes you laugh, and through on-site promotions—handing out Wiener Whistles and an ongoing tryout contest to find the next "Oscar Mayer Kids" to star in a TV commercial—the brand establishes itself as fun and kid-friendly. The unforgettable theme song, which the kids all sing at tryouts, drives home the brand personality:

> *I wish I were an Oscar Mayer Wiener,*
> *That is what I'd truly like to be,*
> *'Cause if I were an Oscar Mayer Wiener,*
> *Everyone would be in love with me!*

When a kid goes home after seeing the Wienermobile and having his big moment onstage singing the Oscar Mayer wiener song, do you think that Mom can serve anything other than an

Oscar Mayer wiener ever again? Not a chance. All other hot dog brands may now leave the building.

Goodyear Tires has developed a brand personality through its fleet of Goodyear Blimps. How can a thing that just hovers in the air have a personality? The brand has crafted its persona by becoming synonymous with "Big Event"—if it's happening, the blimp will be there. You know that you are at a special event (hence, *you're* pretty special) if the blimp has made an appearance. These airships have become a part of Americana. The company drives sales by offering rides on the famous airship with the purchase of a set of new Goodyear Tires when it's in town. Who wouldn't want to hang out and be seen with the blimp? It's cool. Kind of like sitting courtside at a Lakers game with Jack Nicholson.

BORROWING A PERSONALITY

In high school, there are some kids who are popular because they captain the football team or they're incredibly good-looking. Then there are kids who are popular because they're best buddies with the football captain or they date the really good-looking girl, and maybe they sort of look and act the same way.

If a brand has a hard time establishing its own personality, it can employ the same strategy that worked in high school; it can become desirable by association. Take a look at Dr. Pepper. Competing with gargantuan advertising budgets in the soft drink category, Dr. Pepper has a hard time convincing consumers ages eighteen through thirty-five that it has its own unique appeal suited particularly to them. So instead of struggling to create its own image, the brand developed highly visible partnerships with TV programs that have a young and contemporary personality— *Melrose Place, Beverly Hills 90210,* and *Party of Five.* Within this hip context, the brand offers unique prizes like trips to Hollywood for private cast parties or cameo walk-on appearances in the shows. These promotions have been very successful in helping Dr. Pepper develop a relationship with the viewers of these programs, most of whom watch all three shows religiously each week.

Sprite employs a similar tactic, leveraging the personality of the NBA to support a bold, in-your-face attitude for its brand. In the summer of 1996 the brand executed an international promotion that allowed foreign consumers the chance to come to the United States and hang out with the USA Dream Team, the best NBA players on the planet: Grant Hill, Hakeem Olajuwon, Scotty Pippen, Karl Malone, John Stockton, Gary Payton, Shaquille O'Neal, David Robinson, Charles Barkley, Reggie Miller, Mitch Richmond, and Patrick Ewing. Each Sprite winner received an all-expenses-paid trip to the States; had a private breakfast with Dream Team head coach Lenny Wilkens; attended a "closed door" practice; and had the opportunity to meet all of the players, get their pictures taken with each player, and have personalized autographs signed by the players (Charles Barkley even played pick-up games with the young kids!). Finally, the winners watched a Dream Team game from prime courtside seats. In several countries, this promotion drove Sprite volume to all-time highs and effectively helped build the Sprite brand personality.

CONTINUITY PROMOTIONS

Continuity promotions—ones that require a series of purchases—are tricky, but they can be highly effective and well worth the trouble. Airlines are the kings of continuity promotions with their Frequent Flyer programs. Before these programs, consumers had no incentive other than price to differentiate between carriers. They'd shop for their desired destination and choose the lowest rate. But the Frequent Flyer programs compelled consumers to develop loyalties to airlines. Suddenly, consumers were earning credits toward travel when they used their credit cards, purchased a full tank of gas, or stayed at a hotel—activities they would have performed anyway. Awards were adjusted to create the belief that free tickets were attainable *if* consumers concentrated their efforts on one airline. This shrewd promotion allowed the big carriers to escape the low-fare race to some extent and develop a loyal consumer base.

You'll often find continuity programs in fast-food chains such as Taco Bell and McDonald's, which offer game pieces that must be collected during several consecutive visits in order to win. These promotions work especially well in this venue because the typical fast-food consumer eats out several times each week. Continuity promotions provide an incentive for the consumer to return to the same restaurant during the promotional period, instead of eating around.

In fact, nearly any product or service that consumers typically use frequently, or actively seek out alternative products to, can benefit from continuity promotions. Radio stations run them all the time, using their top running shows to advertise promotions that will be announced later in the afternoon, when consumers are less likely to listen. Even banks have joined the continuity game, offering special services like "personal bankers" to encourage consumers to satisfy all their banking needs in one location, instead of shopping around at the many aggressive credit unions and mortgage companies that have cropped up. They know that if they make loan applications and IRA planning easy, they have a better chance of keeping you close to home.

PROPRIETARY PROMOTIONS

Another way to capture competitive advantage is to offer the consumer something highly desirable that she can get *only* through your brand. Coca-Cola rang up a huge success with a promotion that distributed the Official Olympic Ticket Application booklets for the 1996 Summer Games in Atlanta. These booklets were the *only* way consumers could order tickets to the Games, and the only way consumers could get one was by going to a Coca-Cola display in their local grocery store. Consumer research had indicated that 22 percent of American families wanted to attend the Olympics in Atlanta the following summer. Even in such faraway places as Portland and Seattle, interest was high.

On May 1, 1995, Coke began the distribution of the booklets, and to the amazement of everyone, consumers started lining up in front of some grocery stores as early as 4 A.M. to be the first to get their hands on the applications. At stores throughout the United States—from Phoenix to Boston to San Francisco and all points in between—thousands upon thousands of consumers descended upon stores. Most locations looked something like the post office at 11:45 P.M. on Tax Day, April 15! In only twenty-four hours, the promotion distributed more than 1.5 million booklets!

Only in the brand team's wildest dreams did they think that the promotion would be so successful. Grocery store share for

Coca-Cola increased +9 percent during the month (a *huge* jump in what is traditionally a very competitive marketplace where a 2 percent share gain is a cause for celebration). Giant Coke displays were in virtually every store, and for the most part, Pepsi was silenced for the month, despite the fact that they launched their traditional summer promotion at about the same time.

To Pepsi's credit, it rebounded the following year with a tremendous summer promotion that included each of the Three Ingredients of Greatness: a unique and desirable prize, a fair chance to win, and it was easy to play the game. The promotion was an under-the-cap twist and win game, offering a continuity promotion with the chance to win "Pepsi Stuff." The Grand Prize was an opportunity for celebrity sports superstars to come to your house "to play." The TV spot featured basketball star Shaquille O'Neal, NASCAR driver Jeff Gordon and NFL football star Deion Sanders all roughhousing and having fun with a twelve-year-old boy in his bedroom. Suddenly the boy's mother enters and scolds him, saying, "How many times must I tell you to not bring home celebrity athletes to play?" Shaq then says "OK, let's go to *my* house," and off they go! This was a fantastic promotion that allowed kids the chance to fantasize about winning and worked well for Pepsi all summer long in conjunction with the continuity element that allowed kids to collect points when purchasing Pepsi products that could be used to get Pepsi Stuff.

PROMOTIONS THAT ARE HALF-RIGHT

There's almost nothing I hate more than to see a pretty good promotion that could easily have been an extraordinary promotion if only the marketing team had observed the Three Ingredients of Greatness.

AT&T is a good example. Each year during the NBA Finals, AT&T executes a promotion that selects a single consumer to shoot baskets during halftime at one of the NBA Finals games for a chance to win $2 million dollars. The promotion is called "The AT&T $2 Million Dollar Shootout." Registration is simple: the consumer just calls a number shown on the TV screen during commercials.

AT&T successfully addresses two of the Three Ingredients of Greatness (unique and desirable prize, easy to enter), but fails to make you believe you have a chance to win and that *you* will be selected. They've got it two-thirds right, and it's a good promotion. But it's not *great*.

How could they improve the promotion and make it *great?* Several ideas come to mind. What if AT&T borrowed some of the techniques perfected by Publishers Clearing House (remember, it's OK to steal ideas!) and created a mailing that would go out to each person who registered by phone that includes:

- a set of official rules for the shootout
- an itinerary of the NBA Finals (potential dates)
- a notification to the contestant that if selected he or she will receive a videotape of the event from AT&T. No need to worry about setting up their VCR.
- 3-point shooting tips from the NBA All-Star Game's 3-point champion
- an AT&T calling card with a picture of an NBA star. Every time the consumer uses the card, he will be registered again for another chance to win.

Any contestant who uses his calling card five or more times will receive a second mailing that includes materials that make him or her feel even closer to the jackpot, including:

- a registration form for their preferred flight arrangements/preferred airline/preferred hotel to stay in at the Finals
- publicity release forms and advertising release forms
- a request for the name of the contestant's bank
- a request for the preferred method of delivering the money that's won (direct deposit, certified check, etc.)
- a reminder that every long-distance call on AT&T improves the odds of winning

And finally, instead of the current method of selecting and notifying the winning contestant—in which AT&T holds a drawing and then calls the winner on the phone to notify him or her, and the public has no clue who won until the person walks out onto the court to shoot at the NBA Finals Game—AT&T should make the selection itself a highly anticipated and talked about event. How? Hold the drawing to select the winner, but keep the person's identity secret for a week. Through a series of TV spots airing nightly during the NBA Playoffs on TNT and NBC, slowly reveal the chosen contestant.

Start by showing a United States map, highlighting the region of the United States the winner lives in. The next night, highlight *three states,* stating that the winner lives in one of these states. The next night, highlight the contestant's *state.* Then highlight *ten cities* in the state. Then *three cities.* Then *the city,* and finally reveal the winner with a celebration event in that city, which airs during the Playoff Game Half-Time show that has all of the registrants from that city in attendance as honored guests. Over a one-week period (seven days), the promotion would send consumers into a tizzy, thinking they had won—or that they may know the person who has won if it's not their state/city!

That's how AT&T could make it a great promotion instead of one that's merely good. By the way, if anyone from AT&T reads this and wants to implement the ideas, remember the book is copyrighted! I'm easy to work with though. Just send a check and we can talk!

THE GOLD STANDARD

THE OCTOPUS PLANNING MATRIX

Let's assume you've done absolutely everything right. You've focused on your strategy, you've researched the competitive environment, and you've come up with a brilliant idea that incorporates the Three Ingredients of Greatness.

Don't stop there. Once you've got your hands on a really dynamite promotion idea, your challenge is to give it the biggest bang possible. That means exploiting every conceivable means of extending its reach and effectiveness. The only way you can be sure you're maximizing the power of your promotion is to analyze its possibilities in the Octopus Planning Matrix.

The matrix is so named because when laid out on paper it resembles the form of an octopus. It begins with your core idea, the "head" of the matrix, and then creates extensions, or "legs," that can support the core idea in a variety of channels and extend its reach among both retailers and consumers.

The best way to illustrate the idea is to develop a promotion using the Octopus Planning Matrix. Let's imagine for a moment that we are developing a *hypothetical* promotion concept for M&M's Chocolate Candies. We first need to know what the brand positioning strategy is, so let's *make one up:*

> For consumers ages five through twenty-four, M&M's Chocolate Candies are sweet and delicious treats that colorfully brighten your day!
>
> That's because M&M's multicolored candy-coated milk chocolates (both in plain and peanut variety) are fun to eat and provide a playful pick-me-up!

The consumer benefit the brand wants to communicate is that M&M's "colorfully brighten your day." This is the core strategy that all brand promotions must support. The qualities supporting the "colorful brightening" benefit are fun and playfulness.

The next challenge is to dream up a promotion concept that meets the criteria in the Three Ingredients of Greatness: the promotion must be unique, unlike anything else around; it must make consumers believe that they have a good shot at winning; and it must be easy to enter. Of course, it also must stimulate sales, so let's assume that we need to execute the basic promotion via the packages of M&M's candies, and that we're planning our promotion for the key Easter holiday period, when retailers are most likely to display and feature candy products.

In real life, the brand team would probably go off to brainstorm and hire several promotion agencies to try to develop an idea for them, playing the odds that with enough people working on it, somebody will come up with a usable idea. But we'll jump ahead and assume that we've got a plan that everybody likes.

The promotion will be called, "M&M's Great Color Caper." The premise of the promotion is that a renegade bunny, a mischievous cousin of the Easter Bunny, broke into the M&M plant and mixed five wild new colors of M&M's under the cover of darkness, then dumped over 100 million of these colorful counterfeits into the packaging processors. M&M's is collecting all the evidence to bring that bad bunny who perpetrated this preposterous predicament to justice. The bunny has left behind incriminating evidence: paw prints on the wrappers. M&M's is posting a reward of $1 million dollars for any consumer who collects paw prints in each of the five bogus colors and sends them in to the M&M's Candy Detectives.

First of all, notice that the Three Ingredients of Greatness are all addressed: the promotion is fun and unique, something that *only M&M's* could do; it allows *all* consumers to think that they have a good shot at winning (since every wrapper contains paw prints); and it's easy to play the game. Furthermore, every consumer receives wild new colors mixed in her candies, which reinforces the fun and playful tone of the brand, and the renegade bunny character can become a central display figure at retail.

With the renegade bunny as the core promotional idea, we are now ready to begin extending the promotion through the Octopus Planning Matrix:

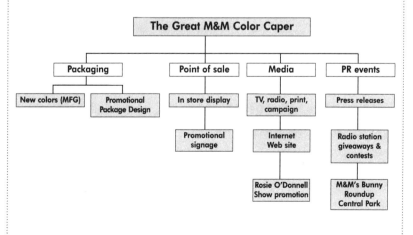

For each box within the planning matrix, you must develop a specific plan of execution to cover all your bases. For example, under packaging, you have two things to worry about: developing new art for the packages that communicates the promotion (and the colored paw prints inside), and working with manufacturing to develop and mix the wild-colored M&M's into the promotional packages. Under PR, you'd develop press events and promotions for radio stations and create a major event to rally attention to the promotion—like maybe sending the renegade bunny out for store appearances or "fugitive sightings" (with rewards for the consumers who spot him). Maybe you do a deal with the U.S. Postal Service to have fugitive bunny posters hung near the infamous FBI Most Wanted Lists inside each branch!

Notice how everything in this plan supports the strategic positioning statement for the brand. The wild new colors highlight the benefit, "colorfully brightens your day." The concept is fun and can be executed with energy and creativity at retail. This is how you create great consumer promotions!

Secrets of the Game

Top companies develop consumer promotion plans that extend far from just the retail store environment. They use the promotion as a means to create radio station tie-ins, stage PR events, rally employees, and develop unique opportunities with the retail trade.

USING PROMOTION AGENCIES TO DO YOUR THINKING

Many big companies off-load their promotion ideation to promotion agencies. This is a terrible mistake. Most agencies simply develop an array of promotion concepts, then they pack them up and shop them around to dozens upon dozens of companies. Never buy a ready-made off-the-shelf promotion from these carpetbaggers. It will violate the first of the Three Ingredients of Greatness—to have a unique and captivating idea. Princess Diana never shopped off the rack, and neither should you. Your competitors could show up at retail with the same idea. Don't let your promotion agency do your thinking for you.

Not that promotion agencies don't have value. They do, but the best way to use them is to involve them in the brainstorming process, and once you get the great idea, let them help you execute it. That's when agencies are the most valuable, in execution.

TAKE IT TO THE PROMISED LAND

If I could communicate only one idea about consumer promotions it would be: *Avoid the sea of sameness.* Your goal should be to explore uncharted territory, to create something unique and special, something that *only* your brand can do, that breaks through the clutter and captures consumer attention.

If you want a promotion idea that will give you just a 1 or 2 percent lift, offer a price discount and save the time and energy of everyone in your organization. *Life is too short to work on 1 percent or 2 percent ideas.* Consumer promotions can be +10 percent solutions if you get out of the box and do something great! Go ahead and think like Don Quixote—dream the impossible dream. You'll be surprised where it takes you.

CHAPTER SUMMARY:

- Often, consumer promotions aren't given the time and attention they deserve. If done right, they can serve as a catapult for your business.
- Consumer promotions must be grounded in strategy. They must support the brand positioning strategy in some way.
- Lazy marketers often commit one of the Four Plagues of Consumer Promotion:
  - *Been There, Done That*—Repeat promotions over and over again.
  - *Sleeping Sickness*—Tiresome and overused tactics.
  - *Trinkets & Trashitis*—Over-valued premiums.

- *Oddsitis*—Offering high odds of winning and lousy prizes.
- All successful consumer promotions have the Three Ingredients of Greatness:
  - They have a unique premise, different from everything else that others have done, with a highly desirable prize.
  - They make you believe you have a good chance (or fair chance) of winning.
  - They are simple to enter.
- Promotions are a great way to craft a personality for your brand (i.e., Oscar Mayer).
- Sometimes a great way to get a personality is to borrow one from some other entity that you can link to.
- Continuity promotions work well in frequent-purchase product categories.
- Proprietary promotions that have huge consumer demand are the ultimate objective.
- The Octopus Planning Matrix is a terrific tool to use to help plan an integrated promotion plan.
- Don't buy promotions "off the rack" from promotion agencies. Use them to help you execute, not do your thinking for you.

The Secrets to Effective Sports Sponsorships

ATTACHING YOUR NAME TO BIG-
TIME SPORTS IS EXPENSIVE
STUFF—HERE'S HOW TO MAKE IT
PAY OFF

W HEN I WORKED FOR PROCTER & GAMBLE, I was asked to evaluate the Hawaiian Punch brand's annual sponsorship of an NHRA Funny Car. The brand was pouring $1.5 million into the race team each year in order to maintain the sponsorship and wanted to be sure it was worth the money. I had only two questions to answer: (1) Does the sponsorship effectively target and motivate Hawaiian Punch consumers, increasing their brand preference and consumption of Hawaiian Punch; and (2) is the brand sales/marketing team effectively leveraging the sponsorship with the trade and consumers to create advertising and promotions that sell incremental cases of product to justify the annual price tag?

Instinctively I questioned whether drag racing was a good fit for a kids' beverage brand whose target audience was moms with kids ages two to twelve. But this was supposed to be a quantitative assessment, not a gut reaction, so I met with the manager in charge of the sponsorship to hear his rationale. To my surprise, I found him enthusiastic to the point of near ecstasy about the results. He raved about trade hospitality tents at each racetrack and the top-level grocery managers who annually attended the events. He pulled out studies of fans at the racetracks and their awareness of Hawaiian Punch as a car sponsor. He produced dozens of photo albums to show Hawaiian Punch signage at the different racing venues and in impressive retail displays. He proudly carpeted his desk with photos of the Hawaiian Punch Funny Car parked outside grocery stores surrounded by consumers peering into the engine and admiring the paint job.

Going into the interview I had been skeptical about a sponsorship that didn't seem to make a lot of sense; how on earth could drag racing sell more Hawaiian Punch to moms? But as I sat across the table from the manager crowing about the promotion, I wondered if perhaps I had been prejudicing my analysis by the fact that I'm personally not a drag racing fan.

I was hopeful and upbeat following the meeting, and ready to see the Funny Car promotion in action. I booked flights to a few of the cities on the NHRA racing tour, creased the brim of my Hawaiian Punch Funny Car hat, and prepared to catch racing fever. But a round of store checks in the very first market quickly cooled my expectations. I was disappointed by the lack of promotional activity outside of the track facility. One or two grocery stores were set up with big Hawaiian Punch product displays—a great photo-op for the local sales rep—but these were a scant minority of our retail customers. The remaining soft drink retailers I visited gave no indication that an NHRA event was in town or that Hawaiian Punch had anything special going on at all. I began to grow suspicious of the incredible results being circulated by the sponsoring brand manager. Clearly, more investigation was required.

I went back to the office and studied case sales by month in each of the markets where the race circuit had traveled over the preceding two years. Consistently, Hawaiian Punch shipments were 20 percent to 50 percent higher in each market when the tour came through town. That was great news—and possible evidence that the promotion was working! Unfortunately, the sales figures in the month *after* the race told a different story. Without fail, shipments plummeted to nearly nothing, regardless of the market. Hmm. I looked at the salesmen's market reports. The reps would claim huge successes attributed to the NHRA event one month, then lament competitive activity, union strikes, or even rainy weather and frog infestations as factors in killing sales the next month.

Frog infestations? Something was beginning to smell fishy. I didn't have to be Sherlock Holmes to deduce that the sales reps were sending huge shipments to the retailer stockrooms during the month of the race to make the sponsorship look good on paper. After the event, the retailers were left with a surplus of Hawaiian Punch to sell off; they wouldn't need any more product for four to six weeks. That was the real reason shipments died in the postrace month.

As I continued the analysis, the hard facts all corroborated that the sponsorship didn't sell more than a few extra cases of Hawaiian Punch each year, and that most of the $1.5 million sponsorship was wasted. As I had initially suspected, the drag racing tie-in didn't convince moms to buy more Hawaiian Punch. Why, then, was the brand manager so personally invested in creating the illusion that it did? Because he was an NHRA racing nut, and it was through his personal interest in drag racing that the sponsorship originally came to be. He was using the brand's money to finance his personal sports fantasy and live out his dream of being a big-time race team owner.

WELCOME TO FANTASY ISLAND

Unfortunately, the motivation behind Hawaiian Punch's involvement with the NHRA sponsorship is not all that unusual. In fact, fulfilling personal agendas is perhaps the most common reason sports sponsorships are funded. Sports properties understand the lure of the childhood dream and their sponsorship pitch often sounds like something from *Fantasy Island*: "Here we can make all of your dreams and fantasies come true." Major sports properties actively market personal dream fulfillment for their sponsoring check-writers to entice them to shell out millions upon millions of dollars for sponsorships—and the beneficiary individuals at the sponsors gladly pay it.

For example, the NASCAR sponsoring pitch doesn't stop at consumer impressions and audience demographics. As a sponsor you get special perks, like attending race car driving school and perhaps taking a few practice laps around the track before a big race. NBA teams sweeten their deal by offering major sponsors the chance for photos with the star players on the court; private coach's luncheons; and VIP treatment at the games, complete with white-tablecloth dinners at a private dining room inside the stadium. NFL teams ply sponsors with sideline passes, luxury boxes, the ability to attend "closed" practices, and premium parking. They even take their top sponsors to the Pro Bowl in Honolulu each January. The list of sponsor privileges associated with any sports property is long and appealing.

Becoming a major sponsor of a sports property using corporate money is a terrific way for any Saturday's Warrior wanna-be to become an instant high-roller, and the sports properties are adept at making anyone with access to large corporate checkbooks feel like he is a bigwig franchise owner.

TO SPONSOR OR NOT TO SPONSOR; THAT IS THE QUESTION

A legendary inside joke that circulates within Coca-Cola is a statement attributed to a senior vice president who was asked how Coke determined *what* and *what not* to sponsor. He stated: "We have a very simple philosophy to follow. If it moves, sponsor it. If it doesn't move, paint it red and slap a Coca-Cola logo on it."

A few years ago, that was a very close description of Coke's sports strategy. Today, even aggressive event sponsors like Coke and Budweiser have taken a step back and developed new thinking about how to best use sports sponsorships to effectively drive sales and enhance consumer brand preference.

Hundreds of corporations shell out millions of dollars each year to attach themselves to sports properties. More often than not, they end up wasting their money. Why? Often it is because they have purchased the sports sponsorship for the wrong reasons.

Let's examine some of the popular fallacies offered as rationale to buy into sponsorships.

Fallacy #1: *There is high attendance at the games, so advertising at the stadium is reaching a lot of consumers.*

If in-stadium advertising is the primary rationale for purchasing a sponsorship package, don't do it. The fans inside a stadium are merely a pimple on an elephant's rear end compared to the vast number of consumers in any given market that you must motivate to move the sales needle. Even if a team claims attendance of a million fans over the course of a season, the vast majority of them are the same people (season ticket holders) coming back again and again.

One popular pro franchise calculated that its 15,000 season ticket holders attended about 80 percent of the home games each season, so despite a total attendance figure of almost a million fans for the year, only around 250,000 different fannies actually churned the turnstiles. Typically, if you start with the season attendance figures for any sports property and divide by three, you'll end up with the approximate number of individuals who attend the games. This is the figure you should use when determining the advertising effectiveness on a cost-per-thousand basis. When you run the numbers, you'll quickly realize that in-stadium advertising is not cost competitive with virtually any form of standard media.

A second reason not to advertise in stadiums is the inability to communicate your brand message in that venue. Usually your only signage option is a static billboard big enough for your corporate name. Boring. Consumers don't notice and they don't care to see your corporate logo. This is a completely ineffective form of advertising—in fact, one of the Six Deadly Sins!

Fallacy #2: *I'm supporting the hometown team, and consumers like companies that offer support within the community.*

Quick, somebody grab me a Kleenex, I think I'm getting a little choked up. Pleeeze! This sappy reasoning applies only if you live in a small college town like Logan, Utah, and spend your money buying a sponsorship of the Utah State Aggies or supporting the high school gymnasium scoreboard fund. If you are entering a partnership with a big-time sports property, consumers know you're doing so for commercial reasons, not as a community rally towel. Besides, many of the teams don't have a whole lot of community spirit themselves, judging from how often they and their players move around.

Fallacy #3: *My company is a winner, and if we associate with winning sports properties through sponsorship packages, consumers will make the connection!*

Sorry, but no consumer I've ever met makes that kind of correlation. Have you ever heard anyone say, "Gosh, the so-and-so's are world champions, and that 'Bank of Bigness' is their top sponsor, so I bet they're the best bank in the world!" The only people who believe that are the managers inside the bank who popped for the sponsorship—and who are probably admiring the signage from prime sponsor seats!

Fallacy #4: *Athletes work hard to achieve greatness. My company works hard to please our customers. My company and this sports property is a sponsorship match made in heaven!*

Sorry, but Avis has already got the line "We Try Harder" trademarked. The hard work connection is not proprietary. Everybody works hard, so unless your core brand positioning strategy is one in which effort and hard work are consumer benefits, or is used as rationale in your "reason why," this line doesn't work.

Fallacy #5: *I've looked at my consumers' lifestyle data, and the consumers of my product have an interest in playing and watching this sport. I'm just going where my consumers are! Whatever they are interested in, our brand is interested in supporting.*

Lifestyle correlation analysis (this correlates activities consumers of your brand tend to migrate toward and helps identify sports where a large percentage of your consumers show interest) can be a great starting point for looking at potential sport sponsorships but should not be used as the final decision maker. Just about every lifestyle report I've ever seen shows consumers are interested in NFL football, NCAA football and basketball, and the NBA—for products as different as toilet paper and perfume. This is a reflection of the sports interests of American society in general, not a unique insight into the minds of purchasers of Hunt's canned tomato paste.

You don't need lifestyle data to know that products with a primary purchaser of women ages eighteen through fifty-four will show high correlations to figure skating, gymnastics, NFL football, college football, and the NBA and WNBA. Products with a target audience of men ages eighteen to fifty-four will skew to the NFL, NBA, college football and basketball, NHL hockey, Major League Baseball, boxing, and the PGA. But before you jump into an affiliation, think long and hard about how the sponsorship might support your brand positioning.

I've seen junior marketers work themselves up until they are frothing at the mouth in excitement over correlations in lifestyle data. Remember, numbers and data tell only part of the story.

RELEVANCE AND BRAND LINKAGE

There are very good reasons to buy into sports sponsorships, but to make the decision rationally you must separate yourself from the romance of the sport and consider the property as a unique *media* and *promotional vehicle*. Sorry for bursting your bubble, but that's all a sports property is. It's just another media and promotion outlet with a few extra perks built in.

Secrets of the Game

When considering whether to buy into a sports sponsorship, ask these three key questions:

1) Are a large percentage of my consumers interested in this sport property and can I reach them through it?

2) Is there a *relevant and rational strategic link* between this property and my brand positioning strategy? There must be some way the sponsorship can support or bring to life one or more of the consumer benefits enumerated in the brand positioning in a unique and captivating way. Note: You should figure this out and lock down on the strategic and creative idea before you buy the sponsorship!

3) Will a sponsorship package with this property provide an effective and cost-competitive media/promotional vehicle?

Failure to create a relevant and meaningful link between the brand positioning strategy and the sports property is where most brands stumble coming out of the gate. A sponsorship will work effectively only if you have a clear and convincing connection.

Let me demonstrate. Pretend for a moment that you are the brand manager for John Deere lawnmowers. Let's assume that brand positioning strategy is as follows:

> For men ages twenty-five to fifty-four, mowing with a John Deere will make you and your lawn the envy of everyone in the neighborhood.
>
> That's because John Deere mowers use a patented microblade cutting system. Each blade of grass receives not one but three clean and even razor-sharp cuts. This patented system ensures mowing perfection, making neighbors green with jealousy.

All marketing plans, including sports sponsorships, must support this brand positioning strategy. So let's concentrate on sports played outdoors on grass like baseball, football, and soccer as potential tie-in partners.

Since virtually all lawnmowers are bought during the spring and summer months, we'll assume you are considering sponsoring Major League Baseball. Your potential strategy for a baseball tie-in is:

> For male baseball fans, Major League Baseball teams exclusively use John Deere lawnmowers because they know that when fifty thousand of their fans are coming to cheer, they can trust their John Deere to make the ballpark lawn look its very best.
>
> That's because John Deere mowers use a patented microblade cutting system. Each blade of grass receives not one but three clean and even razor sharp cuts. This patented system ensures mowing perfection, making ballplayers proud to step out onto the field of play.

The baseball strategy supports the core brand strategy, and does it with a meaningful and relevant link to baseball—not with the game, but with the lawn the game is played on! This strategy strikes the consumer cord, because the grass at ballparks is always mowed with beautiful straight lines that make guys sitting in the stands wish their lawns could look that good. It is a solid strategic platform from which to build a terrific sponsorship plan.

Keep your John Deere brand manager hat on for a moment longer. You just received a pitch from the committee from the Fiesta Bowl to become that New Year's Day college football game title sponsor. Just think, the game could be called "The John Deere Fiesta Bowl." Lots of TV coverage. What do you think? Should you go for it? Think about it before reading on and see if you can figure out a few reasons either pro or con.

Hopefully, you can see that the right answer is . . . Don't even consider it. First, you are the brand manager for John Deere lawnmowers, not the John Deere Company, so your job is to promote your lawnmowers and not the company name. Second, while the game is played in Phoenix on a grass field, it falls on January 1st, not close to the buying season for lawnmowers or most John Deere products (spring/summer). While I'm sure that some people might get John Deere products as Christmas gifts, my guess is that 90 percent or more of John Deere sales occur in spring/summer. If you want to win The Marketing Game, you must concentrate your marketing efforts when consumers are out buying product, not during the off-season. Just think, how successful are Christmas ornament sales in July?

IT COSTS A LOT MORE THAN YOU THINK!

After the creation of a relevant and meaningful strategic platform, the second critical task is the development of a marketing plan; how you plan to utilize the sponsorship to affect consumers and generate sales.

The marketing plan objectives should:

1. increase consumer brand preference; and
2. outline how the brand sales/marketing team will effectively leverage the sponsorship with the trade and consumers to create advertising and promotions *that sell incremental product units to "pay out" the sponsorship price tag.*

Many companies assume the money they shell out for sponsorship rights makes up the bulk of their promotional spending. They're wrong.

Secrets of the Game

For every dollar you spend acquiring sponsorship rights, plan to spend another $8 to $10 on advertising, trade, and consumer promotions to generate enough "bang" to effectively move the sales needle and influence consumers.

This secret is the key to avoiding wasted sponsorship spending. Most companies don't budget much else beyond the sponsorship fees, so they can't effectively take advantage of the rights they've purchased. They nickel and dime the promotions on the back end, where the real sales opportunity lies.

TAKIN' IT TO THE STREETS

To make sports sponsorship worth its price tag, you have to move it out of the narrow reach of the sports venue and into the big, wide-open consumer marketplace. Unless your product is sold inside the arena, spending more than about thirty seconds thinking about what happens within those walls is spending too much time. What happens at the venue is pretty much inconsequential to the big picture—it's just advertising, and limited advertising at that. What you should spend your time thinking about is how to use the sponsorship to create better packaging, bigger in-store displays, and more powerful consumer and trade promotions. That's where you make your money!

> ### Secrets of the Game
> Develop your marketing plan *before* you buy any sponsorship, to ensure that you will have the contractual rights to execute a plan that builds your business.

Once you have signed your sponsorship deal, the sports property has you cornered. They have your money and they are moving on to find other checkbooks. If you don't lock down the rights you'll need to execute your big ideas *before* you ink the agreement, you'll likely never get the authorization to do anything new and different.

I was stuck in just that predicament with USA Basketball when I worked for Coca-Cola. Sprite had purchased a sponsorship of USA Basketball for the 1996 Olympics that was very restrictive in sponsor rights. For the USA Men's Dream Team '96, I wanted to create a promotion that would allow Sprite consumers the chance to get up close with the team—to "Hang With

232 / THE MARKETING GAME

The Dream Team." My wild idea was to run consumer promotions in several countries where winners would come to the United States and be honorary assistant coaches of the team—attending a private Dream Team practice, getting pictures and autographs with the players, and then sitting near the team bench at a game.

As we pitched the promotion to the NBA and USA Basketball, they of course hated the idea and said "No way." We had already signed our sponsorship deal, so they had no incentive to say yes. To them, it looked like a lot of extra work for money they already had in the bank.

I really wanted to run the promotion, so I circumvented USA Basketball and the NBA and signed Lenny Wilkens (the head coach of the Dream Team) to a personal services contract *prior* to his being named the Dream Team coach. My personal services contract with him gave me the rights to execute the promotion through him in the event he was named head coach. Since my contract was with Coach Wilkens directly and was signed before he was named head coach, USA Basketball could do nothing to stop me, as his contract with USA Basketball held a clause stating that all of his personal endorsement contracts were grandfathered in to his USA Basketball deal. I changed the name of the promotion to "Hang With The Coach," but other than that, the promotion was executed as I had envisioned. It was an incredible international success, involving consumers from Mexico, Australia, Germany, and Japan. Sprite volume grew by double digits during the promotional period.

Secrets of the Game

Don't simply accept a ready-made sponsorship package; execute *your* ideas that will drive sales for *your* brand. You have to tell the sports property what *you want to do!*

THE GOLD STANDARD

BUILDING A COMPREHENSIVE MARKETING PLAN

To illustrate how a comprehensive sports property marketing plan can work to achieve outstanding results, let me share with you the plan executed by Coca-Cola in support of the 1996 Summer Olympic Games. This far-reaching marketing effort was the largest campaign ever undertaken by any company in world history, with global marketing spending of around $450 million. The sponsorship cost was $40 million, so Coca-Cola spent roughly $11.00 in marketing costs for every $1.00 paid in sponsorship fees.

It seems incomprehensible that a marketing effort this expensive could ever generate enough incremental sales volume to justify the spending, but it did. Results of the campaign were outstanding. In the eight-month window in which Olympic promotions were executed, global Coca-Cola volume rose +9 percent, overall corporate profits rose +22 percent, and Coke's stock price increased +36 percent. How did they do it?

First, Coke built a solid strategic platform that was consumer relevant. The campaign was entitled "For the Fans," suggesting that drinking Coca-Cola refreshed the fans of the Olympic Games and renewed their Olympic Spirit. The relevant and meaningful connection between Coca-Cola and the Olympics was between the product and the fans: "Cheering Is Thirsty Work." Drinking ice-cold, refreshing Coca-Cola would help keep the fans in good voice to cheer for their national athletes and local heroes.

This strategy positioned the brand as it should; in the stands and in homes, refreshing everyday consumers as they enjoyed watching the Olympics. It wasn't about the athletes. The advertising and promotional materials all featured fans of the Games in realistic situations, cheering for the athletes and enjoying the events surrounding the Olympic Games.

Since the strategy was fan focused, all pieces of the marketing plan needed to support the concept that Coca-Cola would refresh/enhance/add enjoyment to the Olympic experience for everyday consumers throughout the world. We hoped that when the Olympic Games were over and the flame extinguished, consumers would turn off their TVs, lean back in their Barca Lounger chairs, and say, "I really enjoyed these Olympic Games, and Coca-Cola was a big part of that." We didn't expect them to say it out loud, naturally, but that's the impression we wanted to leave.

Starting with the "For the Fans" positioning, we began to search for powerful, innovative ways of extending the positioning into consumer venues, both at the Games and in their homes.

Secrets of the Game

The marketing plan must include "big" ideas that can be used anywhere, but must also allow for the development of local and customer-specific customized programs.

Some of the big ideas from the corporate Olympic marketing group included:

- Distribution of 35 million official Olympic Ticket Application booklets in the United States via Coca-Cola product displays. This gave all fans in the United States an equal chance to order Olympic tickets and attend the Games. It was supported with a consumer promotion on Coca-Cola twelve-pack cartons, offering families the chance to win free trips to the Olympic Games.
- "Who Would You Choose To Carry The Olympic Flame?" a global consumer sweepstakes to nominate fans for selection as one of ten thousand Official Olympic Torchbearers in the 1996 Olympic Torch Relay.
- The 1996 Olympic Torch Relay, presented by Coca-Cola. This eighty-four-day journey across the United States provided the ability for local Coca-Cola bottlers to execute grassroots marketing

in over fifteen hundred cities, towns, and villages along the relay route. It allowed twenty-five hundred Coca-Cola consumers the opportunity to carry the Olympic flame as it wound its way toward Olympic Stadium. Torch Relay promotions were executed in sixty-five foreign countries in addition to the United States.

- The creation of Coca-Cola Olympic City, a $29 million high-tech Olympic theme park in downtown Atlanta. This attraction let consumers feel what it was like to be an Olympic champion, allowing them to compete "virtually" against Olympic stars such as Jackie Joyner-Kersee, Grant Hill, and others. It gave fans an understanding of just what amazing feats of athleticism it takes to set Olympic records, from Carl Lewis's long-jump record to the Olympic records in a variety of sports. Over 650,000 consumers attended Olympic City in its 100 days of operation.

- Coca-Cola Radio, which brought seventy-five of the world's most listened to radio stations to Coca-Cola Olympic City to broadcast live during the Games. Top disc jockeys from around the globe gave their listeners back home an up-close-and-personal feel of what it was like to be a fan attending the Olympics, bringing home the fun from Coca-Cola Olympic City.

- Coca-Cola Olympic Champions, a series of over five hundred personal appearances by current and former Olympic athletes, including such notables as Nadia Comaneci, Bart Conner, Pablo Morales, Sergei Bubka, and dozens more, allowing Olympic fans worldwide the opportunity to meet and talk with these notable champions up close and personal.

The second key part of the plan was to translate these big ideas down to the local level. Our account managers and sales teams throughout the world created regionalized, and sometimes retailer-customized, promotional extensions that celebrated the personalities and local pride of each market.

While Coca-Cola Olympic marketing campaigns were rendered in over 132 countries, no two markets executed the same plan. Each country developed a unique blueprint customized to best address the specific interests and needs of its own Olympic fans.

Coke marketing managers in each of the different countries could choose to tap into the big ideas or they could pass on them—the choice was theirs. Each country took into account the interests and aptitudes of their fans to ensure that the plan would be captivating and consumers would enjoy the Coca-Cola promotions. In Brazil, the plan focused on soccer and volleyball; in Thailand, the effort was exclusively built around the sport of boxing; in Australia, the focus was on swimming and basketball.

Despite the hundreds of different promotional executions throughout the world, the "For the Fans" strategy united all countries behind one Coca-Cola theme and one Coca-Cola creative look. The flexible structure allowed each country to execute promotions in whatever way it saw fit for its fans. It worked.

Secrets of the Game

Think globally. Act locally. Design your sponsorship program to address both a broad market and regionalized interests to extract the most value from your sponsorship rights!

SPORTS BLOOPERS AND SPONSORSHIP BLUNDERS

No writing on sport sponsorship would be complete without an homage to the truly terrible and pathetic entries in the sports sponsorship hall of shame.

In the category of horrible sports signage, the loser is AT&T, which designed a scorer's table sign for NBA teams that was a caricature drawing of the legs of those seated along courtside. Silly, yes. Effective, no. Seeing cartoon legs doesn't make me think of calling long distance.

As for dynamite sports promotions, the Chicago White Sox baseball club wins the title for its infamous "Disco Demolition Night," in which the plan was to blow up a mountain of 1970s disco records between games of a doubleheader. An interesting idea, but it literally blew up in their face, littering the field with pieces of plastic shrapnel and forcing the cancellation of the second game.

The award for carpal-tunnel sports promotion goes to every sports franchise that runs those insidious "Dot Races" or mutant variations on their scoreboard every night.

The sniffing fumes award goes to all airlines that have purchased the naming rights to NBA arenas: United Center (Chicago); Continental Airlines Arena (New Jersey); US Air Arena (D.C.); America West Arena (Phoenix); and The Delta Center (Salt Lake City). Here's a question: How do you relevantly link a basketball arena with an airline? Answer: You can't! Flush! No wonder fares are so high, when the airlines think naming an arena after themselves is a good use of their marketing dollars!

The winner for most graffiti in a sports venue is a tie between all NHL hockey teams who litter advertising across the dasher boards surrounding the ice rinks, and World Cup, which does the same with its soccer fields. This pervasive signage clutters up the stadium and makes the sport look cheap. There is so much advertising that no fan can possibly be positively affected. It gives me a headache just looking at it.

And of course, our grand-prize winner! This brand spends $40 million dollars to become an Olympic sponsor and then, as far as I can tell, does very little to support the effort! They commit one of the Six Deadly Sins of Advertising by buying courtside signage at NBA arenas to show off their corporate logo! This big-spending loser is . . . John Hancock Insurance!

SPORTS AND THE LITTLE GUY

Sports properties can be a wonderfully fun and incredibly effective vehicle for helping to market your product to consumers in a unique and provocative way, providing you find the right link between your brand and the sports property when creating your promotions. While my commentary here is focused on major sports, virtually any sports property can be used effectively as a marketing tool if the proper strategic links are in place—from sponsoring a local Little League team to the high school or local college football team. In fact, in some towns in Indiana, you'd be a fool *not* to sponsor your local high school basketball team. The same goes for high school football in Texas.

Local sports are often a far more effective tool for reaching your consumer base than the larger sports leagues. It's all about relevance to *your* consumer. You need to find sports that your consumers are interested in, then develop a way for you to tap into that interest for the benefit of your product sales.

CHAPTER SUMMARY

- Sports properties are adept at making sponsors feel like quasi-owners of the franchise, plying them with a far-flung menu of innovative and exclusive perks.
- Many sport sponsorships are bought for the wrong reasons. There are five fallacies of sport sponsorship:
   #1: The high attendance at games makes venue advertising a great buy.
   #2: I'm supporting the home team, and consumers like companies that offer support within their community.
   #3: By associating my company with winning sports franchises, I'll convince consumers that we, too, are winners!
   #4: My company works hard. Athletes work hard. We share a commonality that will be a great foundation for sponsorship.
   #5: My research indicates that our consumers are interested in this sport. I'm just going where my consumers are.
- Sport sponsorship, like all consumer promotions, must relevantly link to the core brand positioning.
- Sport sponsorship should be looked at as just another media and promotional vehicle.
- Your sponsorship should drive enough incremental product sales to "pay out" the cost.

- Top marketers budget $8.00 to $10.00 for every $1.00 they spend on acquiring sponsorship rights for their associated consumer promotions.
- Develop your marketing plan for the sport property *before* you buy the sponsorship to ensure that you get the rights to execute what you want to do.
- In rural areas, local sports teams (high school and college) can be even more effective investments than major sports properties.

Concealed Tactics for Leveraging Alliances

MAKING PARTNERSHIPS WORK
FOR YOU

S TRATEGIC ALLIANCES ARE A KISSIN' COUSIN to sport sponsorships. Like sport sponsorships, alliances are formal partnerships between your product and highly visible properties such as charities or nonprofit organizations or entertainment properties such as blockbuster movie releases, concert tours, and television programs or special events. The right partnership can help your brand to capture a unique position in the consumer mindset and differentiate your product from competition, which explains their high popularity as marketing tools.

Alliances usually fall into one of two camps. *Cause-related marketing* involves campaigns created as fund-raisers for charities and nonprofit organizations such as Special Olympics, Save The Rainforests, Feed The Homeless, or Help Find A Cure For The

Disease du Jour. *Popularity marketing* borrows the imagery, personality, and notoriety of a hot entertainment property for your brand. Popularity properties are most often blockbuster movies; major concert tours like The Rolling Stones, Elton John, or Garth Brooks; and top-rated TV programs or special events such as The Miss America Pageant or The Academy Awards.

CAUSE-RELATED MARKETING

Charities and nonprofit organizations are the usual partners in cause-related alliances. Although alliances can, and should, have many different promotions and PR efforts attached (refer to the Octopus Planning Matrix in chapter 14), this type of alliance is usually executed at the store level as "Buy my product and we'll donate x cents to the cause for each purchase you make."

From the consumer's point of view, these promotions are a terrific deal. All she has to do is buy a product that was probably already on her shopping list (although she may need to switch to a different brand) and suddenly she is elevated from the status of a mere shopper to a social benefactor. She walks away from her purchase feeling good about her choice and about the quality brand that "cares."

Now put on the hat of a marketing manager. Why do *you* think brands hook up with charities and nonprofits? If your answer is to be good corporate citizens and to generate funds for needy organizations, you're about half-right. Yes, good citizenry is part of the reason why they do it, and they obviously benefit from positioning themselves as the Lone Ranger, fighting for the greater good of needy causes (unlike those other faceless greedy corporations). But good works, or even a good reputation, are almost never the primary motivator. Most brands adhere to the old notion that charity begins at home, and every tie-in, charitable or no, is measured for its ability to stimulate sales and increase profits. The brand manager bets on the consumers' attachment to the charity or cause to compel them to purchase the product.

The value of the donation to the nonprofit or charity is usually minuscule compared to the brand's profit on each extra product sale. If the tie-in can generate any extra sales at all, the company banks a handsome incremental profit *and* looks like the good guy by giving to charity—the classic win-win situation! For this reason, cause-related campaigns are that rare marketing tactic with low risk and high potential rewards.

Let's run the break-even numbers of a hypothetical brand to see how a typical donation arrangement works out financially. Assume that in a normal week, Brand X sells 100 units of product.

CONSUMER OFFER: BRAND X WILL DONATE $.10 FROM EVERY PRODUCT PURCHASE TO THE SAVE THE WHALES FOUNDATION.

Retailer cost price:	$3.49		
Brand cost-to-produce:	$2.19		
Brand profit per item:	$1.31		
BRAND BREAK-EVEN CALCULATOR:	UNIT SALES	PROFIT	DONATION
Normal week without offer:	100	$131.00	$0
Break-even with donation:	108	$130.68	$10.80

The break-even point for the brand is a mere 8 percent increase in product sales! For every incremental sale above 8 percent, the brand posts higher profit numbers than it would during a typical week. To put it in perspective, assume that the cause-related marketing campaign generates a modest 10 percent increase in sales for the week. After deducting for the donation, which would equal $11.50, the brand profits would still be $139.15—an increase of 6.2 percent over a normal week!

Even if consumers don't respond to the tie-in by purchasing extra product, the campaign is a low-risk proposition. The worst thing that can happen is nothing at all—sales remain flat—in which case, weekly profits would slip by a mere $10.00 (a profitability decrease of only 9 percent). Even in this worst-case scenario, the brand benefits by wearing the good citizen white hat, which at the end of the day is probably worth the $10.00 in lower profits.

Importantly, the brand knows that many retailers also want to enjoy the halo effect of associating with a compelling charity or cause. A good cause-related alliance may earn free or discounted displays, feature ads, or other in-store marketing support—the discounts of which can be more than the donation itself. You already know how much that type of activity is worth, both in saved costs and incremental sales (see chapter 13).

Procter & Gamble brands all participate in cause-related marketing each year through their corporate relationship with Publishers Clearing House. Twice each year you receive in your home a PCH mailer stuffed full of coupons from a wide variety of Procter & Gamble products: Tide detergent, Bounty paper towels, Sure deodorant, Folgers coffee, Hawaiian Punch fruit drink, Mr. Clean cleaner, and more. The mailing, sent out in late December to arrive in homes between Christmas Day and New Year's Day, pledges support to Special Olympics for every coupon redeemed. But you probably haven't noticed the fine print of the offer, where P&G protects its upside from the promotion by setting a "cap" for the total donation. Once the coupon redemption generates enough donations to reach the maximum contribution, all incremental sales line P&G's coffers, with no donation to the charity.

The Procter & Gamble sales force uses the fund-raising component for Special Olympics and the massive couponing effort to persuade the grocery trade to offer price breaks for in-store displays and feature ads. P&G supplies retailers with handsome promotional signage using Special Olympics logos and imagery. As a result, P&G virtually owns in-store activity at grocery stores for the first three weeks each January. The promotion is so powerfully entrenched in the retail promotional schedule that competitors generally throw up their hands and concede these weeks to Procter & Gamble, steering their marketing efforts to other times of the year. This "charitable" campaign is one of the most profitable in P&G's worldwide effort.

Aha! Just another example of a greedy corporation masquerading as the good guy, right? Not exactly. Charities also love these promotions because they actually do provide free money in the tens of thousands of dollars and free publicity for the cause. Most charities could not function without these corporate partners.

THE GOLD STANDARD

CAUSE-RELATED MARKETING AS A BRAND STRATEGY

Some brands, including Ben & Jerry's Ice Cream and Newman's Own, don't merely execute cause-related promotions; they have institutionalized cause-related marketing as part of their brand positioning strategy. Their commitment to charity conveys to the consumer that their brand is not a heartless and soulless megacorporate greed-and-profit machine, but rather a nurturing corporate citizen that cares about the less fortunate and is dedicated to earning money for good causes. Some of the hype is true. In the case of the Newman brands, 100 percent of net profits are donated to charity.

In the post–Gordon Gekko era (didn't you just love Martin Sheen in the movie *Wall Street*?), when the corporate mantra "Greed is Good" is no longer as conspicuously chanted, many companies have felt pressure both from outside groups and stockholders to give back to their communities and use a portion of their profits for the benefit of special charities or the underprivileged. Creating a brand positioning strategy with a cause-related marketing component is a great way to strategically differentiate your brand from competition and demonstrate to consumers that your company has a long-term commitment to helping others.

In the northeast United States, the Buffalo Bills football team's marketing department helped create a breakfast cereal called Flutie Flakes, named after star quarterback Doug Flutie. All profits from Flutie Flakes go to a special charity to fight autism, which one of Doug's children has. In only four months on store shelves, Flutie Flakes sold over 1 million boxes!

It surprises me that, given the overwhelming success of both the Ben & Jerry's and Newman's Own brands, others have not mimicked the strategy. Not only have most brands failed to institutionalize their cause-related efforts, the only other major company I can think of besides Procter & Gamble that has broadly and commercially executed a cause-related marketing component in its brand promotion plan is American Express. Their annual program "The Fight Against Hunger" donates $.01 for every $1.00 a consumer charges to his or her American Express card when they make a purchase during the holiday season. Because they run this promotion every year, the halo effect from the effort remains with the brand year-round.

Secrets of the Game

When executing a cause-related marketing campaign, commit the plan to the long term for annual execution. These are the rare promotions that bear repetition—in fact, they benefit from it! Consumers need to see the campaign executed again and again over time to make a solid connection between your brand and the charity or nonprofit. If you execute hit-and-run cause-related efforts, you miss the opportunity to elevate your brand's image and reap the long-term benefits of the charitable association.

THE GOLD STANDARD

THE NBA AND CAUSE-RELATED MARKETING

Charles Barkley may not accept the job of role model, but NBA commissioner David Stern realized the power of the sports-hero in reinventing the image of the league several years ago. In fact, he integrated cause-related marketing into the heart of the NBA identity.

Think back to the pre–Larry Bird and Magic Johnson NBA of the mid-1970s. The league was in peril. Most of its notoriety and publicity involved its players' brushes with the law. Rumors swirled of rampant drug abuse. Television stations rarely covered the games. The NBA was so poorly regarded as a sports property that CBS televised the NBA Finals games on tape delay, beginning at 11:30 P.M.

At about the same time that Bird and Magic entered the league, Stern took over for former commissioner Larry O'Brien. Stern used the "Showtime" excitement of Magic and the Lakers along with the good 'ol country-boy image of Bird and the hardworking Celtics as cornerstones upon which to build a new and improved NBA. Soon, games were earning live television coverage again. During each telecast, Stern ran a public service announcement showcasing a star

NBA player preaching about drugs, child abuse, reading, staying in school, and other key messages related to families and youth. Season after season, these low-key, intimate portraits of the players and their Good Samaritan efforts continually reinforce the many ways that the league and its players donate both their time and money to worthy causes.

Over several seasons, the image of NBA players changed from a bunch of oversized and overpaid thugs to a group of warm, concerned activists committed to helping in their communities (Dennis Rodman notwithstanding). The campaign continues to this day. Turn on any NBA game and you'll see these public service announcements. Popular spots currently feature Shaquille O'Neal reading "Shaq and the Beanstalk" in an elementary school library; Karl Malone condemning child abuse; and A. C. Green talking with a young boy about the difficulties of growing up and the importance of relying on friends, families, and teachers for help.

What makes the campaign work is that it's more than just the occasional stirring ad. The league has made a commitment, and asks for a commitment from its players, to actively participate in community-service programs. In addition to its far-flung charitable affiliations, the NBA developed its own proprietary "Stay In School" program, awarding children that live in the area surrounding the annual NBA All-Star Game the opportunity to attend a celebration event featuring top music entertainers and NBA stars during All-Star Weekend. The children earn the right to attend the "Stay In School" event only if they rack up perfect attendance during the school year. The results are amazing. Kids are so highly motivated by this promotion that 98 percent of kids in the area qualify, filling the arena with over twenty thousand screaming schoolchildren each year.

CREATING YOUR OWN CHARITY OR CAUSE

In an episode of the popular, now-defunct television series *Seinfeld,* the character George Costanza (actor Jason Alexander) received a Christmas card from his employer, stating that in lieu of a year-end bonus check, a cash donation had been made in George's name to a local homeless shelter. George was livid; he had been counting on the bonus check. Then he hit on a brilliant idea. He'd print up Christmas cards for all of his friends and coworkers, noting that this year in lieu of a gift, he had made a cash donation in their name to "The World Fund." Of course, there was no such thing as "The World Fund." The only donation George was making was to his own checkbook, and inevitably he was caught in his lie and humiliated.

The episode contained some nuggets of truth. At times, companies, like George, invent their own "causes" instead of tying-in with an existing charity or nonprofit organization. Usually these efforts are developed to fill a real void in the community, like the Ronald McDonald Children's Charities. This legitimate and worthy program was created to help families cope with the unique issues faced when their young children require extended hospital care. The company builds Ronald McDonald Houses close to hospitals for families to stay in, and offers assistance with paying the huge medical bills. In filling this important need, McDonald's also created a tremendously powerful and proprietary charity for the McDonald's Corporation.

But sometimes, companies create nonprofit organizations strictly for marketing purposes. The brand group at Procter & Gamble responsible for the introduction of Citrus Hill Plus Calcium Orange Juice founded and paid for a medical organization to promote the benefits of calcium-fortified orange juice for women. The official-looking endorsement logo was proudly featured on the side of every carton of Citrus Hill calcium-fortified juice.

Ringling Bros. and Barnum & Bailey Circus promotes the heartwarming fact that it supports the nonprofit Center For Elephant Conservation in Florida. In fact, the center is not an independent conservation organization but is wholly owned by Ringling Bros. While the facility does in fact breed elephants, and houses the largest herd of Asian elephants in captivity, the conservatory is not run for completely selfless reasons. It serves as a location to train elephants for the circus and to "retire" performing elephants that are too old to remain on the road.

Is there a rule of thumb that you can use in determining how to select a cause-related organization? Of course; it's one of the Secrets of the Game!

Secrets of the Game

To steal a line from the soft drink brand Sprite, when it comes to charities and nonprofits, *image is every-thing*. It doesn't really matter what cause you choose to support, it only matters how you visually support the connection. You must use powerfully motivating and compelling images.

Think of the commercials that show starving children in Third-World countries. Why are they effective in generating donations? The images of these destitute kids are disturbing to us in our comfortable middle-class homes and neighborhoods! Why is the Jerry Lewis Telethon able to generate millions of dollars each year? Because the program is laced with images of young children struggling with the crippling effects of muscular dystrophy. The telethon intertwines hope for a cure with the devastation caused by the disease, driving the viewer to do the only thing he can think of to help: pick up the phone and pledge a contribution.

IN-STORE ACTIVITY

With cause-related marketing efforts, it is often possible to get the retailer to participate not only with reduced prices for display space and feature activity, but with a visible in-store promotion as well. One highly successful program that Special Olympics offers to its sponsors is what they call an "icon" program. The retailer sells "Special Olympics Medals" at their cash register for a $1.00 donation to Special Olympics. The consumer then writes his or her name on the medal and hangs it on a "Wall of Fame" inside the retail establishment. This is a great promotion for retailers both big and small, from grocery stores to fruit stands to delis.

MOVIE MARKETING: HOORAY FOR HOLLYWOOD

Every day in Los Angeles, young men and women step off the bus from small town USA in search of Hollywood dreams. All their lives they've aspired to be movie stars. They've heard the success stories—how Sandra Bullock was working as a secretary before landing her starring role in *Speed*. They know that it takes only one break and they can start picking out a spot for their star on the Hollywood Walk of Fame.

Many brand managers share the dreams of these young actors. They believe that to separate their product from the competitive pack, they should hitch their wagon and go to Hollywood. They know it takes only one measly break to make their brand a star. One lucky placement, and they could be the next Reese's Pieces.

Product Placement: The Legend of Reese's Pieces

ET, The Extra-Terrestrial did more than simply break every existing theatrical record, it also reinvented the rules of product placement marketing. In case your memory is a little rusty, I'll remind you that one of the many charming quirks of Steven Spielberg's lovable alien was a newly acquired love of Reese's Pieces candies. His enthusiasm was contagious. As soon as the movie hit theaters, kids began clamoring for the candy-coated peanut butter morsels. Stores couldn't keep them in stock. Every last bag disappeared as soon as shipments arrived. The sudden interest even caught Reese's management by surprise, and they scrambled to adjust production schedules to make more candy. The movie exposure put the brand on the map. Before the alien started chomping away, Reese's Pieces was a guppy in the candy ocean. Overnight it became a whale. To this day, the Reese's brand enjoys halo effects with consumers from that promotional tie-in over a decade ago.

The Product Placement Casino

Unfortunately, it's not always that easy to make it in Hollywood. Just as 99 percent of young actors end up waiting tables in restaurants instead of acting, most product placements don't generate much publicity for the brand. Yet knowing that the deck is stacked against them doesn't stop many brands from continuing to shell out big bucks to put their products in Hollywood projects. Each brand manager believes that the next product placement they make will be another Reese's Pieces success story, ensuring their personal marketing legacy for time and eternity.

The truth of the matter is product placement in movies and TV shows is a crapshoot. You have to roll 7s twice to come up a winner. The first and most problematic gamble is the bet that the movie will be a success at the box office, or the TV show will be a hit in the ratings. Despite all the hype and star power, some shows just flat out stink. There isn't any way to predict a clunker. Just about anything Hollywood turns out looks good on paper and in the promotional trailers.

The second gamble relating to product placement is how much exposure your brand will actually receive in the final edit, and in what context. When the studio pitches a project, it describes how your product will be used and by what star. The studio pitchmen lead you to believe that the movie's most climatic moment involves the lead star dramatically clutching a bottle of Coca-Cola, gulping gratefully, and remarking, "Wow, Coke in a glass bottle. It always tastes better in glass."

But pitchmen don't make the films. It's always the director's discretion to shoot the scene any way he or she sees fit. Most of the time, what you've been pitched and sold isn't exactly what shows up in the film. And even if the scene runs as planned, more often than not the scene blows right by and doesn't affect consumers in any meaningful way.

When I was at Hawaiian Punch, I was offered a movie product placement in a Dan Ackroyd comedy. Originally, the studio pitch was for $10,000, but I negotiated it down to 50 free cases of Hawaiian Punch for the cast and crew. I got what I paid for. There was a comment made by Ackroyd of "How 'bout a nice Hawaiian Punch?" while he held the can of product, and that was it. The movie lasted only about three weeks in theaters and is now only seen occasionally on HBO. I was very glad I didn't pay to get the product placed, or I would have had some explaining to do to senior management.

Theatrical Movie Promotions

Given these high risks, in my opinion, creating a promotion concept around a movie product placement is too risky to try to leverage. However, many brands, often fast-food chains, have found avenues for creating promotions tied to a movie's theatrical release. McDonald's always runs a big promotion linked to Disney animated classics like *Hercules* and *Mulan*. They have also run promotions giving consumers the chance to win two free tickets to see hit movies such as *Armageddon* when they buy super-size French fries. Taco Bell loves movie tie-ins, linking to *Godzilla*, *Batman & Robin*, and others. Burger King and Shell Oil gas stations ran promotions with the release of the Fox Studio's animated classic *Anastasia*.

Candy companies like to tie in to theatrical releases. Nestle's likes to make special "limited-time only" candy bars featuring movie characters. For Disney's *Hercules*, they made Herculean-size chocolate bars. It worked quite well.

Movie tie-ins cost big bucks but are effective. The studios view the partnerships as free advertising for their film, so they demand millions of dollars of advertising commitments behind all promotional partnerships. Unfortunately, they are out of the range of marketing budgets for most marketers.

Video Marketing

If you want to win in Hollywood, the surest way is to wait for the *video release*. By the time a film comes to home video, you have all the information you need in hand to make an informed decision—box-office dollar totals, demographic information, sales projections, licensed products' success, and more. I know it's not as exciting as a big-screen premiere, but video tie-ins are far less risky and far more predictable than theatrical promotions—and they're a lot cheaper! You can be pretty sure you'll get what you pay for with a video promotion.

Look at the quality of promotional partners inside a typical video release for a Disney animated classic. *Pocahontas* had a $5.00 rebate with purchase of Nestle products; an additional $5.00 rebate from Disney with the additional purchase of two more Disney videos; a free lithograph offer from Mattel; and a special family vacation offer from Walt Disney World Resorts. These all added value to the cassette purchase for the consumer!

MAJOR CONCERT TOURS: LISTEN TO THE MUSIC PLAY

Most big name acts sell the sponsorship of their concert tours in exchange for a number of complimentary tickets to each performance, signage, and "mention" on ticket stubs and during the show. The sponsor is also usually allowed the rights to use the musicians and their music in advertising. Buying into a partnership with a major act is a great way to differentiate your brand and steal the personality of the performers and the emotions of their music for your benefit. The key to success with concert tours, like major sporting events, is being vigilant to concentrate your marketing efforts outside the arena, in national advertising and promotion.

VISA did an incredible job of leveraging the Elton John USA tour a few years ago. They promoted the sponsorship in credit card statements, in a broad-scale advertising campaign, and in print media. Budweiser sponsors The Rolling Stones every time they tour the United States. Bud has created numerous ads around the band, and even uses the trademark Rolling Stones "tongue" in campaigns not specifically linked to the group's tour. Budweiser tries to closely link the free-wheeling fun and energy of the band within its brand personality in a number of forms of consumer communications.

A benefit of allying with musicians is the ability to hone in and specifically target the demographic appeal of the act in order to craft an effective promotional plan. For example, if you are a brand manager for a product that has a youthful, cutting-edge brand personality, like Mountain Dew soft drink, you wouldn't want to hitch your wagon to the 1970s rock group Chicago. However, if you are managing Dockers jeans, a tie-in with Chicago might be right on target with baby boomers. Musicians usually appeal to very specific demographics, allowing you to zero in with your message and hit the target with your promotion.

The most notable and meaningful differentiation in allying with musicians is the ability to use their music in your advertising. Great music can make an emotional connection and create a bridge like no other art form. Think of the Johnson & Johnson baby commercials using Kenny Loggins songs—they almost make you cry. Or remember the Ray Charles association with Pepsi— "You've Got the Right Stuff, Baby—Uh huh!"

There are both good and bad side effects to sponsoring concert tours. The good is that they run for several months, allowing you to change your execution along the way, to get smarter and smarter about how you promote your brand tie-in to consumers. The bad is that they run for several months—one city at a time. Your marketing campaign becomes a series of local marketing efforts in lieu of one big national effort, increasing the manpower requirements and the cost in order to pull it off effectively.

Another major drawback to concert tours is that the consumer must buy a ticket to attend the show in order to see the majority of your marketing efforts. Even with acts that attract twenty thousand fans to a performance, it's a minuscule percentage of the population in a given city, especially in major metropolitan areas like Los Angeles or New York.

Secrets of the Game

If your brand is lacking a personality, borrow one from a musician and their music. If you hang around with the popular acts, people will think your brand is popular, too!

TOP-RATED TV PROGRAMS: DIALING IN WITH CONSUMERS

For my money, an alliance with a major TV program is the best way to go when looking for marketing partnerships. Good programs attract huge, consistent audiences, and you hit consumers in their living room, with no effort from them.

The major difficulty in crafting a TV program alliance is that you have to pay the producers of the show for tie-in rights as well as any actors you want to feature in your promotion. It can get expensive; Hollywood talent isn't cheap. But the expense is usually worth it, because you know the consumer is getting the message.

Diet Coke and Dr. Pepper have both successfully used TV alliances to promote their brands. Diet Coke and the NBC hit *Friends* combined for a watch-and-win in 1996 (a "watch-and-win" means you watch the show and it reveals how to win the sweepstakes). Dr. Pepper uses the Fox shows *Melrose Place* and *Beverly Hills 90210*. Doritos successfully created a Super Bowl half-time show on a competing network to lure viewers from the game that devastated half-time viewership. Consumers like TV promotions!

> ### Secrets of the Game
> To successfully leverage a TV alliance, create a watch-and-win game linked to game pieces found on your product packaging to drive sales!

Special-event TV programs such as The Miss America Pageant, Miss USA, or The Academy Awards are also great vehicles with which to create a partnership. Any cosmetic or personal hygiene product targeted at women would be crazy not to put together an alliance with the major beauty pageants!

ALLIANCES AND THE LITTLE GUY

So can a little guy play in this big-boy world? You bet. Many entrepreneurs have made a good living off of leveraging alliances and not paying a nickel to do so.

For example, most sports bars leverage a wall of TVs showing sports events to attract their customers. They regularly use the NCAA, NBA, NHL, NFL, and NASCAR as marketing tools without paying anything. Often, restaurants host parties to watch top-rated TV shows such as *Ally McBeal* every Monday night.

Other ways are to just buy imagery associated with the property and hang it around on the walls of your establishment. Want to look like the official bike shop of the Atlanta Braves? No problem. One quick trip to the concession stand can fix you up with everything you'll need.

Want to tie in with the next big concert in town? Go buy a couple of tickets and give them away as an in-store raffle. Put up a bunch of signs alerting consumers to the giveaway. You can get just as big a bang as the sponsor who's paid big bucks.

Want to develop a cause-related marketing program with a charity? No problem. They all are glad to help. Anything that will help raise money for their cause is a welcome endeavor, and you don't pay anything to use their name and logo in your marketing efforts.

GETTING OUTSIDE THE BOX

The trick when creating any strategic alliance is to build a promotion that will captivate and motivate the consumer to participate—hopefully through the purchase of your product! Go ahead and get out of the box—dream up something that really rocks!

CHAPTER SUMMARY

- Cause-related marketing partnerships are a great way to differentiate your product from competition.
- Consumers like companies that have a heart and give back to those in need.
- Cause-related marketing can be a win-win for both the product manufacturer and the charity. There is very little downside risk and great upside potential.
- Brands that have integrated cause-related marketing into their core brand positioning statement (Ben & Jerry's, Newman's Own, Flutie Flakes) have proven successful.
- A long-term strategy of aligning with a cause-related marketing organization can help craft your own company personality (NBA).
- Sometimes companies are successful in creating their own charities (Ronald McDonald's Charities).
- Product placement in movies/TV shows is too risky a proposition to build a marketing effort behind.

- Popularity marketing borrows the equity of a popular entertainment property.
- Movies, TV shows, and concert tours are the most common popularity properties.
- Cause-related marketing and popularity marketing are great ways for small businesses to craft consumer promotions.

What Coke Doesn't Want You to Know about Special Events

SECRET TACTICS FOR GETTING
NOTICED AND STANDING OUT IN
A CROWD

EACH YEAR ACROSS THE COUNTRY, millions of families attend thousands of special events, from festivals, fairs, and celebrations to conventions and sporting events—and at each event a mob of companies is hawking its wares. Sponsors camp out on every square inch of free space, clamoring for consumer attention, waving banners, offering free samples and prizes. Yet at each of these celebrations, one company tends to dominate the scene, rising above the throng. Most of the time it's Coca-Cola. Coke's preeminence at these events is not coincidental. It is the result of years of practice, practice, and more practice to get the system right.

PREPLANNING

Developing a winning special-events formula begins with the pre-planning process. I know, you're probably thinking "this isn't Einstein theory, of course it starts with planning!" But what *you* call planning and what *Coke* calls planning are two very different things.

Coke begins its planning processes *far* in advance of the event. For example, when Salt Lake City was selected as the host city for the 2002 Winter Olympic Games in the spring of 1996, Coca-Cola's marketing department had already visited Salt Lake City to scout billboard locations—*before* the bid was announced! Coke leased all of the prime spots along the interstate highways and close to the airport, sports venues, and key hotels *six years* ahead of the Games. In 1998, their staff began working closely with the Salt Lake Organizing Committee to place Coca-Cola signage in the best locations at the sports venues, to have Coca-Cola product available at all concession areas, and to develop a means to get Coca-Cola banners in as many key locations as possible around the city—*four years* before the opening ceremonies.

While the Olympics are perhaps the most planning-intensive affair on earth, other big-league events like the Super Bowl, NCAA Basketball Finals, The Academy Awards, State Fairs, and Spring Break also require a great deal of pre-event planning. The development process for these events typically begins as soon as the prior year's event concludes, and continues for the twelve-month cycle. It begins with an immediate postmortem of this year's successes and disappointments and brainstorming for the upcoming year, followed by an extensive documentation of the event, which generally takes about two months to write. Next, event officials work with sponsors to develop the new marketing plan, and the process of execution begins in earnest.

ORGANIZATION

Coca-Cola has dedicated an entire department to special events, called "Presence and Signage." Its role is to assign an event specialist to every major special event to oversee both the strategic direction and the mountain of minutiae that goes along with it. The specialist develops the marketing plan, works with the local bottler in the event city, and hires contractors and promotional agencies as needed to help execute the plan.

And while corporate headquarters has specialists assigned to the "big" events, each local bottler usually has several individuals within their shop who are event specialists. They divide up the hundreds of local events that come into their area each year— shindigs as small as the Pleasant Grove Strawberry Days celebration to major State Fairs and everything in between.

Coke takes special events seriously. It never wants to see a consumer drinking anything but a Coca-Cola for refreshment at any big event. Walking around a State Fair or cheering at a ballgame is thirsty work, and Coke wants every thirsty consumer to automatically reach for a Coke. This special-events strategy is merely a logical extension of the brand's overarching ubiquity strategy; Coca-Cola refreshment must always be within an arm's reach of desire.

I was at a meeting once with a senior Coke executive who had ascended the ranks from bottler sales rep to corporate vice president. The meeting invited managers from different corporations to discuss their sponsorship of an upcoming special event and to coordinate efforts. About two hundred people were in attendance. As we were settling in to start the day, an attendee from another company walked into the room holding a 32 oz. Big Gulp cup with "Pepsi" emblazoned on the side. The Coke executive went nuts. His face turned bright red and he stormed out of the meeting, refusing to return until the offending cup was removed and a public apology made by the philistine. That's how serious Coke is about dominating events—including corporate meetings!

DEVELOPING A PLAN

The event plan addresses five key initiatives that enable Coke to "own" events. Does Coke play fair? Not exactly. Coke will use every tactic at its disposal to achieve its objective. Don't get me wrong, Coca-Cola doesn't do anything underhanded, illegal, or immoral, but the behind-the-scenes details are carefully managed and manipulated to ensure that Coca-Cola is first in line for every perk that is available to sponsors at the event, and that Coke receives preferential sponsor treatment. Coke is the eight-hundred-pound gorilla at any special event, and it usually gets to sit wherever it wants.

The five-step plan begins with the development and procurement of all of the possible *points of distribution* Coca-Cola can have at the event for its beverages. Existing concession stands are first priority. Second is finding new locations where Coca-Cola can erect beverage stations or "hawk" product in and around the event, in effect creating new Coca-Cola concession stands. Third is contacting each and every vendor who will be at the event to ensure that they have a supply of Coca-Cola and Coca-Cola branded cups on hand, especially if they are selling food or beverages. These containers are more than just good signage; they actually drive consumption. If a consumer is hot and tired and sees someone walking around with a Coke cup, it fuels the desire for an icy cup of his or her own. Finally, the team searches for locations to install extra vending machines for additional product availability.

Once the quest for beverage locations is exhausted, the attention turns to the second initiative: *event signage*. Coca-Cola wants consumers to see a Coca-Cola advertisement no matter where they are at the event. If the event will have television coverage, Coke ensures that its sign can be identified in the background. Coca-Cola event staff offer free signs and banners to every vendor to use at their locations (of course, the banners have Coca-Cola logos on them). They also canvass the city streets and parking lots around the venue, offering Coca-Cola signs and banners to businesses to extend the Coca-Cola presence beyond the venue boundaries.

An important note: We've already spent a great deal of time discussing why signage at events usually doesn't work to build business. Giant logos typically do nothing to impress consumers. But here's where Coke walks a fine, and brilliant, line. Coke signage is always placed in an area that is either selling the product, so that it actually directs consumers to a purchase, or is in a location that represents the center of activity at the event. It is always associated with fun and refreshment—never just a courtside billboard or incidental backdrop.

This signage strategy is further developed in the third initiative: *brand activation*. This is the overall strategy for how Coca-Cola relevantly interacts with fans at the event in a way that will support the brand strategy. Remember, the brand strategy—refreshment within an arm's reach of desire—contains two major concepts: refreshment and availability. All brand activation efforts are designed to highlight one or both of these brand attributes.

The methods of execution can vary widely. For example, in many theme parks you'll find a Coca-Cola "Cool Zone," an area where cool mist is squirted from overhead pipes with fans blowing to cool off consumers on a hot day. Folks can step into this oasis and cool their bodies, buy an ice-cold Coca-Cola from the bank of nearby vending machines, and emerge totally refreshed, thanks to Coca-Cola. To reinforce its image of being "everywhere that's anywhere," Coke makes itself the center of attention at such major events as the Calle Ocho Festival in Miami each year. Coke erects a huge performance stage in the middle of the action and hires top-flight Latino entertainers to perform. Whatever form it takes, brand activation always focuses on Coke's two primary messages: refreshment and availability.

Next comes *hospitality and hosting*, the schmoozing part of the package. This is an elaborate plan for Coca-Cola to host and provide special attention to their key customers, including account buyers, the bottler, store managers, restaurant marketing managers and anyone else who might have influence on Coke's success at retail. Coke provides for all the needs of its VIP guests, including airfare, ground transportation, hotel accommodations, meals, entertainment, and event tickets. From the moment the guests step off the plane until the moment they get back on, Coke makes sure that comfort is the catchword. Services include delivering luggage directly to the hotel room; access to special VIP lounges inside the hotel for socializing and free meals; special events for spouses; expensive gift bags . . . and the list goes on. At the event itself, special guests enjoy exclusive Coca-Cola VIP lounges and tents with air conditioning and free food and drinks and entertainment. As one Englishman commented after witnessing the lavishness of the VIP effort, "Kings and Potentates have endured shabbier treatment."

While the impression to the guests is that Coke spares no expense, in reality, every dollar is accounted for. The hospitality and hosting effort is a key component of the event plan that makes sure that every Coca-Cola sponsorship reinforces the brand image, not only to the consumer but to the trade customers as well. If retailers enjoy working with Coca-Cola, they are much more likely to favor the brand in their stores or restaurants. This isn't just theory; it's proven strategy. In the long run, the cost of the hotels and the tents and the gift bags is slim in comparison with an all-out bidding war with Pepsi for the same channels of distribution.

The final piece of the planning process is *competitive activity*, and here's where the Coke team earns its reputation for ruthlessness.

During the development of the marketing plan, Coca-Cola sets up a team of marketers to play devil's advocate (the devil being Pepsi) and create a guerrilla ambush plan for the event. The guerrilla team pretends that it works for Pepsi and devises a scheme to infiltrate the event and embarrass Coke. This competitive scenario is incorporated into the marketing plans to ensure that all possible attack points are neutralized before the event takes place.

During the event, Coke sets up swat teams that are constantly on the move in and around the event, searching for any signs that the "blue devil" Pepsi or any other soft drink is trying to crash the party. If the swat team spots a competitive threat, even something as seemingly innocent as a lone can of competitive product on a vendor's cart, the Coke police swarm the offender with event managers to seize the offending can, remove it, and destroy it. The same fate awaits any offending signage that may crop up. If the sign is posted on event property, it is immediately seized. If it is off grounds, the property owner is first approached with an appeal to remove it, then offered incentives to comply. If all else fails, a giant Coca-Cola truck appears to park on the street in front of the sign. Hmm, I wonder how that happened!

Secrets of the Game

An effective event marketing plan (no matter if you are a megacorporation or a small vendor) requires attention to five key areas:

1. Where your product will be available for the public to purchase or sample (points of distribution).

2. How you can obtain a dominant presence through event signage (remember, higher is better!).

3. How you will effectively "activate" your brand at the event, relevantly linking it to your brand positioning strategy.

4. How you can offer special or preferential treatment to your event guests.

5. How you will anticipate and neutralize the threats posed by competitive ambush tactics, and put plans in place to swiftly deal with them if they crop up during the event.

SECRETS FOR STANDING OUT IN A CROWD

Over the years, Coke has managed to develop a huge arsenal of tricks and gimmicks that can cheaply and effectively affect consumers at special events. They are captured by what's know as *The Big Bang* Theory:

1. *Big:* Size matters most at special events. The more space you can take up, the more chance consumers will notice you. Height is critical. Try to *tower* over the event, with signage high in the air!
2. *Audacious:* You've got to do something that nobody else is doing. Go over the top. Have the spirit of P. T. Barnum!
3. *New:* Dream up something that nobody has ever seen before.
4. *Giggles:* Make 'em laugh. They'll remember your name, and your brand, fondly if you give them some unexpected fun.

The Big Bang Theory doesn't mean you should erect a big tent and put on a circus, but the mental models are closely linked. At most special events, people just walk on by, and you have only a short window of opportunity to grab 'em. Like the hawkers at carnivals who beckon you to step inside and see the incredible, unbelievable human pretzel fold herself into a one-foot cube, you must attract the attention of the consumer to get him to stop and stay a while.

Coke employed the Big Bang strategy brilliantly during the 1996 Olympic Torch Relay. The event unmistakably fit the definition of *Big;* it traveled cross-country to over fifteen hundred cities, towns, and villages on its eighty-four-day journey. The entourage that accompanied the Olympic flame covered a full city block, complete with motorcycle police escorts blaring their sirens to signal that the flame was approaching!

Audacious is an understatement. Who else but Coca-Cola would attempt to bring the Olympic Games into all of these different cities, with over ten thousand Coke consumers and "Community Heroes" selected to carry the torch?

The opportunity to watch the Olympic flame travel down the streets in your hometown was definitely *New,* something most consumers have never seen before and probably will never see again.

And the staging of the relay was choreographed to make an indelible impression on those 50 million consumers who lined the streets to watch the flame go by. Ahead of the flame, Coca-Cola employees worked the crowds, warming them up in cheering exercises, passing out miniature American flags, and giving everyone a sticker to wear proudly, stating "I Saw The Olympic Flame." By the time the flame arrived, people were raucous, giddy, and filled with a sense of patriotism, meeting the criteria of The Big Bang Theory for *Giggle!*

SPECIAL EVENTS AND THE LITTLE GUY

Of course, just because Coke spent millions on this event doesn't mean you have to go broke to be a player. Creativity is often an effective substitute for cash. Using few dollars and a little imagination, Hawaiian Punch created a terrific stir at Miami's Calle Ocho event in 1992. Calle Ocho is an event like no other in the world. It is a two-day Cuban festival held each spring on 8th street in Miami, a straight, five-mile stretch of road. Vendors line the streets selling everything imaginable. Stages with live entertainment are positioned every few blocks, sponsored by different corporations or brands. Coke and Budweiser are everywhere, with their trucks parked in the road about every three hundred yards. Over one million consumers pack onto 8th Street to enjoy the festival. It is wall-to-wall people for as far as the eye can see!

Hawaiian Punch realized it could not compete against the huge budgets of Coke and Budweiser and other sponsors to make a splash at this event, so it decided to focus their Calle Ocho efforts strictly on their target: kids. In a modest roadside tent, Hawaiian Punch managers passed out ice-cold cans of Hawaiian Punch to kids for sampling, along with an oversized helium-filled balloon tied to a six-foot string. The balloons were Hawaiian Punch red and sported the brand's logo with the brand character "Punchy." Kids loved them, and they reinforced the brand identity and the spirit of youthful fun. After about two hours of dispensing balloons, the Hawaiian Punch team could look out at the sea of one million consumers and see Hawaiian Punch balloons floating above the crowd, up and down the festival route. Hawaiian Punch was the only event sponsor passing out helium balloons, and the effect was stunning! Everyone saw the balloons, and every kid wanted one. The brand beat Coke at its own game for the price of a few tanks of helium and some big red balloons.

CREATING YOUR OWN SPECIAL EVENTS

Retailers often create their own special events to draw consumers to their store locations. Parking lot sales and carnivals, cheap food and beverages are the usual tactics. Some companies also opt to create their own special events for consumers. In an earlier chapter I talked about the rousing success Oscar Mayer has achieved with its touring Oscar Mayer Wienermobile. The brand effectively uses this tactic to drive home the key to their positioning strategy that kids love Oscar Mayer wieners. Movie studios regularly use premiere events to launch new movies. Brands that sponsor NASCAR racing teams often use the cars as bait to lure consumers to retailer locations where they can see the cars. With all of these success stories to point at, one might wonder if it's worthwhile to create your own events.

Usually, the answer is no. Creating your own special event is a time-consuming and expensive proposition. Unless you can dream up an idea that is truly brilliant (like the Wienermobile), or dead-on strategy, chances are you'll regret having spent time, energy, and money on creating it.

I learned this lesson the hard way when I squandered nearly a $250,000 on an idea I developed for Hawaiian Punch, which took its inspiration from the Wienermobile. I created the "Hawaiian Punch Surfmaster," a hydraulic surfing machine mounted in the back of a pickup truck. The vision was that kids would climb onto the surfboard, get strapped into the "life jacket," and the ride would begin. While surfer music blared, the board would rock from side to side. The rider would have to get into "surf" position in order to stay balanced on the board. When the rider's foot slipped off the side, or if he or she lost balance, the life jacket would snap into a locked position so that he or she couldn't fall, and a stream of water would come gushing from the framework around the truck, soaking the rider while the music blared the 1960s song "Wipe Out." A fun, interactive concept, and right on brand strategy!

The grand plan was to take Surfmaster to two grocery stores each day for a three-hour event. The store would simply agree to put up a display of Hawaiian Punch in order to earn a Surfmaster appearance. We built the machine, bought a brand-new truck and customized it with a great "Hawaiian Punch Surfmaster" paint job, hired two surfer-dude college-age kids to drive the truck and "emcee" the events, and we were ready to go—or so we thought. We soon discovered a few sharks in the promotional waters.

First, the Surfmaster had to endure extensive safety testing. Then, the kids we'd hired to run it had to pass drug tests. Then, the corporate insurance department had to decide whether or not to self-insure or buy event insurance. We had to develop custom point-of-sale materials to promote the events. Finally, we had to schedule the stores for appearances. *Wipe out.* We had taken the word of our sales force that Surfmaster would be a "Big Idea," but nobody had actually checked with a few store managers to see if the "Hawaiian Punch Surfmaster" was something they'd want at their locations. We began soliciting stores and came up empty. Store managers didn't want it taking up space in their parking lot. We offered Surfmaster to over three hundred different stores in the Southern California market, and only six signed up to take it. As a backup plan, we tried touring it to elementary schools and junior high schools during lunch breaks, but school administrators would call police and have us shut down. After three months of operation, the Surfmaster went to its watery grave.

Secrets of the Game

If you are considering developing your own special event or touring attractions:

1. Make sure that you have the "site(s)" where you plan to stage the event(s) secured *before* you create it!

2. Make sure consumers want to attend your attraction.

Don't assume that everyone will see your creation as a wonderful thing that can't be missed!

LOCAL TV AND RADIO SPECIAL-EVENT PROMOTIONS

The best way to get involved with special events is to link to existing events with a proven track record, like college and pro football tailgate parties in the fall. Another great resource is local radio stations and TV stations. Most have long-standing annual events that they stage in their local communities that you can easily tie-in to.

The best thing about TV/radio special events is that there is plenty of media weight to drive consumer awareness. The stations don't want to be embarrassed in their own hometowns, so they promote, promote, and promote some more to make sure a big crowd will be there.

Secrets of the Game

Holiday events such as Fourth of July fireworks and Christmas lights shows are terrific special events with built-in audience appeal. Everybody loves a good fireworks show, and Christmas lights are wholesome outdoor fun. These events are sure bets for success.

RELEVANT BRAND LINKAGE IS KEY

The most important consideration when assessing special-events opportunities is how your participation can relevantly link to the event in a unique, "ownable" way that supports your brand positioning strategy and sells your product. The trick is to make it fun for consumers—be imaginative and dream up something wonderful! Be like Captain Kirk and the crew of the Starship Enterprise and "Go where no man has gone before"!

CHAPTER SUMMARY

- An effective special events program begins with the pre-planning process.
- There are five key elements to an effective event plan:

1. Finding the best points of distribution for your product.
2. Obtaining dominant presence through signage (higher is better).
3. Creating relevant consumer promotions to activate your brand, relevantly supporting the brand positioning strategy.
4. Planning special treatment/perks for your event guests.
5. Anticipating competitive activity and planning how to deal with it.

- The secrets for standing out in a crowd are captured by The Big Bang Theory:

  Big: Size matters most at special events. Height is critical. Try to tower over the event, with signage high in the air.

  Audacious: Do or offer something outrageous and fun. Have the spirit of P. T. Barnum!

  New: Dream up something that nobody has ever seen before.

  Giggles: Make 'em laugh. Everybody wants unexpected fun.

- Be careful in going down the path of creating your own special events. Many companies have big event trailers built that never get used because they can't find places that will take them!

- Local TV and radio stations are terrific partners for special events. Use them wisely to drive awareness!

The Hidden Benefits of Licensing

A BIGGER OPPORTUNITY THAN T-SHIRTS AND COFFEE MUGS

WOULDN'T IT BE GREAT to own a business where people sent you money and all you had to do was walk down to the mailbox and collect the checks? Unless you look good in an orange jumpsuit and like the idea of long-term roommates, you'll have to rule out running a Mafia family or engineering illegal pyramid schemes. So what does that leave you with? The next best thing: licensing.

Licensing as a business is lucrative, relatively easy to maintain, and best of all, legal. When you own a coveted trademark that other companies will pay for the right to use, you can receive checks in the mail on a regular basis for very little effort. It's a pretty cool gig if you can get it.

But more likely, you don't own a valued trademark and instead must ask the question "Is there an opportunity for me to license someone else's trademarks so that I can make a buck?" The answer is *yes*. Yet many marketers avoid the world of licensing, intimidated by the unknown, which exists just outside the borders of conventional marketing. Most haven't had much hands-on experience with licensing, and they don't understand the rules of the game. Their ignorance often leads to missed opportunities and lost profits.

THE KEY BENEFITS OF LICENSING

Licensing someone else's trademarks offers the purchaser two key benefits: enhanced brand imagery and instant brand awareness.

Licenses can increase the value of what otherwise would be 'generic' products. To illustrate the opportunity, I have a CD-ROM in my office created by a company called Creative Multimedia that is a complete guide to Hollywood movies and videos. It contains over twenty-three thousand movie reviews encompassing sixty-five years, along with video clips, vintage photographs, and a variety of other features. It's a nice, informative disk. Now it's quiz time. Which has a higher perceived value and feels more authentic to you as a consumer: "Creative Multimedia's Ultimate Guide To Movies & Videos," or "Blockbuster Entertainment's Ultimate Guide to Movies & Videos"? I hope you selected the latter. Since the Blockbuster name is synonymous with videos, it makes perfect sense for Creative Multimedia to have licensed Blockbuster's name to increase the perceived consumer value of the disk. That's the power of licensing.

Secrets of the Game

If you have the capability of manufacturing and distributing a product, then you're a candidate for successfully using licensing as a marketing tool. Look to see if the perceived value of something you already produce can be increased by overlaying a licensed trademark.

HOW LICENSING WORKS

In its most basic form, licensing works as follows: a *licensor* (someone who holds the trademarks to something) sells another party—who is called a *licensee* —the right to use its logos, brand names, characters, or other proprietary words or images for a specific purpose. The licensee usually pays the licensor a minimum guarantee, plus royalties on every item they sell using the licensor's trademark.

Here's a simple example. Miami Heat Head Basketball Coach Pat Reilly trademarked the phrase Three-Peat. Now, anyone who wants to use that term must get the rights to do so from Coach Riley by paying him a licensing fee. This was a lucrative windfall for him when the Chicago Bulls won their third consecutive NBA Championship in 1998. Every company who used the term Three-Peat—from T-shirts to hats to videocassettes—paid Coach Riley for the licensing rights to do so.

In a more classic example, let's say that you own a small clock company. Your research has shown that there is a consumer demand for office wall clocks featuring the logos of local colleges. Since the schools owns their own trademark rights, you can't just slap their mascot on a clock without risking a lawsuit, so you contact the school's licensing attorney to negotiate a licensing agreement that would allow your company to manufacture and sell a collegiate clock featuring the school's name and logo. The university is the licensor. Your clock company is the licensee.

In a typical licensing agreement, you would pay a small up-front fee (this amount varies by product category), plus a royalty to the university for each clock you sell (the royalty is usually between 10 percent and 15 percent, depending on your negotiation skills). In the licensing contract, the school imposes a minimum performance guarantee, which means that you must guarantee to sell a minimum number of clocks each year in order to keep the license valid. If you fail to sell the minimum number of clocks, the license becomes null and void, and the rights to sell and manufacture clocks bearing the university marks revert back to the school. The minimum sales guarantee protects the interest of the school to ensure you actively try to sell its clocks once they are licensed.

The university also imposes a clause for "creative approval," meaning that it must approve the design of the clock before you can begin manufacturing and sale. This supervisory right ensures that you use the school's trademark correctly on the product and in all advertising. The university checks not only for correct colors, images, and copy but also for proper context; for example, they can't have the school mascot drinking a beer or duking it out with a competitive mascot.

Protecting your interests, the agreement contains an "exclusivity" clause, which means the university cannot license their trademarks to any other wall clock manufacturers. The agreement will probably also specify that the school must agree to display and sell the clock in the on-campus college bookstore and in all alumni catalogs the school produces.

Of course, since lawyers are involved, the actual licensing contract is long, complicated and horribly detailed, but those are the basics of a typical licensing agreement.

WHY WOULD SOMEONE LICENSE THEIR TRADEMARKS TO YOU?

For licensors who own marketable trademarks, each query from a potential licensee brings them to a fork in the road; to sell, or not to sell, that is the question. Keeping the trademark—thus manufacturing and selling the goods themselves—would intuitively seem to be much more lucrative than settling for a licensing fee, since they'd make 100 percent of the profits instead of a mere royalty fee. Greed may lead you to think that unless someone simply cannot make and sell the product themselves, they should never license away their trademarks. But alas, this thinking is wrong!

Let's look at the math to see how the financials stack up in a "make-it-themselves" scenario versus a "license-it-away" scenario. Going back to the college clocks as the example, take the point of view of the university's licensing attorney:

	If School Makes It	If They License Away the Rights
Wholesale price	$ 12.99	$12.99
Cost to produce	$ 8.79	$ 7.79
Gross profit	$ 4.20	$ 5.20
OVERHEAD:	$ 2.33*	$ N/A
University NET PROFIT:	$ 1.87	$ 1.94**

* Overhead calculated as 18% of sales.
** Licensing royalty equals 15% of wholesale price.

Whoa Nellie! There are three key issues to flag. The first issue is the cost to produce the clocks. Since the university isn't in the clock-making business, it will have to hire a contract manufacturer to make the clocks. The contract manufacturer must make a profit, so the school will end up paying more to make the clock than you will pay to produce it in-house.

The second key issue is *overhead*. If the university chooses to manufacture and sell the clocks, it must incur the costs of having someone manage the process, act as a sales force, process orders, and ship the clocks. Since it will have to manufacture a number of clocks at one time in order to hold down the unit manufacturing cost, the school will have to invest money into inventory—the cost of the clocks sitting in the warehouse, waiting to be shipped. The university accountants will also charge "carrying costs," the interest cost of the money invested in the inventoried clocks.

Also key is the fact that the school isn't in the clock business. They have no contacts with any clock stores. Every point of distribution will have to be developed from scratch, a slow and tedious process.

After looking at the potential finances, the option of "make it myself" doesn't look too appealing for the university, compared with "licensing it away" and collecting royalty checks. This example illustrates why licensing is a big business! *Unless the licensor owns the retail channel of sale so that it can claim both the manufacturer's profit and the retailer's profit, it is almost always better to license its trademarks away rather than keeping them and dealing with the added burdens of manufacturing, sales, inventory, and carrying costs.*

Secrets of the Game

'Tis better to license your trademarks away and collect royalty checks than attempt to develop and sell to a retail distribution channel on your own.

THE MICKEY MOUSE LICENSING COMPANY

Disney is the king of licensing. The Consumer Products division of the company earns over $2.5 billion each year. The sales are generated between two different areas: *Disney-owned properties* such as the theme parks, The Disney Catalog, and The Disney Stores, and non-Disney retail outlets, which in effect is *everywhere else*.

The way that Disney approaches its consumer products business is pure genius:

- With the retail channels of distribution that Disney owns—such as the Disney theme parks, The Disney Stores, The Disney Catalog and the Studio Store—Disney manufactures and sells all products in these locations, capturing all profits.
- In all retail distribution channels Disney does not own—like toy stores, book stores, mass merchandisers, and department stores—Disney licenses away these rights to others and just collects a royalty check.

This strategy allows the Mouse to maximize its profits. Just as our example proved that it's better for the university to license away its trademarks for clocks, the same holds true for Disney. It is more profitable and less of a hassle for Disney to license their marks away when they don't own the retail channels and let their licensees manufacture and distribute the products.

THE DISNEY LICENSING STRATEGY

MAKE IT AND SELL IT	LICENSE THE RIGHTS AWAY
All Disney theme parks	All other retailers
The Disney Stores	
The Disney Catalog	
The Studio Store	

To visualize the opportunity, let's look again at a clock example, and pretend this time that we work for Disney. The first column is a clock Disney makes and sells in its parks and Disney Catalog. The second column is a clock licensed and sold in all other non-Disney retailers (Target stores for instance):

	DISNEY PARK CLOCKS	LICENSED DISNEY CLOCKS
Clock retail price:	$24.99	$19.99
Wholesale price:	$ N/A	$12.99
Cost to produce:	$ 8.79	$ 7.79
Gross profit:	$ 16.20	$ 5.20
OVERHEAD:	$ 4.49*	$ N/A
Disney's NET PROFIT:	$ 11.71	$ 1.94**

* Overhead calculated as 18% of sales.
** Licensing royalty equals 15% of wholesale price

Again, there are nuances to the financials, notably the retail price. Disney theme parks and proprietary sales channels can charge more for items because Disney controls the sales environment in its distribution channels. Consumers expect to pay more for an item at Disneyland or inside The Disney Store, but the ambiance and impulse to buy is too strong to walk away, especially from an "exclusive" item.

Another key to the Disney strategy is product development. When you spot a particular item at The Disney Store, in The Disney Catalog, or in a theme park, you won't find it in non-Disney–owned retailers. This strategy prevents consumers from price comparison shopping or thinking that they can go buy the item cheaper at some other store.

In all non-Disney–owned retail outlets, hundreds of different licensees do the actual manufacturing and selling of the Disney products. Disney licensed merchandise is sold in virtually every product category imaginable, from towels and sheets to toys and treats. And that's not only a U.S. phenomenon. In fact, 58 percent of Disney's consumer product sales come from international operations! There's all beauty and no beast in this business. Lots of money and no risk. The Mouse just sits back and collects the checks from the licensees, who do all the work! The one-two punch in Disney's retail strategy makes it the strongest retail brand in the world.

WHEN YOU SHOULD CONSIDER ACQUIRING LICENSES

There are right ways and wrong ways to get into the licensing business. Doing it the right way is part of winning The Marketing Game.

Secrets of the Game

Licensing makes the most sense when your company already manufactures and distributes products, and through acquiring a license for a new trademark, you can expand your business within your existing product category. Licensing should not be used to try to break into new product categories for which you do not have the manufacturing and distribution capabilities.

THE GOLD STANDARD

Hallmark Cards has executed this strategy brilliantly. As the world's largest purveyor of greeting cards, it annually has to create thousands upon thousands of high-quality card designs to address all occasions for which a consumer might be in need of a greeting card. Hallmark was faced with a dilemma: Just how many cards can you make using only flowers and generic illustrations? The answer: not enough to satisfy all consumers' needs. By shrewdly acquiring licenses—Peanuts characters (Charlie Brown, Snoopy, and pals), Winnie the Pooh, Garfield, and others—Hallmark has used licensing to do exactly what it does best, creating new greeting-card product lines that peacefully coexist with their basic nonlicensed greeting cards. This integrated strategy offers the consumer a breadth of selection that guarantees that there is a card available for nearly any sentiment or occasion.

Hoyle Playing Cards executed a smart licensing deal. They licensed the rights to manufacture limited-edition 30th Anniversary Playing Cards for Special Olympics. The new product helped them garner more shelf space in most stores for their playing cards and increased sales, at the same time helping a worthy cause, as $.50 of each sale went to Special Olympics!

When I worked at P&G, we had an incredible idea for a new licensed product line that unfortunately never made it off the ground, but the story is one worth recounting. Our idea focused on the Duncan Hines brand. Duncan Hines's primary business is cake mixes, cookie mixes, and frosting. The brand has several manufacturing facilities dispersed nationwide and a retail distribution network that reaches nearly 90 percent of all grocers—a perfect scenario for expanding the business through intelligent licensing.

We looked at the cookie mix business and ideated for a way to expand beyond Duncan Hines branded sugar cookies, chocolate-chip cookies, and peanut butter cookies through licensing. In our consumer research, we discovered that consumers had a high regard for several fresh-baked cookie brands such as Mrs. Field's Cookies. Most moms expressed a high interest and desire in baking a cookie at home that tasted the same as those available at the "mall" cookie stores.

We met with Debbie Fields and the licensing attorneys for Mrs. Field's Cookies in Park City, Utah, with a concept to license the rights to their name to create a new cobranded premium line of cookie mixes. The product line was to be called "Mrs. Field's Home Recipe Cookies" by Duncan Hines. These mixes would bake into great-tasting cookies identical to the ones you buy inside a Mrs. Field's store. Debbie loved the idea and came up with another great idea for a kids' targeted line called "Mrs. Field's Kids Cookies" by Duncan Hines. These would have all sorts of colorful decorations and ingredients such as M&M's and candies so that moms and kids could spend quality time in the kitchen together, making fun and colorful cookies. The meeting was a love-in, and everyone walked away feeling like this was a partnership made in heaven.

We immediately began making plans to develop the products and packaging and launch them into a test market. We anticipated that these new product lines could grow the

Duncan Hines cookie mix business significantly. Unfortunately, we hit a bump in the road shortly thereafter that derailed our plans. Mrs. Field's attorney wanted a $1 million up-front licensing fee from P&G in order for us to execute a test market. The dollars were unreasonable and couldn't be negotiated down, so the idea was tossed into the trash can and we moved on. It is a crying shame that these products never made it to market. I think they would have been great.

Following the Mrs. Field's disaster, we focused our efforts into a licensed line for Duncan Hines cake mix. My boss and I dreamed up and developed the idea of a proprietary disposable paper baking pan in which shaped cakes could be made at home without the use of expensive metal pans. The shapes could be anything you could imagine: a simple heart, a baseball field, a football, or the face of a cartoon character. As the brand team developed the concept, we found that consumer demand increased significantly when the cakes featured popular licensed kids' characters and major league sports properties.

We went about putting together an array of licenses with several different licensors, a fascinating process. We decided to make our first stop at The Muppet Mansion in New York City to meet with Jim Henson and discuss the opportunity to license Kermit Cakes and Miss Piggy Cakes. P&G had approached Henson a year before with the idea for licensing and creating a brand of kids' soft drinks called Muppets Soda—Kermit Lemon-Lime, Miss Piggy Pink Lemonade, Fozzie Bear Orange Soda, etc. Although Henson thought the idea was cute, he declined the offer, saying that he's always held the position that you don't eat the characters.

He'd been approached in the past with licensing opportunities for everything from Muppet chewing gum to Kermit Toothpaste, Miss Piggy Twinkies to Muppet Popsicles, but he'd turned down all comers. Jim admitted that he'd probably tossed millions of dollars of royalties aside by holding the line on his conviction, but that was just the way he felt. He didn't want people eating his characters.

With that knowledge and anticipating rejection, we baked up prototypes of a Kermit Cake and a Miss Piggy Cake, loaded them onto a plane to New York, and marched into the mansion. We were shuffled upstairs into the conference room, a stately chamber with deep cherry-wood bookcases and a long table extending down the center. Above the head of the table hung a six-foot-tall by four-foot-wide oil painting of Kermit the Frog, and to the left was a large chair that had appeared in *The Muppet Movie*.

When Henson stepped into the room, my boss got right to the point. He said he knew Jim didn't want people to eat his characters, but this idea was such a phenomenal concept that we had to run it by him. His pitch was simple: "These cakes will make every kid's birthday party special." And with that we lifted off the boxes covering the cake prototypes and waited for his reaction.

To our surprise and delight, Henson loved them! He thought the cakes were the coolest thing he'd ever seen, and decided to wave his no-eat rule for the very first time. He agreed with our assessment that kids' birthday parties would be great fun with these cakes, and told his licensing folks to cut a deal. We had bagged our first licensor.

We next met with the various people who control the trademark licenses for Garfield, Major League Baseball, and the NFL. All agreed to let us license their marks for a cake mix. The deal was simple. Whatever we negotiated with Henson, everyone else would get the identical deal. If at any time any licensor received more, we'd up the ante for them all so that everybody always had the same deal. What should have been a nasty and prolonged negotiation wrapped up in just a couple of weeks, and we were able to move ahead with production and test marketing of the cakes.

As soon as the cake mixes hit store shelves in the test market, consumers started buying them by the armful. It was one of the most amazing things I've ever witnessed. I'd see a woman loading five or six packages into her cart, and I'd ask why she was buying all these cake mixes. The typical response was that these cakes weren't being sold where her kids or grandkids lived, and so she was buying them for upcoming birthday parties for their extended families. The

U.S. Postal Service was doing box-office business, shipping cake mixes around the country. In just three weeks, consumers cleaned off of the store shelves what should have been a six-month supply of mixes—with absolutely no advertising other than a flyer dropped off to local homes, supporting the product introduction.

Secrets of the Game

The criteria for identifying and evaluating licensing possibilities is straightforward. You need only to answer one question: "Will the use of this trademark with this product increase its value to the consumer more than it will cost me to acquire the license?" If the answer is yes, go for it.

PRODUCT CATEGORIES THAT INTELLIGENTLY USE LICENSING

T-shirt manufacturers do most of their business—and it's big business—through licensing. Nobody wears a blank T-shirt anymore. I have a friend in Atlanta who owns a small T-shirt–printing business that does several million dollars' worth of business each year, printing shirts featuring everything from Hooter's Restaurants to NASCAR to Coca-Cola. And he's just a small player.

Hanes is savvy in maximizing the power of Olympic trademarks. Hanes is granted the license to produce all Olympic apparel through the Sara Lee worldwide sponsorship package (Hanes is a subsidiary of Sara Lee). Since Hanes makes only the basic garments and doesn't do any imprinting, it sublicenses the rights to imprint apparel using the Olympic trademarks to different T-shirt imprinters (like my friend in Atlanta). Very smart, as it helps Hanes recoup the cost of its sponsorship through the fees it charges for the sublicenses.

Many video-game manufacturers are heavy into licensing. Electronic Arts is one of the best. As the largest producer of sports games, they quickly realized that consumers have a much higher

interest in purchasing NBA Jam Session games than a generic basketball game that doesn't use the trademarks of the NBA or the
marquee name players. The same is true of its popular Daytona
500 NASCAR racing game. The licensed trademark brings added
consumer value that is much more valuable than the cost of the
license. If Electronic Arts didn't acquire the licenses and instead
offered just generic sports games, consumers wouldn't buy. They'd
go get their games from some other manufacturer who does offer
games with the "real" goods—the official licensed products!

FINDING LICENSES

Just about any brand name is available for licensing and can be
acquired for such by contacting the parent company. Licensing
attorneys can also help locate trademark owners and negotiate
deals for you. There are licensing trade shows frequently around
the country. The key to finding the right license is when you
already manufacture and distribute a product, and the acquisition
of a license can help expand your base business by piggybacking
on your infrastructure.

You shouldn't try to get into a new business by licensing—the
risks far outweigh the rewards. If you don't have efficiencies of
scale in manufacturing or distribution, licensing will typically not
provide enough of a profit margin to be successful. The reason is
simple. When you license, you are giving away part of the profits
from the sale to the licensor. Unless the value of the license
increases the perceived value of the product significantly over the
"generic" version, you'll likely not be able to up-charge enough on
the licensed product to fully recoup the cost of the license.
Licensing is a lower-margin business that can be used successfully
to augment your core business.

CHAPTER SUMMARY

- Licensing your trademarks is a great business, especially if
  you own desirable ones. Just sit back and collect the royalty checks!
- Most trademarks are available for licensing. The benefits
  are enhanced brand imagery and instant brand awareness.

It usually makes more business sense for companies to license away their trademarks and let somebody else deal with the business issues.

- The only time it makes sense to *not* license is when you own the distribution channel (i.e., Disney at its theme parks, Disney Stores, and Disney Catalog).
- In a typical licensing agreement, you pay the licensor a small up-front fee plus a percentage on all product sales that use their trademark.
- Licensing makes most sense when your company already manufactures and distributes products, and through the acquisition of a licensed trademark, you can expand your business within the category.

PARTING THOUGHTS

I made a promise to you in the introduction that reading this book was going to change the way you think about marketing forever. My hope is that you have found seeds of ideas that like the Star Trek nemesis "The Borg," have assimilated into your collective consciousness to help you market more successfully, whatever your endeavor.

The Marketing Game isn't very hard when you break it down into simple and clear strategies. Most businesses muck up the process by trying to do too much. The key to success is to develop a clear strategic positioning and build all of your marketing efforts from that strategy.

I hope that through these pages you have seen that major corporations have incredible marketing prowess, but at the same time are human and can make mistakes just like anyone else. The same ideas that work for big companies can work for all companies. No individual knows all the answers or the absolute right way to do things. There are many roads to Tupelo. Some are faster than others, but many will get you there. The same goes for marketing. There are many paths that can get you to the same business destination. The trick is in finding the right paths, but we must always keep in mind that the fun is in the journey.

My aspiration is that you will walk away from The Marketing Game inspired and motivated to do something incredible with your business— determined to be different, better, and special. I hope that in some small way, my thoughts can help you achieve your dreams.

FEEDBACK

I'd love to hear what you think of this book, along with any stories you may develop from having implemented these ideas. I'm also available if you have any questions about The Marketing Game. You can reach me directly anytime via e-mail through our Web site at http://www.themarketinggame.com. I will try to respond in a timely fashion. God bless, and thanks for taking the time to read what I've had to say. I truly appreciate it. I hope our paths will cross in the future.

INDEX

A
Ackroyd, Dan, 251
ACV (All Category Volume), sustained placement requirements in, 62-63
Advertising. *See also* Advertising agencies; Compelling reasons; Marketing; Retail environment; Sports sponsorship
creating, 163
creativity in, 137-138, 163
feature ads, 186
in-store marketing, 186-189
little guys and, 150
media planners and, 149-150
for new products, 127
at Olympic Games, 154-155
reach of, 106
sales volume triggers for, 62-63
sins of
Envy, 159-160
in general, 153-154, 155-156
Gluttony, 157-159
greed, 160-161
Pride, 156-157
sloth, 161-162
Wrath, 162
with sports sponsorships, 230-231
spot, 63
successful, 150
Advertising agencies
advantages of using, 137-138
brainstorming sessions provided by, 17-18
creative freedom for, 144-146
critiquing work of, 147-149
realities of
bigger vs. better, 141
no guarantee of success, 140-141
not research groups, 140
not your partners, 139-140
profit motive, 138-139
relationship with
allowance for creative freedom, 144-146
allowance for development times, 147
authority for expenses, 143-144
creative critique rules, 147-149
honesty and feedback, 149
maintaining control, 142-143
positioning strategy focus, 143
provide stimulus and inspiration, 146-147
success of, 141-142
AFTA, 113
Airlines
continuity promotions, 211
passion points affecting decisions about, 53-54
sports promotions, 237
ticket price sensitivity, 77-78
Alliances. *See also* Consumer promotions
by movie studios, 250-253

cause-related marketing, 241-247
creating charities, 247-249
in general, 241-242
in-store activity, 249
little guys and, 255-256
with musicians, 253-254
Allstate Insurance, 119
American Express, 245
Anger, in advertising, 162
Animation cells, 125-126
AT&T
pricing structure, 100-102
promotions, 213-215, 236
Audience. *See* Target audience
Authority channels, establishing, 12
Auto manufacturers, advertising, 158
Avengers, The, 173
Avis, 226

B
Band-Aid, product mix, 94-95, 97
Beanie Babies, 76, 204
Beatty, Warren, 174
Beer, advertising, 112, 157, 159-160, 195, 204, 224, 253
Ben & Jerry's Ice Cream, 244-245
Berra, Yogi, 120
Best Buy, 129
Big Bang Theory, 265-266
Blocking strategies, for enhancing brand recognition, 131-132
Bradbury, Ray, 70
Braindraining, compared to brainstorming, 18-19
Brainstorming. *See also* Decision making; Ideas
braindraining and, 18-19
exercises
Catalog City, 23
Mind Dumpster, 22-23
Pin Pricks, 24-25
666, 23
Stimuli One-Step, 23
in general, 17-18
imaginative possibilities, 25
preparing for success with, 19-20
session requirements, 21-22
truth of, 22
Brand. *See also* Names
distribution strategy affecting, 127-128
Brand activation, 262
Brand linkage
with special events, 269
to sport sponsorship, 227-230
Brand loyalty. *See also* Consumer preferences
consumer values and, 85-86
developing, 211
passion points and, 51
Brand personality
borrowing, 210-211, 254
creating, 112, 202, 209-210
Brand recognition. *See also* Logos
blocking strategies for, 131-132
Brand teams. *See also* Teams
advertising agency as, 142-143
real-world learning for, 30-31

Branding
communicating with, 60-61, 112-114, 117
for fighter brands, 98-99
premium branding, 99-102
sales environment affect on, 122
Breakfast cereals, 112
Budweiser, advertising, 157, 195, 204, 224, 253
Buffalo Bills, 245
Bulworth, 174
Business plans. *See also* Marketing plans
relation to operating charters, 10
vs. operating charters, 13-15

C
Calle Ocho, 266-267
CapriSun juice, 112
Car-rental agency, mission statement examples, 9
Cars
advertising for, 158
pricing for, 77
Carville, James, 30
Catalina Marketing, 189
Catalog City exercise, 23
Category. *See* Product category
Cause-related marketing. *See also* Marketing
as brand strategy, 244-246
discussed, 241-244
NBA and, 246-247
CDs, compared to tape and vinyl, 67
Channel strategies. *See also* Distribution strategies
for distribution, 126-127
Charities
creating, 247-249
marketing with, 242-244
Charles, Ray, 254
Checkout coupons, programs for, 189-190
Cheerios, line extensions, 68
Chicago White Sox, 237
Circuit City, 129
Citibank, Citishopper service, 49
Citizenship, marketing and, 242-244
Citrus Hill Orange Juice, 35-36, 148-149, 248
advertising, 98-99, 159-160
packaging, 109
Clements, Lisa, 176
Clichés, in advertising, 161-162
Clothing, in brainstorming session, 21
Club cards, 190
Coca-Cola
advertising, 139, 143, 144, 155, 157, 166-167, 170-171, 199-200, 203, 224, 262
Big Bang Theory, 265-266
Diet Coke target audience, 47
distribution strategy, 122-123
logo display, 117
marketing practices, 29-30, 167-168, 196, 212-213, 231-232, 233-236, 251, 255, 259-266

mission statements and
operating charters, 6-8
packaging, 108, 132
product mix, 92-93
Colgate Total, 96, 97
Commodities
competition between, 36-37
as premium brands, 100-102
Communication. *See also* Media;
Public relations
with packaging, 106, 108
power of, 55
through price, 84
Compelling reasons. *See also*
Advertising; Consumer benefits;
"Reason why"
communicating, 41-42, 106
for consumer choices, 86
importance of, 47-48, 161, 202
relation to strategic positioning
statement, 43-44
Competition
analyzing, 29, 32-33, 116
with fighter brands, 98-99
Consumer beliefs. *See also* Passion
points; Value
about advertising, 158
about distribution point, 123
passion point affecting, 49-50
relation to strategic positioning
statement, 43
sales environment affect on, 122
Consumer benefits. *See also*
Compelling reasons
importance of emphasizing,
58-59, 61, 87, 202
incorporating in strategic positioning statement, 47-48
linked vs. unlinked, 96, 97-98
psychological, 48
role of in purchase decision, 90,
106-107
Consumer needs
charting with segmentation
analysis, 90-92
expression and meaning of,
36-38
independent vs. linked, 97-98
marketing significance of, 28
Consumer preferences. *See also*
Brand loyalty
understanding, 89-90
Consumer products. *See also*
Product
pricing strategy for, 79
Consumer promotions. *See also*
Alliances; Trade promotions
brand personality creation with,
209-210
continuity promotions, 211-212
creating with strategy, 202-203
in general, 201-202
half-right, 213-215
Octopus planning matrix for,
215-218
plagues of
been there, done that,
203-204
oddsitis, 206
sleeping sickness, 204
trinkets and trashitis,
204-205
promotion agencies for,
218-219
proprietary promotions,
212-213

sports sponsorships and,
227-230
successful, 206-208, 219
Consumer research
advertising agencies and, 140,
147
assumptions about, 35-36
insight required for interpretation, 31-32
Knowledge Mining for, 32-33
standard methods for, 28
Consumer Strike Zone, product
display in, 129-130
Continuity promotions, 211-212
Coors beer, 112, 195
Corporate conventionalism, creativity and, 20
Costco, 128
Coupons
checkout, 189-190
for consumer promotion, 204
in-store instant, 191-192
smart, 189-191
Creative people
in advertising agencies,
140-141, 144-146, 149
soliciting input of, 20
Creativity. *See also* Fantasy
in advertising, 137-138, 163
bass-ackward, 64
as motivation for advertising
agency, 142
stimulus response method for,
18-19
in think tank environment, 69
Crest toothpaste, 95-96
Crow, Sheryl, 178
Curriculum development, for
brainstorming session, 21

D
DeBeers Diamonds, 132
Decision making. *See also*
Brainstorming
assisted by operating charter, 13
Delta Airlines, 78, 158
Departments
goal establishment for, 5-8
mission statement for, 5-6, 13
at Coca-Cola, 6-8
Diet Coke. *See also* Coca-Cola
target audience for, 47
DirecTV, 86
Discount Outdoor Malls, 124
Disney
advertising, 163, 171, 178
animation cells, 125-126
distribution strategy, 124-125
EPCOT center, 25
licensing, 276-277
packaging, 113-114, 132-133
promotions, 205, 252
video sales, 31, 51-52, 113-114,
124-125, 132-133, 178,
194-195, 252-253
Displays. *See also* Packaging
in retail environment, 186-188,
243
special displays, 132-133
Distribution channel
affecting new products, 62-63,
65-66, 127
product strategies by, 128-129
Distribution strategies
channel strategies, 126-127
choosing, 123

errors in effecting brand,
127-128
exclusivity, 123-124, 125-126
in general, 122
for special events, 261-263
ubiquity, 122-123
Dockers, 253
Doritos, 255
Dow Bathroom Cleaner, 44, 112,
159
Dr. Pepper, 210, 255
Dream Team, 231-232
Duncan Hines, 279-280
DVD players, 66-67

E
Edison, Thomas, 57
Eggo waffles, 161-162
Eisner, Michael, 163
Electronic Arts, 282-283
Elton John, 253
Emotion
in advertising, 162
compared to passion points, 50
Employees
mission statements and operating charters for, 14, 15
workplace goals for, 5, 8, 13
Equality
among competing brands, 36-37
in brainstorming session, 21
ET, 250
Eureka! Ranch, brainstorming
ideas, 18-19, 22
Exclusivity
of distribution channels,
123-124, 125-126
with licensing, 274
Executives, participation in brainstorming session, 21

F
Fantasy. *See also* Creativity
advertising and, 158-159
sports sponsorships and,
223-224
Fast-food restaurant, mission state-
ment examples, 9
Feature ads. *See also* Advertising
retail sales affected by, 186, 243
Feedback, in brainstorming ses-
sion, 21-22
Ferengi business practices, 87
Fighter brands, developing and
using, 98-99
Fitness equipment, 160-161
Flutie Flakes, 245
Folgers coffee
packaging, 114-115, 131-132
PR campaign, 175-176
promotions, 205
response to competition, 32
Food, role in creative process, 20
Franco-American spaghetti,
187-189
Franklin, Benjamin, 57
Frequent Flyer programs, 211
Frozen desserts, 66
Fun
in creative process, 19-20
public relations and, 177-178

G
Garfield, 281
General Foods, frozen desert deba-
cle, 66

General Mills, Cheerios, 68
Gibson, Mel, 173
Goals
  corporate, 3-4, 5
  defining, 12-13
  establishing, 5-8
Goizuetta, Roberto, 122
Goodyear Blimp, 210
Grocery trade. *See also* Retail environment
  new product introduction to, 62

H
Hall, Doug, 18, 22
Hallmark
  corporate mission statement, 4, 14-15
  licensing, 278
Hanes, 282
Hawaiian Punch
  advertising, 251, 266-267
  Calle Ocho, 266-267
  line extensions, 68
  sports sponsorships, 221-223
  Surfmaster, 267-268
Henson, Jim, 280-281
Hispanics, advertising aimed at, 139-140
Hoyle Playing Cards, 278-279

I
Ideas. *See also* Brainstorming
  generating in brainstorming session, 20
  must be able to stand alone, 60, 61
  for public relations, 172, 178
  purchasing for new products, 68-70
  relevant yet unexpected, 43-45, 256
Images. *See also* Advertising
  in advertisements, 157-159, 249
In-store instant coupons, 191-192
Information, for consumer insight, 28-29, 31-32
Intellectual competitive advantage, creating, 28-29
Inventors, 27-28, 57

J
Jell-O Pudding Pops, 66
John Deere, 228-229
John Hancock Insurance, 237
Johnson & Johnson, 254
Jump Start Your Brain (Hall), 18, 22

K
Kellogg's, Breakfast Mates, 65-66
KISS strategy, 97-98
"Kitchen logic," for analyzing consumer benefits, 59-60
Klein, Calvin, 162
Kmart, 31, 129
Knowledge Mining
  consumer research and, 32-33, 37-38
  exercise for, 33-35
Kraft Cheese, 110
Kroger supermarkets, 196

L
Laundry detergent, 109
Lauren, Ralph, 123-124
Leary, Dennis, 162

Lethal Weapon 4, 173
Levi's, 127-128, 162
Licensing
  benefits of, 272
  by Disney, 276-277
  by Hallmark, 278
  considerations about, 278
  in general, 271-272
  how it works, 273-274
  investigating, 283
  product categories for, 282-283
  trademarks, 274-275
Line extensions. *See also* New product development
  new products and, 67-68
  packaging and, 112-113
Little guys
  advertising and, 150
  alliances and, 255-256
  packaging for, 119-120
  special events and, 266-267
  sports sponsorships by, 237-238
  trade promotions and, 194-195
Loggins, Kenny, 254
Logos. *See also* Brand recognition
  on packaging, 117
  placement considerations, 156-157, 193, 225
Loyalty. *See* Brand loyalty

M
M&Ms, 216-218
McCormick's Spice, 196
McDonald's, 139, 209
  charities, 248
  logos, 117
  promotions, 203-204, 211-212, 252
McMath, Robert, 65
Marketing. *See also* Advertising
  by movie studios, 250-253
  cause-related, 241-244, 244-246
  disguised as public relations, 170-171
  in-store, 186-189
  popularity, 242
Marketing costs, in new product development, 63
Marketing development funds (MDFs), procedures for, 185-186
Marketing plans. *See also* Business plans
  Big Bang Theory, 265-266
  for special events, 259-266
  for sports sponsorships, 231-232, 233-236
Martinelli's apple juice, 108
Matalin, Mary, 30
Maxwell House coffee, 131-132
MCI, 100-102
MDFs. *See* Marketing development funds
"Me-Tooism," 67
  in advertising, 159-160
Media. *See also* Radio stations; TV stations
  "free" publicity in, 169, 170-171
  public relations and, 170-171
  restricting contact with, 167
  sports sponsorships and, 227-230
  tagged, 195

Media planners. *See also* Advertising
  working with, 149-150
Melrose Place, 255
Message boards, 193
Miami University, 175-176
Michelin tires, 45-46
Microsoft, monopoly practices, 78
Miller beer, 208
Mind Dumpster exercise, 22-23
Minute Maid Orange Juice, 35-36, 99, 114
Mission statements
  corporate, 3-4
  creating, 8-9
    examples, 11-12, 14-15
  departmental, 5-6, 14
  developing, 3-4
  working, 4-5, 8
Monopolies, 78
Morality, in business, 87
Motivation, 169
Movie studios
  marketing by, 250-253
  public relations of, 172-175
Mrs. Fields Cookies, 279-280
Muppets, 280-281
Music, in creative process, 19-20
Musicians, alliances with, 253-254
MusicLand, 133

N
Names. *See also* Brand
  for new products, 60-61
NationsBank, advertising, 158
NBA, cause-related marketing by, 246-247
Nealon, Kevin, 133
Nestle's candy, 252
New product development. *See also* New products
  in general, 57-58
  idea acquisition for, 68-70
  product concept example, 61-62
  risk and reward in, 70
  secrets of
    consumer benefits focus, 58-59
    good ideas must stand alone, 60
    new products learning, 61-62
    plausible "reason why," 59-60
    product name significance, 60-61
New products
  failure rate for, 58, 62-63
  pitfalls
    bass-ackward creative process, 64
    distribution debacles, 65-66
    line extensions, 67-68
    marketing costs underestimation, 63
    "Me-Tooism," 67
    point of difference requirements, 66-67
    trade hurdles, 62-63
    X-Files, 65
  segmentation strategy for, 95-96
New products learning, bringing to life, 61-62
New Products Showcase and Learning Center, 65
Newman's Own, 244-245

NHRA Funny Car promotion, 221-223
Nike, 209
Nonprofits, marketing with, 242-244

O
Octopus planning matrix, for consumer promotions, 215-218
Olympic Games. *See also* Coca-Cola
advertising at, 154-155, 166-167, 170-171, 259-266, 265-266
Operating charters
benefits of using, 12-13
at Coca-Cola, 6-8
creating, 9-12
elements, 10
examples, 11-12
departmental, 5-6
vs. business plans, 13-15
Ortho Lawn Care, packaging, 109-110
Oscar Meyer
Lunchables, 110-111
Wiernermobile, 209-210, 267

P
P&G. *See* Proctor & Gamble
Packaging. *See also* Displays
brand personality creation with, 112
changes in affecting sales, 52, 64, 114-115
consumer preferences about, 105-106
copy and art for, 106-107
creating preference with, 109-110
developing, 115-117
for distribution channel, 128-129
graphics treatments options, 117
line extensions and family packaging, 112-113
little guys and, 119-120
for public relations, 172
for shipping, 114-115, 117
unique and proprietary shapes, 108
Packaging brief, preparing, 118-119
Packaging strategy, requirements for, 118-119
Passion points. *See also* Consumer beliefs
affecting consumer beliefs, 49-50
identifying, 53-55
role in purchase decision, 50-52
Patents, 109
Pepsi, 195, 213, 254, 264
Personal development, mission statement creation for, 13
Personality. *See* Brand personality
Pin Pricks exercise, 24-25
Pine Sol, 67
Pocahontas, 171, 252
Point-of-purchase sales, 106
Point-of-sale materials, 195
Popularity marketing, 242
Positioning statement. *See also* Positioning strategy
ABCs of, 43-45

art and discipline of, 42-43
for consumer promotion, 202-203, 204
developing, 42, 45-46
consumer benefits, 47-48
"reason why," 48-49
"relevant yet unexpected," 50, 54-55
target audience, 46-47
maintaining focus of, 227-228
Positioning strategy
cause-related marketing and, 245
emphasizing in advertisements, 157
maintaining focus of, 143, 145, 233-234
Premium branding
effect of packaging on, 108
value perception with, 99-102
Premiums, in consumer promotions, 204-205
Press conferences, public relations and, 170-171, 171-172
Press releases, public relations and, 170-171
Price. *See also* Pricing
average, 81
best-value, 86
exact, 79-81
lowest, 84-85, 85-86
relation to profitability, 75-76
relation to quantity, 125-126
relation to value, 83-84, 102, 125-126
variation in, 75-76
Price elasticity, discussed, 78-81
Price elasticity analysis
performing, 79-81
relation to price sensitivity, 78
Price insensitivity, factors affecting, 78
Price perception, 84
Price reductions, in retail environment, 186
Price sensitivity, factors affecting, 77-78
Price wars, competing in, 102
Price/value relationship, transforming, 83-84
Pricing. *See also* Price
Ferengi practices for, 87
Machiavellian, 76-77
sales commission quandry and, 82
through product life-cycle, 86
Prioritization, assisted by operating charter, 13, 14
Proctor & Gamble (P&G). *See also individual brands*
licensing, 279-280
marketing practices, 29, 130, 203, 244
new product introduction, 63, 64, 111
Product. *See also* Consumer products
displaying in retail environment, 129-130
placing in films, 250-251
Product categories
competition within, 36-37
consumer preference issues about, 90
Knowledge Mining exercise for, 33-35
owning, 102

price sensitivity within, 77-78
Product life-cycle, pricing through, 86
Product mix
determining, 90-92
optimizing, 102-103
product categories and, 92-93
Product strategies, by distribution channel, 128-129
"Profit by sku," 131
Profitability
of marketing programs, 186
for new products, 63, 116-117, 198
relation to price, 75-76, 81, 82
retailer concerns for, 116-117
Profitability analysis, affecting product displays, 130-131
Promotion agencies, for consumer promotions, 218-219
Promotions. *See* Consumer promotions; Sports sponsorships; Trade promotions
Public relations
campaign model for, 175
consistency and continuity in, 166-168
Folgers PR campaign, 175-176
fun ingredient, 177-178
in general, 165-166
Hollywood style PR, 172-175
marketing disguised as, 170-171
marketing PR model, 171-172
PR plan development, 176-177
small shop departments for, 168
three incarnations of, 168-169
corporate PR, 169
defensive PR, 169
marketing PR, 169
Publisher's Clearing House, 206-208

Q
Quaker State Motor Oil, 162

R
Radio stations. *See also* Media; TV stations
continuity promotions, 212
special event promotions with, 269
third-party promotions with, 197
Raffles, in-store, 199
Real-world learning
discipline of, 29-30
with Knowledge Mining, 32-33
practice of, 30-31
"Reason why". *See also* Compelling reasons
plausibility criteria for, 48-49, 59-60, 61
Reese's Pieces, 250
Regression analysis, performing, 79-81
Research. *See* Consumer research
Retail environment. *See also* Advertising
capturing shelf space, 130-131, 183-184
creative retailer programs
in general, 193-194
point-of-sale materials, 195
proprietary shelf space, 195-196

tagged media, 195
third-party promotions, 196-197
displays, price reductions, feature ads, 186
marketing development funds (MDFs) procedures, 185-186
product display, 129-130
proprietary retailer programs checkout coupons, 189-190
direct mail smart coupons, 190-191
in-store instant coupons, 191-192
proprietary signage, 193
shopping carts, 193
Robinson-Pattman Act effect on, 184-185, 193, 196-197
Ringling Bros. and Barnum & Bailey Circus, 248
Robinson-Pattman Act, effect on retail environment, 184-185, 193, 196-197
Rolex, 121-122, 123, 126
Rolling Stones, The, 253

S
Safeway, 188-189
Sales commission quandry, pricing and, 82
Sales projections, for new product introduction, 63
Sam's Club, 128
San Francisco Zoo, "Sex Tour," 177
Scalpers, sports ticket purchases from, 75-76
Segmentation analysis, in general, 90-92
Segmentation strategy of Coca-Cola, 92-93
KISS strategy for, 97-98
for new products, 95-96
for new usage occasions, 93-95
Seinfeld, 247
7-Eleven, 121-122
Shelf space. See also Slotting allowances
capturing, 130-131, 183-184
product display on, 129-130
proprietary, 195-196
Shopping carts, advertising on, 193
Shopping malls, 127-128
666 exercise, 23
Slotting allowances. See also New products; Retail environment; Shelf space
circumventing, 199-200
in general, 197-199
for new product display, 62
Small brands, profit expectations for, 131
Smart coupons, 189-190
direct mail, 190-191
Snickers, 160-161
Special displays, merchandising advantages with, 132-133
Special events. See also Sports events
creating, 267-268
little guys and, 266-267
local, 269
marketing at, 259-266
Special Olympics, 249

Spielberg, Steven, 141
Sports events. See also Special events
advertising at, 156-157
Sports sponsorships
blunders and bloopers, 236-237
consumer lifestyles and, 226-227
consumer promotions and, 227-230
costs of, 230-231
fantasy and, 223-224
in general, 221-223, 224-225
in-stadium signage, 225
little guys and, 237-238
local support and goodwill, 225-226
marketing plans for use with, 231-232
relevance and brand linkage, 227-230
winning and greatness, 226
Sports tickets, from scalpers, 75-76
Spreadsheets, running profitability analyses with, 130-131
Sprint, 100-102
Sprite, 210-211, 231-232, 249
Starbucks coffee, 32
Stern, David, 30, 246
Stimuli One-Step exercise, 23
Stimulus response method, for creativity, 18-19
Strategic positioning statement. See Positioning statement
Sunshine Generation, 58
Sweepstakes, in consumer promotions, 206

T
T-shirts, 282
Taco Bell
promotions, 211-212, 252
retail packaging, 111
Tagged media, 195
Target, Disney and, 194-195
Target audience, defining, 46-47, 202
Teams. See also Brand teams
in brainstorming session, 21-22
management of, 3-4
Telephone companies, branding for, 99-102
Texsun orange juice, 98-99
Think tank, for idea development, 69-70
Third-party promotions, 196-197
Tickle Me Elmo, 76
Tide
Liquid Tide, 109
logo display, 117
Time, as commodity, 99-102
Toothpaste, 95-96, 97
Toyota, TV commercials, 44, 50
Trade. See also Retail environment
affect on new products, 62-63
Trade promotions. See also Advertising; Consumer promotions; Retail environment
account-specific, 194-195
beating the system, in general, 193-194
Trademarks, 271-272, 273-274
licensing of, 274-275
Tropicana Orange Juice, 35-36, 99, 159

Truth. See also Advertising; Public relations
in advertising, 160-161
TV commercials. See also Advertising
about cars, 41-42
deconstructing, 46
Toyota cars, 44, 50
TV shows
alliances with, 254-255
brand partnership with, 210-211
TV stations. See also Media; Radio stations
special event promotions with, 269
third-party promotions with, 197
TVs, variations in, 128-129
Tylenol, product mix, 91-92, 97

U
Ultra Downy, 64
Underwear, 89-90
"Usage occasions," developing, 93-95

V
Value. See also Consumer beliefs
compared to price, 77
premium brands and, 99-102
relation to price, 83-84, 85-86
Videos, marketing, 31, 51-52, 113-114, 124-125, 132-133, 178, 194-195, 252-253
VISA, promotions, 155, 253

W
Walmart, 129
Watch-and-win game, 254-255
Wham-O frisbee, 50
Winnie the Pooh, 31, 51-52, 124-125, 178
Working mission statements, 4-5. See also Mission statements